AF449251

The Righteous Demon

The Righteous Demon
A STUDY OF BALI

Clifford Hospital

University of British Columbia Press
VANCOUVER
1984

The Righteous Demon: A Study of Bali

This book has been published with the help of a grant from the Canadian Federation for the Humanities, using funds provided by the Social Sciences and Humanities Research Council of Canada.

Canadian Cataloguing in Publication Data

Hospital, Clifford.
     The righteous Demon: a study of Bali

Includes index.
Bibliography: p.
ISBN 0-7748-0187-5

1. Bali (Hindu mythology) 2. Mythology, Hindu.
3. Purānas—Criticism, interpretation, etc.
I. Title.
BL1205.H67 1984   294.5′13   c83-091464-1

International Standard Book Number 0-7748-0187-5

Printed in Canada

Contents

Abbreviations

AV — *Atharva Veda*
Agni — *Agni Purāna*
Aitareya — *Aitareya Brāhmana*
Bhāgavata — *Bhāgavata Purāna*
Bhaviṣyottara — *Bhaviṣyottara Purāna*
BhG — *Bhagavad Gītā*
Brahma — *Brahma Purāna*
Brahmavaivarta — *Brahmavaivarta Purāna*
Bṛhadāranyaka — *Bṛhadāranyaka Upaniṣad*
Bṛhannāradīya — *Brhannāradīya Purāna*
Chāndogya — *Chāndogya Upaniṣad*
CI-O — Census of India, *Onam: A Festival of Kerala*
CSM — Achyuta Menon, C. *Cochin State Manual*
Garuḍa — *Garuḍa Purāna*
Hariv. — *Harivaṃśa*
HK — Padmanabha Menon, K. P., *History of Kerala*
KDG-E — Sreedhara Menon, A., *Kerala District Gazeteer — Ernakulam District*
Kūrma — *Kūrma Purāna*
MBh — *Mahābhārata*
Matsya — *Matsya Purāna*
NEB — New English Bible
Padma — *Padma Purāna*
Pañca — *Pañcaviṃśa Brāhmana*
Rām — *Rāmāyana*
RV — *Ṛg Veda*
Śata — *Śatapatha Brāhmana*
Skanda — *Skanda Purāna*
TSM — Nagam Aiya, *Travancore State Manual*
Vāmana — *Vāmana Purāna*
Vāyu — *Vāyu Purāna*
Viṣṇu — *Viṣṇu Purāna*

Preface

I have long been interested in the use of negative religious symbols. Such an interest perhaps derives from the circumstances of my childhood. I grew up in a religious community, the Methodist Church in Australia, which adhered to prohibitions not shared by the community at large, or even by other Christian churches. Drinking, smoking, swearing, and dancing were definitely out. And for a girl to wear lipstick was to have her piety called into question.

I remember a vehement argument with an Anglican friend of mine when I was about twelve, concerning the wine used in the Service of Holy Communion. I argued that Jesus had not drunk alcoholic wine. He argued that of course Jesus had drunk alcoholic wine, that one could not live in the area where Jesus lived without the modern techniques of refrigeration and have grape juice not ferment. But we Methodists were so sure of these things that it came as a considerable shock to me to discover later that he was right.

One of the effects of this kind of experience has been to leave me with a long-term interest in the ways in which the people of various cultures have, by the use of positive and negative symbols, set forth values for themselves and their children. From this broad field I have derived a more focussed interest in symbols that are clearly negative for a culture, but under some circumstances also used as positive symbols. A particularly interesting example is that of the demons in Hindu mythology. This work on Bali is, I hope, a worthwhile contribution towards what might be a large scale history of the demonic in Hinduism.

Some initial comments are in order on the methodology of this study and on the question of the audience for whom it is intended. My approach to the subject is technical and detailed but not, I hope, obtrusively so. To enhance the book's readability as much as to illustrate the discussion, I have chosen to include translations of original texts. Since not many of the texts are of great literary merit, I found myself wondering whether I should omit these translations and just concentrate on the discussion. Another possibility might have been to include summaries of the various texts. However, given the very detailed analysis of texts which I regard as imperative to my task, it seemed most appropriate to attempt detailed and fairly literal translations.

The decision to do this still left me with the question of the appropriate relation between the texts and the discussion. I judged it most necessary to use the translations in each section to introduce the discussion of that particular set of texts. An alternative might have been to present all of the texts at the beginning, and then to follow this by a discussion of the relation between them. I think, however, that the method I have used is the most helpful for portraying the development and the ramifications of the stories over a period of about two thousand years.

It seems to me, however, that one may read the texts and commentaries in different ways. In order to perceive the nature of the problem in relation to Bali, I would suggest a reading of the texts (found at the beginning of each chapter) from beginning to end. In order to grasp the full import of the discussion, one might either read the text and the commentary in the order given, reverse this order, or read the text, then the commentary, and finally the text once again.

In part, the question of how one reads this may be related to the question of audience. My hope is that this work will interest both established scholars and less experienced students of religion in India. The suggestions made here about reading and rereading are partly intended to assist students and others who may not be entirely familiar with the material. It is also for this group that I have attempted to facilitate the study of a large number of fairly esoteric texts by including with the index a glossary of names and terms which are difficult to render in translation.

The system of transliteration used here will be on the whole familiar to students in the area. For the names of deities, classes of beings, places, and so on, and for concepts judged untranslatable, I have for Sanskrit and Tamil words, used the most widely accepted form of transliterating to the Latin alphabet. For Malayalam publications, no systematic pattern of transliteration has yet emerged. Since Malayalam contains words of both Sanskrit and Tamil origin, I have used an appropriate combination of Sanskrit and Tamil transliterations. It should perhaps be emphasized that in both Tamil and Malayalam unvoiced consonants are voiced when they follow vowels or other sonants within a word. Thus what is written in the text as "Nampūtiri" is pronounced as it is sometimes written in a Latinated form, "Namboodiri."

Finally, I should like to acknowledge the help of many people towards this project: To the Shastri Indo-Canadian Institute for providing me with a senior fellowship to visit Kerala in 1977–78, particularly in order to pursue the Malayalam side of this project; to Dr. V. S. Sharma of the Department of Malayalam, and Dr. N. Unithiri of the Department of Sanskrit, both at the University of Trivandrum, for considerable help in the translation of Malayalam texts; to Mrs Dorothy Schweder of Queen's Theological College for much typing and retyping of the text; to Dr. Jane Fredeman of the University of British Columbia Press for her overseeing the technicalities of bringing such esoteric material to print; and to many others in Kerala, the United States and Canada who in a variety of ways have helped me formulate the ideas presented here.

I

Of "Demons" and Method

This study of the Asura Bali is the first part of an attempt to examine in detail the role of demons in Hindu mythology. A companion piece in progress is a study of the great Rākṣasa, Rāvaṇa, king of Laṅkā. That I have chosen Bali and Rāvaṇa as subjects for detailed investigation is no accident; they are among the four or five demons whose characters are explored in some detail in Hindu literature.[1] Bali and Rāvaṇa are particularly notable figures for they both draw us into an array of religious forms: both are associated with major festivals and both are represented in image form. Moreover, like Milton's Satan, each of these ostensibly evil figures has not only physical might but high moral and intellectual attributes. Indeed, in certain contexts, each has become something of a hero.

That demons can be heroes is not unknown in other cultures. Frequently there is a kind of underside to a culture, a complex of negative symbols which are taken and made positive by certain cults which themselves thereby act as a counter-culture or alternative sub-culture. Such European phenomena as the Black Mass and witchcraft have been interpreted as functioning, at least partly, in this manner (Wilson, 426–30; Murray).

The position of Bali and Rāvaṇa is different, however, in that as heroes they are positive foci for peoples in specific geographical-cultural areas — Bali primarily in Kerala, and Rāvaṇa in Tamil Nadu. Indeed, in Kerala, if there is a single national hero, a figure whose story is invoked as the ideal of the good life, it is Bali (known in Kerala as Mahābali, "the great Bali").

That it is possible for Bali to represent goodness immediately raises the question whether the word "demon" is an adequate translation for the class of beings to which Bali belongs. The problem becomes more pressing when it is noted that while Bali is of the class called Asuras, Rāvaṇa is a Rākṣasa, and yet both are frequently referred to as demons.

This problem has, of course, been noticed before. Ananda Coomaraswamy(1935a) offered light on the situation by translating "*deva*" and "*asura*" (usually termed "god" and "demon") as "angel" and "titan." In doing so he was effectively reversing the analogies between Indian and Western (that is, Judao-Graeco-Christian) mythological systems that are followed in the more usual translations. That is, whereas "god" draws on the analogy, and a very ancient historical connection, between *deva* (Sanskrit), *theos* (Greek) and *deus* (Latin), and "demon" on the fact that, like demons in Christian mythology, the Asuras[2] tend to stand opposed to the forces of "righteousness," Coomaraswamy draws our attention to the fact that in Hindu mythology Devas are often more like the angels of Christian mythology than the *theoi* of the Greeks, and Asuras are in certain respects closer to the Titans of the Greeks than to the demons of Christians. The Devas of the Epic-Puranic period and even of later periods function often as servants and executors of the will of the Supreme Person, the Lord (usually Viṣṇu or Śiva), or, less frequently, of the Goddess. The Asuras are like the Titans in at least three respects. First, they are of the same "ontological" status as the Devas, for both are pictured in the early materials (for example, *Sata* ii.1.6.6–11) as sprung from Prajāpati, the creator-god, and the Asuras are at times called the elder brothers of the Devas (E. W. Hopkins, 47). Secondly, there is some evidence within Vedic materials that Asuras were at one time a class of "gods" alongside, even superior to, the Devas and that over a period of time they were negativized (Macdonell, 156). Thirdly, both Western and Indian mythologies refer to a fatal flaw, pride — the *hubris* of the Titans and the *abhimāna* of the Asuras

(E. W. Hopkins, 50). Some scholars have called Rāvaṇa a Titan (Shastri, *passim*) because he has a brother Kubera who is in some versions a Deva, and for him too pride is *one* if not *the* fatal flaw. Yet others have identified the Rākṣasas as an equivalent of the Northern-European bogeyman, since the Rākṣasa exercises his power nocturnally, and is frequently pictured as man-eating (*puruṣādin, narāsana*). Hopkins suggests an analogy with the ogre (E. W. Hopkins, 38–39).

A further difficulty in defining the conception of these beings comes from the confusion within the Hindu texts about the various classifications. The Asuras are composed of two family groups: the Dānavas, the children of Danu, who figures as the mother of Vṛtra in *Ṛgveda* 1.32.9; and the Daityas or Daiteyas, the children of Diti. The father of all these demons is the great divine sage Kaśyapa. The major Devas, called Ādityas, are also the children of Kaśyapa by a younger wife, Aditi. Hence the tradition referred to above of the Asuras as the elder brothers of the Devas. In physical appearance and quality, for example, their ability to assume any shape or form or to disappear, and in their use of the superhuman power of *māyā*, they differ little from the Devas. The Rākṣasas seem different in that they are characteristically portrayed as having pointed ears, stiff or red hair, fangs or tusks, thick noses, copper-coloured faces, and long reddish tongues (see E. W. Hopkins, 39 on Ghaṭotkaca). Yet Rāvaṇa is usually portrayed like a Deva as basically human in form, but with many heads and necks (he has ten, hence the epithets Daśānana, Daśagrīva), and numerous arms. Rāvaṇa's sister Śūrpaṇakhā, however, is described by Vālmīki in a typically Rākṣasa form, effectively contrasted with the handsome Rāma (*Rām* 3.17.9–11; Shastri, 2:39):

> Beholding that hero, the equal of Indra, the Rākṣasī was overwhelmed with desire. Rama was handsome, she hideous; his waist was slender, hers thick and heavy; he had large eyes, hers squinted; his locks were beautiful, hers were red; his whole appearance was pleasing, hers repellent. Rama's voice was sonorous, hers strident; he was fair and youthful, she old and haggard; he was amiable, she was sullen; he was self-controlled, she unruly; he was captivating, she odious.

Further complications arise from the fact that in *Bhāgavata*, Kaṃsa, an Asura who has taken the form of a human king, has a sister Pūtanā who is described as a Rākṣasa—even though it is never suggested that the Rākṣasas are of the same family as the Asuras: the Rāṣasas are descended from Pulastya, the fourth son of Brahmā (E. W. Hopkins, 41). In addition certain inconsistencies in the Epics show that the line of demarcation between Asuras and Rākṣasas is not at all clear. Kumbha and Nikumbha are Rākṣasas in *Rām*, while in *MBh* they are sons of Prahlāda, who is himself the son of Hiraṇyakaśipu, a Daitya king.

We have here a very confused situation. No doubt this is partly because the Epics and Purāṇas are repositories of many differing traditions, some highly significant in terms of the mainstream of Indian culture, others idiosyncratic efflorescences.

Is there any way out of this confusion? Can we find a dominant concept here? One way often chosen is to note frequencies of ideas on the assumption that the recurrence of an idea in different texts indicates its importance for the culture that has engendered it. This seems valid, although different texts may have to be weighted differently as sources. A single popular text may say things definitively for a large number of people, while the ideas of a less known one may have influenced others even while the text remains in the background. One would be able to assess the significance of its ideas only through an extended and deep encounter with the people of the culture. Again, a chance mention in an obscure or unimportant text *may* be important in providing a clue to the puzzle of a particular set of symbols. Moreover, such clues may be missed if one looks only at texts, for there may be ideas that are regarded in the culture as so basic and axiomatic that they do not need to be mentioned—but are silently accepted as part of the symbolic field. Only close familiarity with the culture will attune the scholar to such conceptual underpinnings.

Again, how is one to know which chance mention in a text is an excrescence and which is a proper clue? The answer of Lévi-Strauss to such a question would be, I think, to suggest that the question is wrongly put, that in fact nothing is excrescence, since all occurrences within a set comprise clues to the essential meanings embedded within the set. If, for example, one is trying to understand a particular myth, one will be able to see what it is about only if one looks at all extant, variant versions (Lévi-Strauss 1963, 217). On the analogy of variations on a theme in music, Lévi-Strauss argues (1969, 17, *passim*) that the central structure of the myth is merely a framework and the significant problems with which the myth is dealing are to be seen in an exploration of the variations. Lévi-Strauss even goes so far as to argue the importance of a motif in a particular mythical account despite its omission from that version (1969, 137), a position that is highly suspect unless one can be quite sure that the omission is intended.

While I think that the idea of looking at all possible occurrences of a myth is valuable—I shall be attempting a "modified structuralist" approach to Bali in this discussion—there are two major points at which I disagree with Lévi-Strauss, and they are important in the context of this attempt to think generally about demons. The first is that in both music and myth I would want to give much more weight to the central structure than he allows. While the great improvisors among French organists can be given a random set of notes and use such a set as the theme for a dazzling array of variations, nevertheless there are some themes that are inherently more satisfying than others, and for the satisfaction finally obtainable from a theme with variations, the theme is fully as important as the variations. Extending the logic to myths, I would argue that since there are certain set structures that appear to form the base of myths across a wide variety of cultures, there are a limited number of experiences significant for all human beings.

Necessarily, it seems to me that myths draw their power as much from these stock human experiences as from the variations built upon the basic structures. That is, I think the meaning for a culture of a set of mythic variations may be mediated as much via the central structure as by the variations developed around the central structure.

The second point of disagreement has to do with the question I have asked about excrescence and clue. While I think it is important not to decide too quickly what is excrescence and what is clue, what is peripheral and what is central, nevertheless the danger is real that one may thoroughly misunderstand how the symbols of a culture work if one does not ask this question. A valid treatment of a cultural symbol system (or even of a small part of it) cannot be a merely mechanical manipulation of the 10,000 pieces of a puzzle, but requires considerable sensitivity on the part of the investigator.

Such sensitivity comes mainly through immersion in many aspects of the culture. Conversation, a feeling one's way into the religious life of the people concerned, or a study of works of art—all are helpful in discerning central clues, hidden agenda, and in separating these from the merely peripheral.

For a fruitful secondary sally into the world of Hindu demons we have to examine certain classics of Hindu art. The paintings of various schools of the Indian North-West (now mainly the states of Rajasthan, Punjab, Jammu, and Himachal Pradesh) from the seventeenth to the nineteenth centuries (see Archer) provide us with a large number of examples of accepted pictures of demons. Illuminated manuscripts and drawings of mediaeval and reformation Europe provide us with a somewhat parallel Christian heritage (see Hughes, *passim;* Rosenberg, *passim; Tres Riches Heures,* Pl. 91; Simons, 173–80). A comparison of these reveals sets of characteristics which are quite distinctively Christian or Hindu, as well as others which are common to both traditions. Through such a comparison one is able to bring into focus the nature of "demons" in the Indian tradition.

Many of the features that stand out as distinctively Christian can be understood in the context of Christian history or in the contrast between Christian and Hindu developments. One is the focus on the snake and related figures like dragons. The association of the snake with the so-called "fall of man" in Genesis 3, the place of the sea-monster Leviathan in eschatological materials in Isaiah 27.1, and the apparent conjunction of these in the apocalyptic writings in Revelation 12.9 and 13.1 form an adequate basis for the frequent depiction of the demonic in these forms. They also appear to depend upon a common negative response of *homo sapiens* towards reptiles, particularly the snake. That the snake does not appear in a similar symbolism in India is not because Indians are more comfortable with snakes. The fear response is evident there also, but it has been focused differently in the symbolic system. What appears to have been developed as fear-revulsion in the West becomes in India fear-awe. From the well-known story of Kṛṣṇa and Kāliya (see Zimmer 1962, 87) set in the region of Mathurā on the Yamunā, to the custom of the Nayars of Kerala in leaving a section of their land as the domain of the snakes (Krishna

Iyer, 117), the emphasis has been to suggest that these awesome creatures have their place in the world, that they harm only when forced into conflict, and that it is appropriate to appease them. In India, while snakes are considered awesomely dangerous, they are also revered as potentially benevolent. And, if the association of figures like the Buddha, Śiva, and Viṣṇu with snakes reflects initially a building up of their cults upon the substratum of Nāga worship, it also suggests an ultimately benevolent relationship between the snake and the Supreme Person. By contrast, the snake in Christian mythology is rather an aberration, the snake's dangerousness a focus of the aberrant quality of a fallen world—a world which is not as God intended it to be.

A second specifically Christian symbolism is that of the goat. This may be ultimately derived from such Biblical sources as Revelation 13.11 ("Then I saw another beast, which came up out of the earth; it had two horns like a lamb's but spoke like a dragon"), and the parables of the sheep and the goats in Matthew 24, correlating with the sheep-sheepfold-Shepherd symbolism for the saved, the true Israel and God on one hand and suggesting a goat symbolism for the damned and the powers of evil on the other. But the use of the symbol appears to be affected by events of post-Biblical Christian history. As Robert Hughes has pointed out, early Christians took over much mythology from other important religious movements of the Graeco-Roman world, absorbed it, and redirected it. The church was thus able to win battles against competing cults by meeting them on their own ground (see Angus, Nock). The cult of Dionysus remained, however, a powerful continuing force, so that even in the seventh century Theodore, Archbishop of Canterbury, anathematized the practices of the fertility cults. Hughes argues (242) that the importance of the goat symbolism reflects this conflict: "the Church did to Pan what Stalin did to Trotsky—and for precisely the same reasons. It turned him into the epitome of absolute evil, the Lord of Misrule, the devil. The attributes of Pan were given, in art, to the Christian Satan."

In its suggestiveness the goat symbolism is related to another common Christian symbol of the demon—that of the wild man, or the hairy man. Both symbols suggest by implication that the *libido* or sexuality is evil. This reflects an important strand of Christian tradition, particularly related to celibacy (see Ruether).

Yet another motif particular to Christianity is that many

demons have what appear to be the wings of bats. Structurally, they function in contrast to the beautiful, aquiline wings of angels. That there is no equivalent in India is probably the result of differing traditions about the ability of superhuman beings to transcend normal human methods of locomotion. In Christian mythology this ability seems to have been focused on wings; the Hindu picture is more diffuse. A Deva may move through the various regions at will; he may ride in a sky-chariot (*vimāna*) or he may ride on a *vāhana*, an animal vehicle (for example, Brahmā's goose, *haṃsa*; Viṣṇu's mount, the giant eagle-like bird, *garuḍa*).

In contrast with the Christian traditions, specifically Hindu traditions are less notable. Perhaps the most important one is that the demons may take different forms as they wish. They appear sometimes in animal forms (for example, buffalo, crane, a large serpentine figure), (see Spink, 18–21) at times in human form, and occasionally in a form similar to that of a deity.

Nevertheless, there is a general picture of Asuras and Rākṣasas as a class. And what is most remarkable is how similar the characteristic forms are to those of demons in Christian art. The major features common to Hindu and Christian are as follows:

    (a) a body roughly human in shape;
    (b) face — ape-like or canine;
    (c) mouth — accentuated teeth and/or tusks;
    (d) horns (in Indian examples they rarely appear to be goats' horns);
    (e) feet — clawed like those of carnivorous birds;
    (f) eyes — red, staring, leering;
    (g) hair — wild, erect;
    (h) ears — pointed (like goats' or donkeys');
    (i) skin — often repulsive — mottled (Indian) or scaly (Christian).

The similarity of these features suggests that, as a class, the demons function similarly in both mythological traditions. The common combination of animal and human characteristics might lead one to think that what is crucial to this picture is hybridization, or the freakish. Such an interpretation would see the symbolism of the demonic in both traditions as an extension of the way *tabus* work, after the style discussed by Mary Douglas in *Purity and Danger* (54–72). Demons would thus be seen as imagined anomalies.

In both Christian and Hindu cultures, then, demons are projections of such anomalies. But the details of these figures show that there is more to them than that, for in both cases they appear to function as the foci of fear responses. Joseph Campbell has argued that much of the groundwork of mythology is to be seen in archetypical responses which are analogous to innate releasing mechanisms (1:30–49). The common characteristics of demons appear to draw on some of the innately negative responses that humans have towards the savage carnivore (exemplified by teeth, fangs, claws) and towards the demented (suggested by the wild hair and eyes).

There is, however, a difference between the way these demonic forces function in the Hindu context and their use in much of Christian art. Watching Kathakaḷi performances in Kerala I came to realize that while the traditions of make-up there have developed incredible representations of the horrific, the dance forms developed undercut this and effectively "dehorrify" the horrific. In Kathakaḷi, the heroes, divine or human, usually appear first, and they engage in lengthy displays of their prowess. They are master craftsmen and their dancing is beautiful, but after some hours they become a trifle boring. One senses that the audience, apart from the true connoisseurs, is drifting into somnolent or near-somnolent states. But then the demons appear and everybody wakes up, including the children, for this *darśana* of the horrific. And the demons roar on and on, engaging in such a violent display of their prowess that the final effect is more in the nature of a burlesque. Initially menacing, they finally appear rather comical, and even lovable.

Turning again to the paintings, one realizes that here too there is a slightly comical aspect. The medieval Christian imagination seems to have developed the images of danger and madness into a picture of an utterly repulsive demonic realm as an effective method to draw people into the safe embrace of the Church. On the contrary, at least some strands of Indian tradition suggest that the horrific powers should not be taken too seriously.

There is a further aspect to note about the painting of the Indian demons. While groups of demons are almost always presented in the characteristic forms I have described, as also are certain individual demons (for example, Mahiṣāsura killed by the Goddess, or Hiraṇyākṣa killed by Viṣṇu's boar *avatāra*), certain demons are

1. *Viṣṇu's avatāra as a fish*

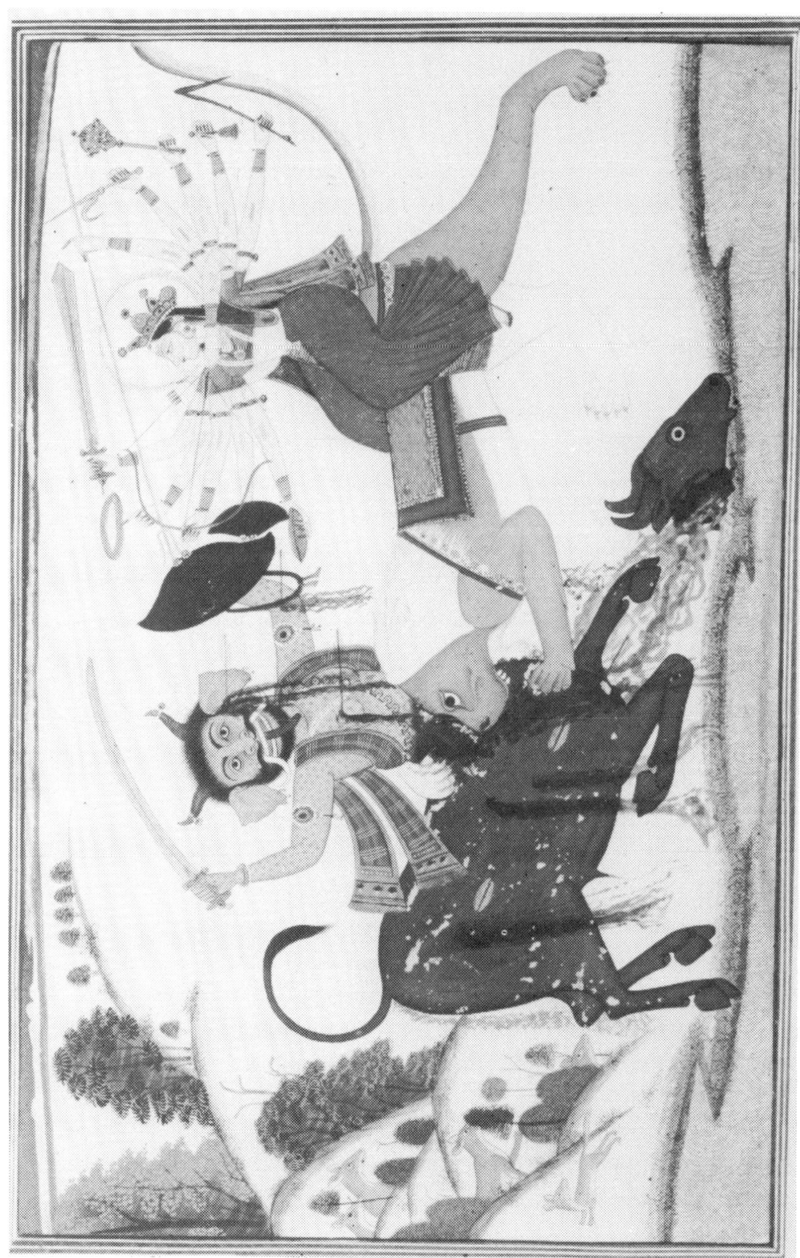

2. *Dūrgā fighting Mahiṣāsura*

never shown in this form. Rāvaṇa, for example, no less awesome than Hiraṇyākṣa, is presented, as we have said, in a form approximating that of a deity. Bali, the subject of our study, appears always as a king. All of which suggests that while as a class (or an intermixture of classes, Asuras and Rākṣasas) demons function in a set manner, certain representatives of these classes have a quite different role, are subject to more detailed characterization and, as a result, the messages they bear to Hindus are much more diffuse. It is the diffuseness in the characterization of Bali that will be explored in this study.

This second look at demons, via works of art, effectively raises for us a further question in relation to methods of study, namely, whether it is appropriate to generalize about Indian demons from such materials. The paintings are a comparatively recent phenomenon. A comparison of these with Persian paintings of the same period (see Anthony Welch, Pl. 10; Stuart Cary Welch, Pls. 4, 5, 9) and knowledge of the extent to which Mughul and thence Rājput painting were affected by Persian painting is sufficient to make one doubt whether the demons of these paintings can in any way be related to earlier views.

The methodological point at issue is one that has occasioned considerable debate in relation to the study of Hindu mythology: to what extent is it valid or possible to think about this material in terms of historical development?

The question of possibility is the more obvious one. It is well-known that materials from Epic and Puranic literature are inordinately difficult to date; so many of the texts are obviously an encyclopedic mix of materials coming from different historical periods. In some cases, the *Devī Māhātmya* section of the *Mārkaṇḍeya Purāṇa* for one, the general milieu of the Purāṇa as a whole is so different from that of the limited and specific section that the latter is obviously an interpolation (Winternitz, 1:565). But often an entire Purāṇa is quite mixed, and unravelling the different milieux and different historical periods becomes an impossible task.

In the case of the Puranic myths there are two further problems. The first is the widespread problem of the obscurity of mythic forms. Myths are often so complex or so strange that it is difficult to know how to interpret them. In relation to some geographical areas and historical periods, scholars know enough about the conditions out of which the myth has arisen to posit a *Sitz im Leben*, a "life situation" in the context of which they can find clues by which to interpret the myth. An area of scholarship where this method has proven very fruitful is the study of the Jewish and Christian scriptures. Not that *Sitzen im Leben* have been established beyond debate; in relation to the New Testament there have been extensive recent discussions about the relative weights of Judaic and Hellenistic backgrounds, about the importance of Zealots (Hengel, Brandon) and Essenes (Hanson, Leaney and Posen), and about the relations between the early Christian community and the Gnostics (Pagels)—as well as occasionally the more extreme presentations of the cross as sacred mushroom (Allegro), and of Jesus as a magician (Morton Smith). But that such debates are seriously possible speaks for a situation which is very different from what has been the case with respect to Indian texts. That is, there is evidence from the Hellenistic world of contemporary interest in accurate historical accounts, particularly among Jews (from whom so much of the relevant material is derived). One might therefore reasonably expect to be able to specify the *Sitz im Leben* of, say, a specific and troublesome statement of Jesus.

In India the situation is vastly different. The lack of interest shown by Indian writers in accounts which are historically accurate is proverbial. Not that there is lack of interest in history, if by the latter we mean the record of humanity's past. But in the stories about humanity, human beings are so often portrayed in interaction with superhuman beings—beings who would have to be identified in empirical terms as "constructs of the imagination"—that scholars have found virtually impossible the task of separating out what is historically accurate (see Pargiter, 1922).

It is perhaps in the absence of historically accurate materials, and therefore of discernible *Sitzen im Leben* for so much Indian literature, that the structuralist approach to the study of myth has recently become so popular among students of Hinduism. Lévi-Strauss's use of the method with materials that cannot be set in any known *Sitz im Leben* or general historical background is highly encouraging for scholars faced with the Purāṇas, which have been notoriously difficult to locate, temporally or spatially. Using Lévi-Strauss's method one is able to ignore—indeed, it is essential to ignore—questions of historical dependency or the priority of one text over another. Rather, all versions of a myth become part of the total field in which the myth works.

One can see from the work of scholars like O'Flaherty (1973) and Biardeau how liberating and, indeed, how fruitful of insights such an approach may be. In part the excitement is derived from "breaking the code." Lévi-Strauss's basic position, which is adhered to throughout his work, is that what one reads at the level of discourse tells one virtually nothing of what the story is really about. Thus, for example, the well-known myth of Oedipus (1963, 216):

> has to do with the inability, for a culture which holds the belief that mankind is autochthonous. . . to find a satisfactory transition between this theory and the knowledge that human beings are actually born from the union of man and woman. Although the problem obviously cannot be solved, the Oedipus myth provides a kind of logical tool which relates the original problem — born from one or born from two? — to the derivative problem: born from different or born from same? By a correlation of this type, the overrating of blood relations is to the underrating of blood relations as the attempt to escape autochthony is to the impossibility to succeed in it.

If one knows the Oedipus myth, one cannot but be surprised by this interpretation. And, beyond that, the creative scholarly mind is likely to be quite excited. What fun can be had with a 2000 piece jig-saw puzzle!

The sceptic, however, wonders whether the scholarly results have anything at all to do with the cultural phenomena being investigated. The most cogent expression of such scepticism vis-à-vis Lévi-Strauss appears in Clifford Geertz's discussion of *Tristes Tropiques* and *La Pensée Sauvage.* In a finely ironic piece he analyses the anthropologist in terms of the Hero Quest. The hero leaves his ancestral shores and journeys into another darker world, a world full of surprises, tests, and revelations. He returns, resigned and exhausted, to ordinary experience, with a deepened knowledge of reality.

Yet this deepened knowledge is not a revelation but a riddle. The anthropologist can understand those men contaminated by his own culture; those who are uncontaminated remain virtually unintelligible. A problem of method such as this might bring the anthropologist to despair except that it makes an approach other than personal involvement a possibility. The anthropologist can stand back and construct out of the particles and fragments of the debris (Geertz, 27-28):

> a theoretical model of society which, though it corresponds to none which can be observed in reality will none the less help us towards an understanding of the basic foundations of human existence.... It is not by storming the citadels of savage life directly, seeking to penetrate their mental life phenomenologically (a sheer impossibility) that a valid anthropology can be written. It is by intellectually reconstituting the shape of that life out of its filth-covered "archaeological" remains, reconstructing the conceptual systems that, from deep beneath its surface, animated it and gave it form.
>
> What a journey to the heart of darkness could not produce, an immersion in structural linguistics, communication theory, cybernetics and mathematical logic can.

Geertz, in this gentle satire, is arguing that a Lévi-Straussian "reconstruction" is essentially unrelated to the realities of the life of the culture being discussed. A structuralist approach, however, does not necessarily lead to the sort of theory unrelated to facts as Lévi-Strauss develops, a theory that actually assumes ignorance of the facts. Often, it seems to me, people are not unaware of the coding systems involved in their symbolisms. In a study of conflicting symbol systems related to disputes about the wearing of an "upper cloth" by low caste Christian women in nineteenth-century Kerala (Hospital, 1979), I found that central clues were provided by those articulating the Christian and Hindu positions. For the British Christian missionaries the covering of the breasts had to do with modesty, and they assumed that the wearing of an upper cloth by the Christian women was a sign of the modesty that resulted from their being Christian. For the Hindus, however, the uncovered breasts of low caste women was a symbol of their respect vis-à-vis the upper castes, the point being noted by one author that the upper class Nayar women also remove the upper cloth on entering a temple, or when going into the presence of a member of the

Travancore royal family (Mateer, 62). So they assumed that the wearing of an upper cloth by Christian women was a mark of disrespect and rebellion.

Similarly, it seems to me that an intelligent and articulate Hindu would have no difficulty with many of the findings of Wendy Doniger O'Flaherty (1973) concerning the modalities of sexuality and asceticism in Hindu society in general and in the exploration of these in the myths about Śiva. Yet I have difficulties with O'Flaherty's approach in two main areas. First, while her study is awesomely erudite and full of minute details about Hindu life, the final picture is really very generalized and rather simple (315).

> The ancient Indian knew well the Faustian lust for the full experience of the most diverse possibilities of human life; the Buddha saw this thirst as the cause of all human misery, but the Hindus did not dismiss it so easily. They recognized a constant tension between the desire to sample every aspect of experience and the desire to exhaust at least one by plumbing its extreme depths. Thus every human action involves a choice, and every choice implies a loss.
>
> In the sphere of human society, the choice implicit in this conflict was simply denied by the caste system with its doctrine of *svadharma*, one's particular duty in life: each person could perform one role fully and must let the rest go untried, at least in this existence. But these frustrations are relieved in the myths, where Śiva embodies *all* of life, in *all* of its detail, at every minute. He alone need make no choice; through him all of the conflicting challenges are accepted at once. In reading the myth, we too embrace the preciousness of life; we, too, lose nothing. Yet even the myths cannot fully slake this thirst; hence each story is told again and again, each time with new detail — a new character, a different episode, an expanded description — for no single myth can capture all the richness; each is merely a hint, a promise, a symbol of all that life can be.

I wonder whether the situation is not far more complex than this. If one thinks of an analogous situation in the case of Europe, a discussion of European views on celibacy and sexuality would be considered suspect if it cited indiscriminately from twentieth-century Irish anti-clericalism, sixteenth-century Lutheran anti-Catholicism, twentieth-century Australian Protestant anti-Catholic attacks on the morals of priests and nuns, and the finely-honed satire of Geoffrey Chaucer.

I am perhaps overstating my case; O'Flaherty does at times talk about the ideas of specific groups or specific texts (for example, the Vedas). Yet for much of her discussion the *Sitz im Leben* or even the general milieu of a text under discussion is ignored. The total effect of this is to make one wonder whether generalizations about "the Hindus" as in the above citation have any validity. There have been numerous strands to the Hindu tradition, many of which make one wonder whether the Buddha's vision of "thirst as the cause of all human misery" would not after all be a more adequate characterization of "the Hindus" than O'Flaherty's picture.

My second difficulty is related to the first: just as O'Flaherty ignores contexts, so also does she often ignore time periods. If one accepts even the general picture of an interaction between Aryan and pre-Aryan in the cultural mix of classical Hinduism, then one cannot assume such cultural continuity between Brāhmaṇas, Upaniṣads, Epics and Purāṇas that one can use them all together to talk about Hindu culture. One cannot *assume* that the meaning of a symbol used in the Brāhmaṇas can elucidate the meaning in a late Purāṇa, or vice versa.

My skirmish with O'Flaherty is not an attempt at detraction; her achievement is enlightening, at times brilliantly insightful and, undoubtedly *because* of the structualist approach, highly refreshing. Yet I am convinced that a more exacting method must be developed for the investigation of a mythic *corpus*. And my first principle is related to what I have had to say about the structuralists. While it may be impossible to find a specific *Sitz im Leben* for a particular mythic account, it would be reckless to ignore the question. If we cannot know a specific *Sitz im Leben* we can often discern a more generalized milieu — from a single textual account, from a group of similar texts, from what we know of accounts of parallel myths of the same historical period and, at times — though considerable caution is needed here — from other parts of the work in which the account is incorporated.

What I mean by milieu will become clearer as the work progresses. Initially it may be defined as a set of symbols which cohere into a more or less unified cultural complex. Thus I would regard the period of the Brāhmaṇas as exhibiting predominantly one milieu in which life is focused on the correct performance of numerous sacrifices. A few texts of the period point towards a new milieu, one seen also in the early Upaniṣads, where interest has shifted from the actual performance of the sacrifice to speculations about the hidden dimensions within which the sacrifice becomes efficacious — with a further blossoming of a more general speculation about the nature of reality. It seems to me not unreasonable to make an attempt, by careful attention to detail, at placing a text in a particular milieu.

By so placing individual texts, we should find it possible to trace the history of a myth through a series of textual modifications. Wilfred Cantwell Smith has argued that an approach which freezes a culture into a system is invalid and uses the concept of "cumulative tradition" to suggest that we would do well to make ourselves aware of the continually changing quality of human tradition (Smith, 1963, 139–53). Following his reasoning I have come to believe that it is not less interesting to see the ability of a myth in its modifications to carry new and different messages, than it is to discern the message of the totality of the myth in all its modifications. This direct perception must necessarily begin with the task of detecting phases in the development of a myth. In order to do so, this study draws a distinction between three different myths related to Bali, which have been designated as A, B and C. C is found only in Kerala, and in only one text. B is found only in *MBh* in two versions, though the *Yogavasiṣṭha* contains what could be regarded as a modification of B. A is found in numerous versions and it is to this group that the basic method has been applied.

I began this study by translating all available texts of the myth. I then attempted to isolate significant basic units from all texts. The result, given in Appendix B, is a total of 177 such units. Deciding what is a "significant basic unit" is not always easy. At times it is one sentence; at other times it is a section of verses that stand together as a unit, for example, a hymn. In general it is anything recorded — an action, an object, a motif, or a symbol — which adds materially to the telling of the myth.

The units are then tabulated against all available texts. The texts are arranged in roughly chronological order, this being determined by the time frame of the field generally accepted among scholars of Epics and Purāṇas. The tabulation makes it clear that some of these basic units are shared by virtually all texts, while others are shared only by two or three. Particularly when a group of texts share two or three units absent from all other texts it seems reasonable to talk of a "family relationship" among such texts. About two texts with such a family relationship it could be said either that one has borrowed from the other, or that both have borrowed from a third text, no longer extant, or that, given the importance of oral tradition in India, both have drawn on a generalized but limited (to a particular area, a particular time period, etc.) oral tradition.

Also, within such a "family" one could well find a text which contained further units unique to it. Of such a text it could be said that certain of such units could not have arisen without the prior existence of other units in the family. It becomes reasonable on such a basis to see a further *phase* experienced within the family.

It is, however, necessary to distinguish clearly between phases and milieux. One may see that a group of texts from about the same period bear in common a number of new elements beyond those found in an earlier phase. Some of these new elements taken together signal a new milieu, contributing substantively to that new milieu. Others of these new elements constitute merely conventional additions. On the basis of these observations it becomes possible to conceive of a text which, though it clearly belongs to a new phase of the myth, containing as it does a significant number of elements shared with other texts of that phase, yet does not participate in or contribute significantly to the new milieu to which other texts of that phase belong.

It is also in principle possible that at a particular phase of the development of the myth—that is, in a particular period—one might find two different family developments, each a significant contribution to the development of the myth, each participating in a different milieu. Thus, for example, in the second phase of the myth one might have two different milieux, each different from the milieu of Phase I.

In fact, I find that, until the later stages of development of this myth, accounts from the same phase tend to share a similar milieu. Thus, I have placed in Phase 2 a set of texts from the middle Puranic period, namely, accounts in *Hariv. App., Matsya, Vāmana, Kūrma,* and *Agni.* All of these except *Agni* are part of a milieu (which I call Milieu 2) different from the milieu to which the earlier, more primitive Phase 1 texts belong. The *Agni* text is clearly part of Milieu 1, the milieu common to Phase 1 texts, although it shares so many significant basic units with other Phase 2 texts that it has to be placed with them.

Using the method I have outlined, I have isolated five phases of Myth A, the central myth of Bali. The first phase (which I examine in Chapter 2) comprises the following set of texts from the Epics and early Purāṇas: *MBh* 12.326.74–76; *MBh* 3 App.1 (lines 63–82); *Rām* 1.28.1–11; *Vāyu* 2.36.74–87 = *Brahmāṇḍa* 2.73.75–86; and *Harivaṃśa*, Harivaṃśaparva 31.68–92. In this phase the predominant milieu for the portrayal of Bali identifies demonic beings as constituting a threat to *dharma,* such a threat being eventually overcome by an *avatāra* of Viṣṇu (in the case of Bali, the Vāmana or Dwarf *avatāra*).

The second phase (dealt with in Chapter 4) comprises a set of texts from the middle Puranic period: *Agni* 4.5–11; *Harivaṃśa App.* 42B; *Matsya* 244–46. These are reproduced almost verbatim in *Vāmana* SM 2–10; *Vāmana* 48–52; and *Kūrma* 1.16. Many of the details of the new significant units of this phase reflect the details of Myth B (discussed in Chapter 3), and found in two versions; *MBh* 12.216–18 and 220–21. All texts of this phase (except, as already intimated, *Agni* 4.5–11) belong to a new milieu in which Bali is portrayed quite positively, even being shown as arriving at devotion to Viṣṇu. Complementing this change, there is evidence in these texts of a thorough exploration of the interrelations between goodness, prosperity, devotion and *dharma.*

The third phase (Chapter 5) is constituted of *Brahma* 73, *Bhāgavata* 8.15–23, *Padma* 6.226–267 and *Bṛhannāradīya* 10–11. These bear significant new details in common, with some important modifications of the Phase 2 accounts. The portrayal of Bali as devotee is now quite strong, and there is a clear focus on the motif of the Lord's feet which affects the portrayal of Bali and is also given a parallel development in the account of the origin of the Ganges. The *Bhāgavata,* while belonging to the general milieu of this new phase, is a highly original and telling portrayal of Bali as devotee.

The fourth phase (Chapter 6) comprises five versions of the

myth found in the *Skanda* (1.1.17.286–1.1.19; 5.1.63–1.10.270; 7.1.114; 7.2.14–19; and 7.4.19) which is dated quite late among the Purāṇas. All of these except 7.1.114 contain details that reflect a knowledge of Phase 3 motifs. The texts are all idiosyncratic so that it is impossible to detect a common milieu for this phase. A number of them, however, show an interest in special festivals related to the myth. It is particularly the relation of Dīvālī to Bali that calls for major exploration here.

The fifth phase (dealt with in Chapter 7) is represented by three versions from modern Kerala (from books by K. M. George, K. Jacob, and George Woodcock). These involve a tie between Bali and Kerala's Ōṇam festival, and a portrayal of Bali's rule as a golden age in Kerala's past. Important for seeing the development of characteristic motifs of this phase is the popular Malayalam ballad *Mahābalicaritam*, which contains a brief version of Myth A set within the much longer story that I have called Myth C.

Chapter 8, "Bali Comes West," could also be seen as part of this fifth, modern phase of the myth. The single significant literary text, Robert Southey's poem "The Curse of Kehama," presents a cameo appearance of Bali (Baly) in which the old story is told in a form similar to that of Phase 1, but containing some details shared with texts from Phase 4 and from modern Kerala. There is also a striking new link with the ruined city of Mahabalipuram.

Also part of this modern phase are Western critical studies which look at Bali, and these could be seen as constituting a new milieu of the myth. In all earlier versions, new milieux are mediated via a retelling of the myth. Now, however, second level critical discussion of a Western historicist approach becomes important. And this monograph concludes with the argument that such critical discussions, including the present one, are part of the ongoing life of the myth in its vicissitudes.

It is high time, however, that we moved from the discussion of generalities. In order to bring into focus the major shifts that have occurred in the import of the central myth of Bali, I can do nothing better than to set down side by side two texts. The first is characteristic of the earliest stages of its development in the Epic-Puranic materials, and the second one of the recent versions from the state of Kerala.

3. *Viṣṇu as Dwarf-Trivikrama*

Text 8
[*Agni* 4.5b–11]

Formerly in a war between the Devas and Asuras the Devas
were defeated by Bali and his followers and driven out of
heaven. They sought refuge in Hari. He quelled the Devas'
fears, and having been praised by Aditi and Kaśyapa, he was
born to Aditi as a dwarf. He went to the sacrifice of Bali who
was sacrificing with his wealth at Gaṅgādvāra, and he sang a
hymn of praise. Hearing the dwarf reciting the Vedas, the
giver of boons, Bali, though obstructed by Śukra, said to the
Dwarf: "Tell me what you desire, and I will grant it to you."

4. *Mahābali*

The Dwarf said to Bali: "Grant me as fee, land for three steps." "I will give it to you," said Bali. When water had been poured on to his hand, the Dwarf was no dwarf, and earth, the mid-region and the sky were his three steps. And Hari sent Bali to Sutala, and gave the triple-world to Śakra. And Śakra, along with the other Devas, praised Hari and was happy as lord of the world.

Text 23
[K. M. George, 210–12]

Long long ago a king named Mahābali ruled over Kerala. He was generous and kind. Life was very happy for everyone. The Kerala ruled by Mahābali was like heaven and that made the Devas jealous. The result of this was that Viṣṇu descended as Vāmana, a dwarf, who begged Mahābali for a gift of the land he could cover in three steps. And the generous king granted his request.

Immediately the Dwarf became so large that he was able with two steps to win earth and heaven. For his third step he placed his foot on the head of Mahābali and pushed him down to Pātāla. But before going down to Pātāla, Mahābali asked Viṣṇu for a boon: he asked for permission to visit his people once a year. This was granted and accordingly the day when Mahābali visits Kerala is Ōṇam in the month of Ciṇṇam.

These accounts, separated by centuries, offer a sharp contrast both in plot and in attitude. On the one hand there is Bali, a purely negative figure, enemy of the gods, readily disposed of by Lord Viṣṇu. On the other, Mahābali, "the great Bali," good king of Kerala whose visit to his people each year is the happiest and most festive period of the Malayalis' year. It is this contrast that forms the cultural puzzle on which the present investigation centres.

2

Myth A, Phase 1, Milieu I

The earliest mention of Bali in Indian literature is in the *Mahābhāsya* of Patañjali who is usually dated by scholars around the second century B.C.. Kane notes (4: 1, 130) that: "On Vārtika 6 to (Pānini) III.1.26 the Mahābhāṣya gives two examples 'Kaṁsam ghātayati' (meaning 'he tells the story of the slaughter of Kaṁsa') and 'Balim bhandayati' (meaning 'he narrates the story of the imprisonment of Bali')." The earliest recountings of the central story appear in the *Mahābhārata*. They represent the first phase of the myth and are presented below.

This central myth relating to Bali could be seen, of course, as primarily the story of Vāmana, the Dwarf, who is one of the *avatāras* of Viṣṇu. But the numerous transformations of the story suggest that the story is at least as much Bali's as it is Vāmana's. The reason why this is so is itself a point for contemplation.

Text 1
[*MBh* 12.326.74–76]

The great Asura Bali, the powerful son of Virocana, will arise

and cause Indra to fall from his kingdom. When the triple
world has been stolen by him despite the opposition of the husband of Śacī, I will take birth as the twelfth son of Aditi and
Kaśyapa. Then I shall restore the kingdom to Indra, of infinite
glory. I shall return the Devas to their positions, O Nārada,
and Bali I shall cause to dwell in the region of Pātāla.

Text 2
[*MBh* 3, Appendix I No. 27, lines 64–82]

The lotus-eyed Lord took another form for the welfare of the
world, and was carried in the womb of Aditi as the son of Kaśyapa. After a thousand years, she was delivered of that superhuman embryo; the child was of the hue of the rain clouds,
had shining eyes and the body of a dwarf. He carried a staff
and a waterpot and his chest was adorned with the Śrīvatsa
mark; the Blessed One wore matted locks and the sacred
thread and appeared in the form of a child. Then that glorious
one went to the sacrificial enclosure of the lord of the Dānavas
and with the help of Bṛhaspati he joined Bali's sacrificial ritual.
Bali seeing that one in the form of a dwarf was pleased and
said, "I am glad to see you, O Brāhman. Tell me what you
want."

Thus addressed by Bali, the Dwarf answered, "Greetings."
Then smiling he said to Bali: "Grant me, O Lord of Dānavas,
three strides of land." Then the gracious-minded Bali granted
this to that Brāhman of boundless energy, and that most wonderful divine form of the striding Hari quickly took the worlds
with three strides. And the eternal god Viṣṇu gave the earth to
Indra. This appearance which has been proclaimed is called
"Vāmana." The Devas thereby became manifest and the
universe was called "Vaiṣṇava."

Text 3
[*Rām* 1.28.1–11]

1   Then when Rama of immeasurable prowess asked about that
    forest, Viśvamitra, that one of great *tejas*, began to answer him

thus: "This was formerly the *āśrama* of the noble Vāmana, O Rāma. It is called 'Siddhāśrama' because it was here that one of great *tapas* fulfilled his purpose. At that time Virocana's son, King Bali, conquered the Deva hosts, including Indra and the Maruts; and renowned throughout the three worlds he set up his kingdom. And while Bali was performing a sacrifice, the Devas, with Agni at their head, came to Viṣṇu in this *āśrama* and said: "Virocana's son Bali is celebrating the highest sacrifice. While this sacrifice is still incomplete, accomplish your purpose: Since he gives whatever they ask to those who turn to him, he will surely give you everything you ask for. Employing your *māyā,* for the welfare of the gods, assume dwarf-hood and achieve the highest good, O Viṣṇu. This through your grace will come to be called 'Siddhāśrama.' When your deeds have been accomplished, O Lord of Devas, depart from here, O Blessed One."

9   So this glorious Viṣṇu was born from Aditi. Assuming a dwarf-form he came to Virocana's son. Then begging three strides he received them from Bali. And intent on the welfare of all creatures, he, the world's Self, strode out of the worlds. Having by his power restrained Bali, that one of great *tejas* gave the triple world again to the great Indra, making it again subject to him.

Text 4

[*Vāyu* 2.36.74–87a = *Brahmāṇḍa* 2.73.75–86]

74   In the seventh Treta Yuga when the worlds were controlled by Bali and the triple world had been seized by the Daityas, the Dwarf came as Viṣṇu's third appearance. Contracting himself in his limbs, he went, preceded by Bṛhaspati, to the place where the chief of the Daityas was sacrificing. And the Lord, that joy of the family of Aditi, becoming a Brāhman at this auspicious time, said to Bali the son of Virocana, "You are the king of the triple world. Everything is established in you. You should grant to me the space covered in three strides." "I grant it," said King Bali, Virocana's son; and considering him to be just a dwarf he was very pleased.

Then that Dwarf, the Lord, that best of Brāhmans, with

three strides stepped over the sky, the mid-region and the earth — this entire universe. That celebrated one, the Self of all beings, with his own *tejas* outshone the sun, illuminating the four quarters and the intermediate points of the compass. The powerful Janārdana shone forth, illuminating all the worlds, and stole away both the Asura's prosperity and the three worlds. And he led the Asuras, with their sons and grandsons to the region of Pātāla. Those cruel ones, Namuci, Śambara and Prahlāda, were routed by Viṣṇu and scattered to the four corners. Mādhava, who is all the great elements and the Self of all beings and Time in its entirety, revealed to the Brāhmans there that wonder. He revealed himself: that the entire universe is in his body. There is not anything in the world which is not pervaded by that illustrious one.

Devas, Dānavas and humans, seeing that form of the Lord, were all stupefied and infatuated by the glory of Viṣṇu. And Bali, with his relatives and friends, was bound with great cords, and the entire family of Virocana was sent off to Pātāla. Then powerful Janārdana made Indra the ruler of all immortals.

The general milieu (Milieu 1) into which these texts fit centres on the most important role of demons — Asuras (Daityas, Dānavas) and Rākṣasas — in Hindu mythology over at least 3000 years, that is, as opponents of the Devas. The basic structure of hundreds of accounts involving gods and demons is best described as a conflict motif. In its most developed form it is found in a great number of Epic-Puranic myths, and particularly in the accounts of the major *avatāra*s of Viṣṇu:

(1) A demon or company of demons usurps the power of the gods, taking control of the worlds.

(2) The demons upset *dharma*, and the worlds stand on the brink of chaos; creatures are beset by fear.

(3) The gods seek refuge in the supreme person (variously Viṣṇu, Śiva, Śakti).

(4) The Supreme Person acts in response to their plea in such a way that, sooner or later, the demon is slaughtered, or at least overcome.

(5) The gods and other creatures are restored to their rightful

places and there is peace and prosperity again in the world.

A. *Devas and Asuras in the Brāhmaṇas and Upaniṣads*

In order to understand how this works it is important to go back to the precursors of such stories, the conflicts between the Devas and Asuras recorded in the Brāhmaṇas, and behind those the conflict between Indra and Vṛtra, which appears to be the most important myth for those who composed the *Ṛgveda Saṃhita*.

The claim of W. Norman Brown (1942) that the conflict story is a cosmogonic myth rather after the style of that of Marduk and Tiamat in the Mesopotamian text "Enūma Eliś,"[1] has been accepted by most scholars. It is, after all, to be expected that a conquering people like the Aryans might perceive the establishment of the cosmos as the act of a great military hero. While Ingalls (1968,553) has called into question the depiction of the Ādityas as liberals and Vṛtra and his associates, the Dānavas, as conservatives, most scholars accept in general the scenario of the conflict and its sequel given by Brown in his analysis of the *Ṛgveda* (Brown,96):

> The battle was fierce, and even Indra received serious injury when Vyaṃsa, who is Vṛtra (1.32.5), broke his jaw (4.18.9). But Indra in turn broke Vṛtra's jaw (10.152.3; 1.52.6) and his face or nose (1.32.6), split his head (4.17.3; 1.52.10), and in general crushed and slew him and left him lying there [*amuyā*]. His weapon was the vajra, and with it he pierced twenty-one mountains (8.96.2), burst the bellies of the mountains (1.32.1), which means that he split open Vṛtra.

After the victory,

> He released the Waters (1.32.2), generated the sun, the sky, the dawn (1.32.4) or, as stated elsewhere, he and Soma made the dawn shine, led forth the sun with its light, supported the sky, spread out Mother Earth (6.72.2; cf. 10.62.3; 2.13.5),

having struck away Vṛtra from them (1.51; 1.52). Or, again, having slain Vṛtra, he proceeded to creation (2.15.1ff.). He is, therefore, called *viśvakarman* (8.98.2; 9.63.7) 'All-Maker, Creator,' and Lord over all creation (8.98.2; 10.153.5). He created by setting the worlds apart and starting the sun on its revolution (6.3.5; 8.36.4; 10.29.6; 10.54.3; 1.62.4–6).

In later sections of *RV*, other creation stories made their appearance (though they were not always spelt out in detail in *RV* hymns). Four motifs appear important: the arising of *sat* from *asat*;[2] the origin of the world from a golden egg or embryo (*hiraṇyagarbha*) set on the Waters;[3] connected with the latter, the idea of the creative power of *tapas*, so that development of the differentiated cosmos is conceived as a kind of self-incubation by *hiraṇyagarbha*;[4] and the origin of various parts of the universe from the dismemberment and sacrifice of a great cosmic being (*puruṣa*).[5] Later creation stories from the Brāhmaṇas to the Purāṇas (which still form the basis for traditional Hindu views) have comprised various combinations of these with some additional developments (Brahmā as creator, the lotus replacing and incorporating *hiraṇyagarbha*).[6]

The result was that the story of the conflict between Indra and Vṛtra ceased to be a cosmogonic myth. The conflict motif, however, did not lose its importance. It merely shifted focus. The Brāhmaṇas continually narrate conflicts between Devas and Asuras, but the emphasis falls upon the sacrificial rituals, so that it is by virtue of the power gained through sacrifice that the Devas always manage to overcome the Asuras.

Frequently in the *Pañcaviṃśa Brahmaṇa* it is by the power of a particular chant received from Prajāpati that the Devas defeat the Asuras (*Pañca* 8.31; Caland, 167–68):

The gods and the asuras contended for [the possession of] these worlds. The Gods resorted to Prajāpati; he gave them this *sāman*, [saying]: 'By means of this *sāman* ye will be able to drive them away.' By it they drove them away from these worlds. Because they drove them away (*akālayanta*), therefore it is [called] the *kāleya*.

The context in which this is set is frequently found in the Brāh-maṇas. By the performance of certain sacrificial rituals, or by the uttering of certain powerful words, or by the knowledge of the power inherent in such sacrificial rituals or utterances, the sacri-ficer is able to obtain prosperity. He gains wealth in the form of thriving cattle (*Pañca* 8.9.4, 13.6.7); he causes the rain to fall; he repels evil (*Pañca* 13.5, 13.23); and he escapes harm (*Pañca* 12.5.23).

The accounts of the conflicts between the Asuras and the Devas serve as legitimating or "charter" myths (see Kirk, 59) for phase after phase of the sacrificial ritual. The efficacy of the ritual actions of the sacrificer is established not on any pragmatic basis but on the basis of what was done in the past by the Devas. The stories unfailingly conclude with the assertion that what was won by the Devas through this *mantra* or that ritual act will also be won by the sacrificer.

The Devas, of course, never failed to win eventually. Both the "boo-hurrah" image of O'Flaherty (1976, 64) and Long's game model (see esp. 203–5) which O'Flaherty cites favourably (61) as a way of understanding the Brāhmaṇa stories, miss the essential point that the Devas and Asuras are not evenly balanced. From the constant repetition of the pattern of these myths it must be assumed that the Devas will win. There are many such charter accounts where the Asuras do not figure at all—only the Devas, performing the effectual ritual. When the Asuras are introduced they function essentially as a foil to the Devas.

There are two major patterns in the Brāhmaṇas that illuminate the different aspects of the relation between the Devas and their opponents. The first pattern has the following elements:

(1) The Devas and Asuras contended, strove together (*praspṛdhive*).

(2) The Asuras were in ascendency (winning worlds, sacrifice).

(3) Devas performed ritual actions, uttered mantras, etc. and/or Asuras made crucial mistakes.

(4) The Devas won (sacrifice, worlds).

(5) Postscript: Whoever knows this, and sacrifices thus, wins. . . .

Variations on this pattern can be observed in the following examples:

(a) "With the Asuras was the whole sacrifice. The Devas saw the *yajñayajñīya*. By means of the words: 'by sacrifice on sacrifice in honour of Agni' they took from them the *agnihotra*: by the words 'and by hymn on hymn in honour of the skilful'; the full-and-new-moon sacrifices; by the words: 'continually we will extol the immortal Jātavedas', the seasonal sacrifices, and by the words 'as a dear friend I will extol', the sacrifice of *soma*." (*Pañca* 8.6.5; Caland, 176–77)

(b) "He recites (the eighth *sāmidhenī*): 'Agni we choose as messenger!' Now the Devas and the Asuras, both of them sprung from Prajāpati, were contending for superiority. When they were thus contending, the *gāyatrī* stood between them. That *gāyatrī* was the same as this earth, and this earth indeed lay between them. Now both of them knew that whichever she would side with, they would be victorious and the others would be defeated. Both parties then invited her secretly to come to them. Agni acted as messenger for the Devas; and an Asurarakṣas, named Saharakṣas, for the Asuras. She then followed Agni: he therefore recites, 'Agni we choose for messenger', because he was the messenger of the Devas. — 'As Hotṛ the all-knowing, him!'" (*Śata* 1.4.1.34; Eggeling, 1:176)

(c) "The Devas and the Asuras, both of them sprung from Prajāpati, were once contending for this sacrifice, which is their father Prajāpati, the year: 'Ours it (he) shall be!' 'Ours it (he) shall be!' they said.

Then the Devas went on praising and toiling. They saw these fore-offerings and worshipped with them. By means of them they gained (*pra-ji*) the seasons, the year; they deprived their rivals of the seasons, of the year: hence the fore-offerings are victories (*prajaya*), for, assuredly, *prajaya* is the very same term as *prayāja* (fore-offering). And in the same way the sacrificer wins by means of them the seasons, the year; deprives his rivals of the seasons, of the year. This is the reason why he performs the fore-offerings." (*Śata* 1.5.3.2–3; Eggeling, 1: 144)

(d) "Now, the Devas and the Asuras, both of them sprung from Prajāpati, were contending for this sacrifice — their father Prajāpati, the year — saying, 'Ours he shall be! Ours he shall be!'

Then the Devas went on singing praises and toiling. They devised this Agniṣṭoma feast, and by means of this Agniṣṭoma feast they appropriated the entire sacrifice and excluded the Asuras from the sacrifice. And in like manner does this sacrificer, by means of this Agniṣṭoma feast, now appropriate the entire sacrifice, and exclude his enemies from the sacrifice: therefore he celebrates the Agniṣṭoma." (*Śata* 4.2.4.11–12; Eggeling, 2: 301)

On looking at these accounts, we find that elements (1), (3), (4) hardly vary; (5) may often be understood, not needing to be spelt out every time. The fact that (2) is only occasionally part of the structure becomes significant when we set (2) against the structure we have outlined as standard in the Purāṇas, for it is clear that there has been a major shift in emphasis by the time of the Purāṇas. In the Brāhmaṇas the Asuras are opponents who may or may not win for a time. In the Epics and Purāṇas there is much greater emphasis on the initial victory of the Asuras and the effects of that victory.

In this first pattern from the Brāhmaṇas, then, we have the legitimating of the sacrifice on the basis of a conflict myth — or, better, legitimating it by the use of a metaphor of battle, in which there is a certain see-sawing of fortunes, but one that, eventually, by use of the right weapon or technique, the Devas win.

The second pattern also derives from the conflict situation but is less extended than the first:

(1) The Devas (sacrificing?) were afraid of attack from Asura-rakṣas or Rakṣas.

(2) The Devas performed a certain ritual.

(3) The Devas thus warded off the attack, became free from danger.

(4) The sacrificer performs this ritual for similar purposes.
Again some examples are helpful.

(a) "He offers it continuously; for at that time the Devas were afraid lest the Rakṣas, the destroyers, should come there after them! They saw that continuous libation in order to prevent the destructive Rakṣas from coming after them: hence he offers it continuously." (*Śata* 6.3.1.5)

(b) "They stand on the south side; — for the Devas at that time were afraid, lest the Rakṣas, the destroyers, should smite their sacrifice from the south. They saw that thunderbolt, yonder sun; for this horse is indeed yonder sun; and by means of that thunderbolt they drove off from the south the Rakṣas, the destroyers, and spread this sacrifice in a place free from danger and destruction. And in like manner does the sacrificer now by means of this thunderbolt drive off from the south the Rakṣas, the destroyers, and spread this sacrifice in a place free from danger and destruction." (Śata 6.3.1.29)

(c) "The Adhvaryu then says to the Hotṛ, 'Recite to the fires being led forward!' For at that time when the Devas were setting out to spread the sacrifice, the Rakṣas, the destroyers, sought to smite them, saying, 'You shall not sacrifice! You shall not spread the sacrifice!' Having made those fires, those bricks, to be sharp-edged thunderbolts, they hurled these at them, and laid them low thereby; and having laid them low, they spread that sacrifice in a place free from danger and destruction." (Śata 7.3.2.5).

From these examples one can see that (4) is often implicit, as (5) was in the former pattern. The conflict situation here is one in which the Devas are in possession of something crucial but are subject to attacks from enemy storm troopers. The compound Asura-rakṣas is interesting in that it could be regarded as a *dvandva*, and thus refer to a group comprising two classes of opponents, Asuras and Rākṣasas; or it could be a specific class of Rākṣasas (if the compound is a *karmadhāraya*). Within the context in which it occurs, however — Asura-rakṣas and Rakṣas are found almost exclusively in this type of conflict situation — it seems most likely that Asura-rakṣas refer to a group of Asuras who are "guard-scouts" of the Asura army. This image of an attacking army neatly fits into the metaphor of conflict that is applied to the sacrificial ritual. From this picture it seems that the Rakṣas, as well as guarding their own territory, engaged in incursions into enemy territory. The development of the term *rākṣasa*-marriage, in which the woman is carried off by force, and, if necessary, her male relations are killed (see Hara), fits that pattern.

In the context of the ritual, what appears to be the meaning is that there are potentially weak points in the ritual structure, as in the following example:

Hence if the Hotṛ recites by half-verses, let the Adhvaryu respond at each half-verse; and if he recites by *pādas*, let him respond at each *pāda*. For whenever, in reciting, the Hotṛ draws breath, there the Asura-rakṣas rush into the sacrifice: there the Adhvaryu closes it up by means of the response, so that the destroyers, the Rakṣas, cannot rush in; and thus he destroys the world of the sacrificer's enemies. (*Śata* 4.3.2.6)

Much of the exactness and detail of the ritual is designed to guard its basic efficacy. The scenario used as a legitimation of such carefulness is that of an army guarding and strengthening the strongholds against possible or actual enemy attack.

It is worth noting in passing that a number of verses in the *Atharvaveda* depend on one or other of these structures, though the myth is not given in detail and the focus of attention is the magical use of amulets and the like.

Indra placed them upon his arm in order to overthrow the Asuras. Indra did eat the *pāta* plant in order to overthrow the Asuras. (*AV* 2.27.3–4)

With the weapon with which the Devas drove away the Asuras, and with which Indra led the Dasyus to the nethermost darkness, with that, O Kāma, drive far away from this world, those who are my enemies! (*AV* 9.2.17)

With the *varaṇa* the Devas warded off the onslaught of the Asuras day after day.
This *varaṇa* upon my breast, the kingly, divine tree shall smite asunder my enemies, as Indra the Dasyus and the Asuras. (*AV* 10.3.2,7)

A number of myths from the Brāhmaṇas have specific details which are important in the stream of ideas flowing from the *Ṛgveda* through the Purāṇas.[7] Thus, ·besides the more generalized accounts of conflicts between Devas and Asuras, the ancient battle between Indra and Vṛtra is also utilized in the Brāhmaṇas in similar fashion (*Pañca* 12.13.4; Caland, 303):

Indra, saying: 'I will slay Vṛtra,' resorted to Prajāpati. To him Prajāpati gave this *anaṣṭubh* devoid of energy; by means of this verse Indra did not vanquish Vṛtra; because, being unvanquished, he roared [*vyanadat*], therefore the *nānada* [*sāman*] has its name.

This account concludes with Indra's conquest of Vṛtra with the help of Prajāpati.

Śata too has some accounts of the slaying of Vṛtra by Indra. In one Indra is victorious by means of the full-moon sacrifice (*paurnamāsa*) (*Śata* 11.1.3.5) and in another by means of a cake offering (*purodāśa*) (*Śata* 5.2.3.7).

There are two other accounts of particular importance in specifying the relationship of Bali and the Dwarf. In one it is recounted how the Devas won by means of a trick. The Asuras had routed the Devas and were in control of the three worlds, but the Devas, with Viṣṇu the sacrifice at their head, went to the Asuras, who granted them as much earth as Viṣṇu was able to lie upon. Viṣṇu is pictured in this story as a dwarf, but he is also the sacrifice, and he wins for the Devas the entire earth (*Śata* 1.2.5.1–7).

The second text utilizes another motif that becomes integral to the myth of the Dwarf and Bali — the *RV* tradition of Viṣṇu's three strides. But it is now linked with the theme, so common in the Brāhmaṇas, of the Devas winning over the Asuras. (*Aitareya* 6.15; Keith: 270):

> Indra and Viṣṇu fought with the Asuras; having conquered them they said 'Let us make an arrangement.' The Asuras said 'Be it so.' Indra said, 'So much as Viṣṇu three times traverses, so much be ours; let the rest be yours.' He traversed these worlds, then the Vedas, then speech.

In both of these there is a utilization of another motif that is common through the Brāhmaṇas and early Upaniṣads: that by means of the appropriate action the Devas win *all*. In the former it is the earth; in the latter the three worlds (which appear in these materials to represent the entirety of the universe of space). In this second piece other common totalities are added — the Vedas, and speech. (See *Chāndogya* 2.23.2–3 for a similar association of the worlds, the Vedas and speech.)

The question of good and evil, which O'Flaherty poses in relation to Devas and Asuras in the Brāhmaṇas, is important if we are to understand later developments. The first thing necessary is to ask whether the word "evil" is appropriate in this context; or if one must use it, what one implies. In the Christian case the concept of "evil" as it relates to negative human experiences and acts is highly

unified. It also takes on cosmic proportions (the "problem of Evil")
by virtue of its relation to the concept of God, who is also conceived of as unified and of cosmic proportions (though the latter is
something of an understatement). That is, the concept of evil develops the form that it does in Christian theology by virtue of the
defining of God as "perfectly good", as a corollary of which, among
other things, a strong opposition of good and evil is seen. In India
such a unified conception of negative forces is rarely seen. In cases
where the concept of God is similar to that of Christians, for example, in the theology of Rāmānuja, there are other features, such as
the doctrine of *karma*, that dissipate the problem of negative human experience (Carman, 176–79).

In considering the relation of the Asuras to evil in the period of
the Brāhmaṇas, one needs to look carefully at the context in which
we might find a concept or concepts approximating that of "evil".
In terms of the materials we have looked at above, we can say that
the Asuras represent a threat to the good life, a life of material
prosperity given symbolic focus in the three worlds, a life distinguished by supremacy and winning. The correct use of the
sacrifice on the part of the Devas adequately puts to naught this
threat. But the threat remains, and hence the necessity of a continuing careful attention to the cosmically potent sacrificial activity.

But then there is a secondary threat, hypostatized in the Rakṣas, that the potency of the sacrifice might be lost. The threat to
winning can be active again at a weak point in the defences of the
sacrificial system, so great care is needed to shield the chinks in the
sacrifice's armour.

Still, within the context of the practice of sacrifice, even with the
threats lurking in the background, the effects of the repeated variations of the Deva-Asura myth is to assure the sacrificer that the
sacrifice, properly performed, will stave off all threats. Prosperity
is assured for the Devas in the myth.

One can see the very interesting effects of this in an important
piece of speculation about the origins of the Devas and Asuras. I
cite the latter part of the cosmogonic myth recorded in *Śata*
II.1.6.1–11, the part relevant to our discussion (Winternitz, 1:224).

> [Prajāpati] placed reproductive energy into himself, and with
> his mouth he created the Devas.... After he had created

them, he saw that there was, as it were, daylight [*divā*] for him, and that is the divinity of the Devas, that after he had created them, he saw that there was, as it were, daylight for him. Now he created with the breath of life which is below, the Asuras.... And after they were created, he saw that there was, as it were, darkness. He knew: "Truly, I have created evil for myself, as there was darkness as soon as I had created them." And even at this early stage he smote them with evil, and their day was then already done. Therefore it is said: "It is not true what is reported of the battles between Devas and Asuras, partly in narratives [*anvākhyāna*], partly in legends [*itihāsa*], for at that time already Prajāpati smote them with evil, at that time already their day was done.".... After he had created the Devas, he made the day out of that which was light, and after he had created the Asuras, he made the night out of that which was dark. So there now existed day and night.

Here the negative experience of the sacrifice-prosperity complex personalized in the Asuras is extended in two different directions. In one, the vital breath of life (*prāṇa*) is polarized into a positive breath from the mouth and a negative (evil?) breath from the anus; this is then correlated with the polarization of Devas and Asuras, so that the Devas are created from the mouth of Prajāpati, and the Asuras from the negative breath. And then a further correlation is made with light and darkness.[8] Thus a radical negativizing of the Asuras has been achieved via body symbolism and the ready symbolism of day and night — all given a cosmic dimension.

This establishment of the Asuras in a negative mode is used to account for one of the ways in which the Asuras function in the sacrificial complex. They function negatively vis-à-vis the Devas because they originated negatively vis-à-vis the Devas. But then there is a further step which accounts for the other way they function. Having realized that he had created "evil", Prajāpati rendered them "evil": that is to say, having created something negative, like a bad smell, he rendered them negative, ineffectual: "already their day was done." Thus it can be said, as this text asserts, that the accounts of the battles between Devas and Asuras are not true — in the sense that one who knows of their origins knows that the Asuras cannot win. What one can perceive from the repetitive patterns of the myths about the Devas and Asuras is now accounted for in more cosmic and metaphysical terms.

In all of this, the concept of evil is very imprecise. Further light on it comes from an early strand of the Upaniṣads. In two parallel versions of a conflict between Devas and Asuras (*Bṛhadāraṇyaka* 1.3 and *Chāndogya* 1.2) victory is won by the Udgītha associated with the breath (*prāṇa*) in the mouth.[9] Before the victory is won, the Udgītha is associated in turn with the breath (*prāṇa*) in the nose, with speech (*vāc*), with the eye or sight (*cakṣu*), with the ear or hearing (*śrotram*), and with the mind (*manas*), and in each case the Asuras pierce (*vidh*) it with "evil" (*pāpman*).

In each case this *pāpman* is explained. The two texts treat it slightly differently. In *Bṛhadāraṇyaka* the key word is *apratirūpa*: "unfit, improper, inappropriate." *Pāpman* is the unfit thing that one speaks, smells, sees, hears, or imagines. In *Chāndogya*, in each case a contrast is used following the pattern: "Therefore with it one smells both the sweet-smelling (*surabhi*) and the ill-smelling (*durgandhi*) for it has been pierced with *pāpman*" (1.2.2). Thus, in relation to each of these "senses" there is a distinction between positive and negative characteristics:

smell	*surabhi* (sweet-smelling)	*durgandhi* (ill-smelling)
speech	*satya* (true)	*anṛta* (untrue)
sight	*darśanīya* (fit to be seen)	*adarśanīya* (not fit to be seen)
hearing	*śravaṇīya* (fit to be heard)	*aśravaṇīya* (not fit to be heard)
thought	*saṃkalpanīya* (fit to be conceived)	*asaṃkalpanīya* (not fit to be conceived)

In their speculation on the nature of reality as breath, these passages are similar to another in which the centrality of *prāṇa* is established and in which there is probably the implication that *prāṇa* is the true nature of the Ātman (*Chāndogya* 5.1.1–15). But one can see here also the beginnings of the systematizing that comes to its full height in the Sāṃkhya *darśana*, specifically in the class of *jñāna-indriyāṇi*, the organs of sense. However, only three of these (the nose, the eye, and the ear) are found in these Upaniṣadic passages. *Vāc* becomes one of the five *karma-indriyāṇi* (organs of action) in Sāṃkhya, and *manas*, the thought organ, stands alone alongside these other organs as clearly different from both groups.[10]

With respect to these early Upaniṣads, then, we can say that the senses, the faculty of speech, and the faculty of thought are perceived as infected with the possibility of positive and negative experiences. And except for the area of speech (where the characteristic word is *anṛta* = untruth), *pāpman* appears to connote something experientially unpleasant rather than some moral or ritual fault or error.

The crucial point in the discussion of *Chāndogya* 1.2 is that because the power of the breath is exclusively located in the mouth, the power is not divisible into positive and negative experiences. The Devas, who revere OM as the breath in the mouth, acquire all its potency, leaving no room for the negative Asuras in the hierarchy of power.

In these speculations, then, the negative association of the Asuras with the "breath from below" is carried a step further in a more general identification of Asuras as the origin of negative, unpleasant experiences. This, in turn, nominates them as negative symbols in a number of different contexts.

The contexts in which the Asuras compose the negative mode change from phase to phase of Indian religious history. Thus, the conflict situation of the Brāhmaṇas can be made the locus of a new message in the Upaniṣads. In *Chāndogya* 8.7–12, Indra as the leader of the Devas, and Virocana from the Asuras resort to Prajāpati for wisdom about the true nature of the Self (*ātman*). Virocana is satisfied with a superficial answer; Indra persists until he arrives at the true wisdom. Thus, as a new religious way develops, again the Devas are identified as the winners through their persistence in the (new) correct path.

B. The Conflict Motif in Epics and Purāṇas

In Epic and Puranic literature, the conflict motif is again employed. The threat to the Devas is more real, however, than in the Brāhmaṇas. A fairly standard pattern emerges. By some means — often through *tapas* — an Asura or a group of Asuras or some other demonic beings obtain extraordinary powers and eventually are so powerful that they are able to take over the control of the worlds from the Devas. Sometimes they are granted a boon by Brahmā, thereby becoming virtually invulnerable. Brahmā often appears a little foolish in this, though he is acting in accord with his nature in rewarding those who engage in a strict asceticism (*tapas*) (Hopkins, 175).

The result is that the Devas are routed. They resort to Brahmā, and together Brahmā and the Devas resort to the only one who is able to help. In Vaiṣṇava texts this is generally Viṣṇu, and in Śaiva texts, Śiva. In *Bhāgavata*, a typically Vaiṣṇava Purāṇa, for example, Śiva is resorted to on only two occasions — for the destruction of Tripura,[11] and for consuming the poison *hālahala* at the time when the primeval ocean is being churned. And even then, in each case the story is told in such a way that it serves to glorify the Blessed Lord Hari rather than Śiva (*Bhāgavata* 7.10; 8.7).

The dual role of Brahmā as helper of the ascetic demons and helper of the Devas is interesting as a pointer to discrepancies between different religious systems. *Chāndogya* 8.7–12, as we have seen, shows the Asuras as losers at the Upaniṣadic method. But according to later texts, one religious duty emphasized in the same Upaniṣad, *tapas* (see *Chāndogya* 2.23.1), is frequently acquired by Asuras or Rākṣasas, with troublesome results. In many cases the conflict of Devas and Asuras comes to be centred on the relation between *tapas* and *dharma*, with *bhakti* as an adjunct to *dharma*. But the fuller ramifications of this are best explored in the context of the idea of *avatāra*. Let us turn to a preliminary exploration of this.

1. *The Context of Avatāras*

One of the earliest clear references in Indian literature to what appears as a "doctrine" of descent (*avatāra*) — though the term is not used — appears in *BhG* 4.6–8.

Although I am unborn, and my Self is immutable,
and though I am Lord of creatures,
yet resorting to *prakṛti*
I come into existence [*saṃbhavāmiy*] by means of my own *māyā*.

> For whenever there is a decline of *dharma*, O Bhārata,
> and a rising up of *adharma* —
> then I send myself forth.
>
> For the protection [*paritrāṇāya*] of the good,
> for the destruction [*vināśāya*] of evil-doers,
> for the sake of the establishment of *dharma*
> I come into existence [*saṃbhavāmi*]
> in age after age.

At its most basic level this may be just a way of explaining how the one who is in human form talking as Kṛṣṇa to Arjuna can be the supreme being. However, there is also the suggestion that this is not a once-for-all appearance — Kṛṣṇa comes into existence in *yuga* after *yuga*. This is consistent with the Hindu view of cosmic history as a cyclical process, and also with the idea of transmigration or re-birth. With the latter idea, a direct link is made in *BhG* 4.5. Kṛṣṇa says:

> Many a birth have I passed through,
> And you have also.
> I know them all.
> But you do not know yours.

The mention of a number of appearances in somewhat casual fashion suggests that the tradition of *avatāra*s may have been accepted for some time in Kṛṣṇaite or Vaiṣṇava circles. It is important also to note that there is a specific purpose for Lord Kṛṣṇa's coming into existence: to destroy the wicked, to protect the righteous, and thus to establish *dharma* again.

The earliest list of *avatāra*s are found in *MBh*. At one point in the *Nārāyaṇīya*, it is said that Bhagavān creates many forms (*rūpāny anekāny*) for his appearances (*prādurbhāva*) (*MBh* 12.337.35). But the early lists are quite short. In the *Nārāyaṇīya* there are two such lists, one enumerating four appearances, and the other, six. The list of four follows immediately (v.36) from the statement about "many forms." They are Varāha (the Boar), Narasiṃha (the Man-lion), Vāmana (the Dwarf), and Mānuṣa (the Human). (In each case here an adjectival form is used; the substantive forms,

Varāha, Narasiṃha, and Vāmana, come to be regularly used as the names of God in the respective incarnational forms.)

This seems to be the original nucleus, for a similar list is found in *MBh* 3.100.9, and there are no shorter lists in extant materials. The other list in the *Nārāyaṇīya* replaces "Mānuṣa" by three— Rāma in the Bhṛgu clan; Rāma the son of Daśaratha; and Kṛṣṇa, referred to as "the appearance in Mathurā" (*MBh* 12.326.77–78). The list also places the three human births in relation to *yugas*— Rāma of the Bhṛgus in the Tretāyuga, Rāma Dāśarathi at the junction between the Tretā and Dvāpara *yugas*, and Kṛṣṇa between thē Dvāpara and Kali *yugas*.

The writers are interested in explaining the reason for the manifestations of Nārāyaṇa. In 12.337, the reason is that Brahmā has created so many creatures, including Daityas, Dānavas, Gandharvas, and Rākṣasas that the earth is oppressed with the burden. And many of these beings, having acquired *tapas*, receive the most excellent boons (v.30). Puffed up with pride, they oppress the hosts of *suras* (that is, the Devas) and the Ṛṣis. The purpose of Nārāyaṇa's several appearances is the removal of the earth's burden (*bhārāvataraṇam*), which is to be achieved by the chastening (*nigrahena*) of the wicked, and by the supporting (*pragrahena*) of the righteous.

In the other *Nārāyaṇīya* section (12.326), of which our Text 1 is a part, the reasons for the various descents differ, though certain patterns emerge. In each case there is a demon to be slain, except in the case of Rāma of the Bhṛgus, who exterminates the Kṣatriyas. In each case there is a possibly moral or dharmic aspect. Hiraṇyākṣa is arrogant on account of his strength (v.73: *balagarvita*); and Hiraṇyakaśipu is a destroyer of sacrifices (v.73: *yajñaghna*). Bali has confiscated the three worlds (v.75). The Kṣatriyas are abounding in power and possessions (v.77: *samṛddhabalavāhana*), while Rāvaṇa is horrific (*ghora*), the thorn of the worlds (v.81: *lokakaṇṭaka*). Often it is emphasized that these appearances are of value for all: the raising of the earth by Varāha will be for the welfare of all creatures (v.71: *sarvabhūtahitāya*); Kṛṣṇa and Arjuna will consume Kṣatriyas for the good of the world (v.9: *lokakāryārtham*).

At this point, then, the most basic ideas related to the incipient *avatāra* doctrine concentrate on the idea of a continued support of and concern for the well-being of the world and the creatures within it—a concern that is particularly related to the notion of order or *dharma*. These aspects also utilize very nicely the Vedic mythology of Viṣṇu. Viṣṇu's three steps for the prosperity of the three worlds, and his form as Dwarf in *Śata*, where he aids the Devas in defeating the Asuras, are now combined in the *MBh* picture. Other ancient stories are utilized in similar fashion, but what happens to them is evidence of what has sometimes been called "Vaiṣṇava syncretism." The Boar (Varāha) *avatāra*, for example, which is one of the forms in the basic list of *MBh*, is in *Śata* 14.1.2 a form assumed by Prajāpati in order to raise the earth from the primeval waters. The Matsya or Fish form, which becomes one of those frequently mentioned in Puranic texts, is also found in *MBh* (3.185) as is Kūrma (the Tortoise) (1.16.10–11), but neither is associated with Viṣṇu. Only later are these forms incorporated into the expanding system of *avatāra*s. The Buddha, who is included among lists of *avatāra*s relatively late, also appears to be interpreted in a way which is characteristic of Vaiṣṇava syncretism—a syncretism which also includes a decidedly sectarian intent. In *Viṣṇu* (3.17–18) there is an account of the appearance of the Buddha as an illusory form emitted by Viṣṇu in order to deceive the Daityas; this is clearly an attack upon the Buddhists, for they are being depicted as demons who have been misled by false teaching. This attitude persists through much Puranic literature (see *Bhāgavata*, 2.7.37), though in some late texts the Buddha is pictured in a much more positive light as an *avatāra* who out of compassion for animals rejected the Vedic sacrifices (see Miller,71).

Even though the situations that call forth an *avatāra* are quite diverse, they do bear in common a threat, a danger—to the worlds, to the Devas. It seems natural, then, that the role of the Asuras in the Brāhmaṇas should be repeated in these texts. The presence of Asuras and Rākṣasas is not invariable, though by the time one arrives at an advanced stage of the stories, such as one sees in *Bhāgavata*, the only two of the ten *avatāra*s accepted as major where the threat is not constituted by demonic beings are Paraśurāma (the threat is the Kṣatriyas) and Kalkin (who will overcome the Mleccas).[12] Thus the Fish retrieves the Vedas stolen by Hayagrīva, the king of the Dānavas (Bhāgavata 8.24.8). The Boar battles with the Daitya Hiraṇyakṣa (3.18.6). The Tortoise *avatāra* is undertaken in order that the Devas may be able to acquire the *amṛta,* the nectar of immortality, by churning the ocean of milk; the Asuras also help, but are tricked by Viṣṇu and are prevented from obtaining the nectar. The Man-lion tears apart Hiraṇyakaśipu, and the Dwarf recaptures the three worlds from Bali. It is also said that the birth of Kṛṣṇa takes place because the earth is burdened by a host of Daityas who are born as kings on earth (10.1.17; 1.13.48). In *Viṣṇu* (5.1.22–23) a number of Asuras who later appear in the story and are killed or overcome by Kṛṣṇa are mentioned at the beginning of the story: Kaṃsa, Ariṣṭa, Dhenuka, Keśin, Pralamba, Naraka, Sunda, and Bāṇa. In the Buddha form, the Lord uses trickery in order to lead the Asuras (*devadviṣam*) away from the Vedas; he teaches them *aupadharmya,* false doctrine (2.7.37).

But the relating of *avatāra*s to Asuras, etc. is only part of a complex of causes for descents. One can see this best if one looks at a range of accounts of one *avatāra,* the Boar.

2. *Symbolic Context of Varāha*

There are two main stories related to Varāha. The first is set at a time when the earth is sinking down into the primordial waters and Viṣṇu, in the form of a boar, raises the earth again and re-establishes it. The second is of the demon Hiraṇyākṣa who fights with the Boar and is eventually slaughtered.

MBh, in the critical edition, has only the account of the raising of the earth [12.202], as also the *Matsya* (247–48). *Agni* (4.1–3), on the other hand, recounts only, and very briefly, the story of Hiraṇyākṣa. The *Hariv. App.* [13] and *Bhāgavata* both have accounts of the two stories.

The cause of the submerging of the earth differs from account to account. In *Viṣṇu* it occurs at the beginning of this *kalpa* when the world is being re-created. The universe comprises a mass of water and the earth is submerged in water. Prajāpati (the relationship between him and Brahmā is not quite clear, though Brahmā is called the one having Prajāpati as Lord) desires to raise the earth and so takes the form of a Boar, as he had formerly taken form as Matsya, Kūrma, and so forth (*Viṣṇu* 1.4.8).

In other accounts, however, the earth is weighed down by the mountains. The *Hariv. App.* and *Matsya* accounts are very similar at this point. There are said to be three major agents of the sinking of the earth — the weight of the mountains (*Hariv. App.* 42, line 121; *Matsya* 248.6), oppression by Dānavas and Rākṣasas (*Hariv. App.* 42, line 144; *Matsya* 248.54), and the *tejas* of the Lord. In explanation of the latter, it is said in *Hariv. App.* that the celestial waters flowed down on to the earth, and bearing the *tejas* (presumably here meaning "energy, power") of the Lord, they pushed the earth down to Rasātala. In *Matsya* also (248.9) the earth is described as "oppressed by the *tejas* of Bhagavān."

In these accounts, then, there is a heaping together of various explanations for this calamity: on the one hand a naturalistic explanation, in the weight of the mountains; then a typical relating of the calamity to the oppression of the world by demonic beings; lastly, and most strangely, a suggestion that is not really developed, that there is something inherent in the relationship between God's power and the world which caused the resultant instability.[14]

In the *Bhāgavata* account the context is, as in *Viṣṇu*, the creation of the universe at the commencement of the Varāhakalpa. Svayambhu Manu asked Brahmā to provide a place for him and his offspring since "the earth which was the home of all creatures has been submerged in the great flood."

Brahmā placed his confidence in the Lord from whom he has sprung, and from his nostrils came a tiny boar, and in a moment it stood in the sky and increased to the size of an elephant. This boar, being then praised by those dwelling in various heavenly regions, Janaloka, Tapoloka, and Satyaloka (v.25), raised the submerged earth on his tusk.

Despite the setting of different backgrounds, all these accounts agree in the central event of the story — the raising of the earth from Rasātala by means of the boar's tusk.

According to *Viṣṇu*, when the earth has been raised, it rests upon the waters "like a great boat" and does not sink "on account of the flatness of her body" (*vitatatvāt tu dehasya:* 1.4.46). In *Viṣṇu, Hariv. App.,* and *Matsya* there follows a mention of the ordering and dividing up of the earth. In the case of *Matsya* it is given in one short statement (248.78): *pṛthivīpravibhāgāya manaś cakre* "He decided to make divisions on the earth". In *Viṣṇu* (1.4.47,49) the account is more detailed:

Having made the ground level,
the Blessed Lord, the One without beginning, the Supreme
    Lord,
heaped up the mountains on the earth
in proper order.

Then having properly divided up the earth
into the seven continents
he, as formerly, created the four worlds,
this world and the others.

Viṣṇu then moves into the further creation by Hari, "the Blessed
Lord having four faces." The phrase thus suggests that Viṣṇu
takes form as Brahmā the creator.

In these accounts, then, there is some lack of clarity as to the origin of the earth's instability, but there is no doubt at all that the
central decisive act of the Lord in taking the form of a boar is the
consolidation of the earth, giving it stability and order.

As we have seen, one major story of the Boar is centred on the
raising of the earth from the primeval ocean. The inclusion of the
demons in this account is a later development, for in the earliest
accounts of the Boar, before it is associated with Viṣṇu, there is no
mention of demons. The raising of the earth is part of a story of
creation. *Taittirīya Brāhmaṇa* (1.1.3.5) has this story:

> The universe was formerly water, fluid. With that water Prajā-
> pati practised arduous *tapas,* saying "How shall this universe
> be developed?" He noticed a lotus-leaf lying on the water. He
> thought, "There is something on which this lotus-leaf rests."
> Having assumed the form of a boar, he plunged beneath it.
> He found the earth down below. Breaking off a portion of her,
> he rose to the surface. He then spread it out on the lotus-leaf.
> (See also *Śata* 14.1.2.11)

It is difficult to determine exactly how developments take place,
but it is obvious that the inclusion of the demons in the account of
the raising of Earth either reflected or gave rise to the other major
story associated with the Boar. In *Agni* (4.1–3) there is a very brief
account of the Boar:

Agni said:
I will describe the descent of the Boar
for the destruction of evil.
Hiraṇyākṣa was the lord of the Asuras,
and having conquered the Devas
he settled himself in heaven.

Viṣṇu was praised by the Devas
who went to him.

He became a boar, with the form of the sacrifice,
and he slew that thorn, the Dānava,
together with the Daityas.

Accomplishing the protection
of *dharma,* the Devas, and so on,
Hari then hid himself.

Hariv. App. 42 gives basically the same account, but in much greater detail. In this account, the effects of Asuric domination are likened to the conditions at the time of dissolution; the Asura army is likened to Death in the dissolution at the end of a *yuga* (line 227). There is a very vivid account of the battle in which the Devas are conquered, and a similarly detailed picture of the slaughter of Hiraṇyākṣa by the Boar.

When the battle is over, the Devas acknowledge their devotion to Hari: "We desire to serve your feet." If in *Agni* the Boar is described as "accomplishing the protection of *dharma* and Devas" (*dharmadevādirakṣākṛt*), in *Hariv. App.* he is seen as giving instructions to the Devas concerning their duty in protecting the world and in effectively rewarding the virtuous — ascetics or those who are truthful, heroic, generous — by allowing them to enjoy heaven. The Boar also instructs the Devas in punishing the evil — the lustful, the avaricious, the atheistic — by sending them to hell (lines 610ff).

3. *Symbolic Contexts in Bhāgavata*

The *Bhāgavata* version of Hiraṇyākṣa draws upon motifs similar to those in *Hariv. App* and *Agni.* Thus, the Daitya so terrified the

Devas that they hid themselves "like snakes terrified of Garuḍa (*tārkṣyatrastā iva ahayah*)" (3.17.22). He is seen by Brahmā as one who commits offences against, and produces fear in, the Devas, Brāhmans, cows, and all innocent creatures (3.18.22). Again the metaphor of the thorn (*kaṇṭaka*) is used. But the portrayal here is related to what one finds in other parts of *Bhāgavata*, where *dharma*, the Vedas, sacrifice, *yoga*, rites (*kriya*), knowledge (*jñāna*), and *tapas* all have Vāsudeva as their source or goal (1.2.28–29); where Brāhmans, cows, Vedas, *tapas*, *satya*, control (*dama*), peacefulness (*sama*), faith (*śraddhā*), generosity (*dayā*), and so forth are all forms of Hari (10.4.41). One finds a similar portrayal of the Daityas surrounding Kaṃsa, who vow to slay the Brāhmans, the readers of the Vedas, ascetics, those engaged in sacrificing, and cows (10.4.39–40). These Daityas are pictured as enemies of *sanātana-dharma*. Similarly (8.24.5):

> The Lord assumes forms
> desiring the protection
> of cows, Brāhmans, Devas, *sādhus*,
> and also of the Vedas,
> and of *dharma* and *artha*.

One can see here a tendency to group together positive symbols from various phases of the development of Hindu culture and to paint the Asuras as a threat to or the enemy of such beings or ideals.

Another way in which the threat is portrayed in the *Bhāgavata* is through the ominous portents which attended the birth of Hiraṇ-yākṣa and his twin brother Hiraṇyakaśipu from Diti (3.17.4): "The earth, along with the mountains, shook. All the quarters were aflame." The description runs the gamut of inauspicious signs and portents — meteors, comets, strong winds, darkness; disturbances on ocean, lake and river; cries of jackals, dogs and asses; birds leaving their nests, animals excreting faeces and urine together, cows giving blood as milk, clouds showering pus; images of gods weeping, trees falling down without any wind to uproot them.

The conclusion that people draw from these great portents is what one might expect: they think it is the inundation of every-thing (*viśvasaṃplava*) — presumably at the time of dissolution.

A similar picture of horrific sights arises in the midst of the battle between Hiraṇyākṣa and the Boar. This time they are products of Hiraṇyākṣa's *māyā*. They have a similar effect upon those watching; everybody is terrified and thinks that it is the dissolution of the universe. Also, when Hiraṇyākaśipu engaged in *tapas* (7.3.4–5),

> As a result of his *tapas*
> from the top of his head
> a fire with smoke arose.
> It burnt the middle, the upper and the lower worlds,
> consuming everything.
> The rivers and oceans were agitated,
> the earth with its continents shook.
> The stars and the planets fell down,
> and the ten regions were ablaze.

These three images move in somewhat different landscapes, so it is clear that the *Bhāgavata* poet does not think consistently in any one pattern about the origin of these portents. They may be due to a kind of cosmic sympathy, or they may result from the Asura's *māyā* or *tapas*. One thing stands out clearly, however, and that is that the ascendancy of such horrific creatures is accompanied by terrifying events within the cosmos.

All of this is part of a series of contrasting symbols evident in the portrayals of the *avatāra*s and their demon opponents. Thus, in contrast to the association of evil portents and horrific events with the Asuras, there is an association of auspicious signs and beautiful conditions with the presence of an *avatāra*. When Hari was born in the dwarf-form as Kaśyapa's son, (8.18.4):

> The quarters and expanses of water were calm,
> creatures were happy,
> and the seasons were abundant with riches.
> The sky, the mid-region, and the earth,
> the gods, the cows, and the twice-born,
> were overjoyed —
> and so were the mountains.

And while the birth of Hari makes all the world joyful, the powers of the world complemented by the stars and planets who shed their influence render his birth auspicious (*dakṣina*). In addition, the hosts of the heavens and other regions—Apsarās, Gandharvas, Siddhas, Munis, Manus, Devas, Pitṛs, Yakṣas, Rākṣasas, etc.—all sing and dance in praise of the Lord (8.18.8–10). Later, when Kṛṣṇa is born, the conditions within the universe are expressed in virtually identical terms (10.3.1–8).

Similarly, when Rāma is king, the world is at its best, and whatever Rāma's subjects desire is provided. There is no pain or sorrow or fear, nor even death for those who do not desire it (9.10.13–14). And when Kṛṣṇa is in Vṛndāvana, we are continually reminded of the paradisical conditions that accompany his presence. Even creatures with a natural enmity—the lion and the lamb, as it were—live together peaceably (10.13.59–60).

This contrasting in *Bhāgavata* of conditions attendant upon the ascendancy of the Asuras and of Hari serves to give a cosmic scope to the Lord's battle with demonic powers. Thus Brahmā prays the Boar to conquer and slay Hiraṇyākṣa and establish the worlds in peace. When the Asuras are in power, the entire universe is out of joint and everything is in danger. The defeat of the Asuras sees a return of peace and happiness and prosperity, and the auspicious signs at the birth of the Lord are a prefiguring of this.

The praise of all creatures at the time of Hari's birth as Vāmana is also paralleled by the frequent paean of the praise of the Lord by all beings at the time when he defeats the Asuras. In the Varāha story, the main hymn occurs when the Lord is raising the earth, and the central emphasis is upon the Lord as the sacrifice. At the time when Nṛsiṃha has torn to pieces Hiraṇyakaśipu, many different groups of beings join in a hymn of praise to the Lord. The hymn of each group is intimately related to its *dharma;* each praises the Lord, it appears, because it has been restored to its most characteristic duties (7.8.40–56). Indra, for example, notes that the portion of the sacrifice belonging to the Devas has been restored to them, and the prosperity of the Devas, expropriated by Hiraṇyakaśipu, has been restored. The Siddhas, who had lost their *siddhi*s, because Hiraṇyakaśipu had taken away their powers by virtue of his superior power, praise the Lord because he has destroyed the Asura who was so insolent on account of his achievements.

In his *avatāra*s, then, Viṣṇu is pictured in much Epic-Puranic writing as the great cosmic hero, the winner of cosmic battles against forces which are *adharmic,* which upset cosmic stability, which endanger the three worlds and the creatures within them, which trouble and terrify the good, and which are at enmity with the representatives of true religion. He is a military hero, the Viṣṇu presented iconographically with discus and mace, the Kṛṣṇa who as a child kills many demons, and then after killing the tyrant Kaṃsa, becomes king, and engages in many battles against other kings — who, we are reminded, are also Asuras who are overburdening the earth.

Viṣṇu is the maintainer of *dharma,* the protector of the good. And therefore he is the one who protects those who call upon him. The *Bhāgavata* account of Indra's defeat of the Asuras (6.8) includes a prayer for protection addressed to the Lord. The request is for protection in every situation of life. A large number of the names by which the Lord is addressed refer to the *avatāra*s, while most of the others refer to his weapons.

One of the most interesting stories of protection is that in *Bhāgavata* of the elephant who is caught in the jaws of a mighty crocodile and takes refuge in the Lord. His prayer for deliverance moves ·gradually into the expression of a desire not for deliverance within the world, but for deliverance in its ultimate sense of *mokṣa.* This is a movement which is characteristic of the way Vaiṣṇavas have read the great heroic deeds of the Lord in his *avatāra*s. Somewhat paradoxically, the major implication that can be drawn from the Lord's deliverance of the world from the forces of disorder and instability within the cosmos is that he is able to rescue the devotee from the cosmos entirely.

I have referred extensively to the *Bhāgavata,* a relatively late text which, as we shall see below, has another significant dimension to add to the approach to inimical beings. In its expansiveness the *Bhāgavata* offers many sidelights on the pattern in which the treatment of Asuras in relation to *avatāra*s becomes part of a portrayal of a painful threat to the stability of the universe, to the right order of things, to the place of the Devas, to the appropriate reverence for Vedas, Brāhmans, cows, etc.

Most of the major *avatāra*s eventually come to be linked with Asuras or Rākṣasas. That this happens relatively late in accounts of the Fish, and that in the *Bhāgavata* account of Kṛṣṇa there are

more Asuras added beyond what is given in *Viṣṇu* and *Hariv. App.*
suggests that there might have been an increase in the tendency
towards "demonizing" the accounts.

One other feature of these Puranic elaborations should perhaps
be noted. The picture in the Brāhmaṇas of a series of contests
between the Devas and Asuras is developed into a Puranic tradition of twelve wars between the Devas and Asuras. *Matsya*
47.41–54 lends further definition to the tradition by naming each
war (some of the names deriving from Viṣṇu's *avatāra*s), and by
relating to each of several wars a major Asura who is slain or
defeated. In tabulated form the tradition appears thus:

WAR	NAME	VERSE	ASURAS ASSOCIATED	VERSE
1st	Nārasiṃha	(42)	Hiraṇyakaśipu falls	(46)
2nd	Vāmana	(42)	Bali bound	(46)
3rd	Varāha	(43)	Hiraṇyākṣa slain	(47)
4th	Amṛtamanthana	(43)	Prahlāda	(48)
5th	Tārakāmaya	(43)	Virocana slain	(48)
6th	Āḍībaka	(44)		
7th	Traipura	(44)	Dānavas	
8th	Andhaka	(44)	Asuras, Piśācas, Dānavas	
9th	Vṛtraghātaka			
10th	Dhātra			
11th	Hālāhala		Vṛtra	
12th	Kolāhala			

A notable feature here is that this is quite different from the
more usual order in which these Asuras succeed each other: Hiraṇyākṣa, Hiraṇykaśipu, Prahlāda, Virocana, and Bali.

C. Bali—Myth A, Phase 1

Within this general context of developing portrayals of the *ava-*
*tāra*s it is now appropriate to look at the specific Phase I accounts of

Bali and Vāmana. A tabulation of basic units occurring in these accounts is given in Appendix B. Obvious from the tabulation are:

(1) Text 1 is very brief, gives few details.

(2) Only two of the five units of Text 1 are found in Text 2.

(3) All five of Text 1 units are found in Text 4, as also all eleven units of Text 2, suggesting that the writer of Text 4 either knew and drew on both these texts or carefully presented a comprehensive account of the myth as it was at that stage of development.

(4) If one puts together events that are recorded at least three times in the first four texts (and that means virtually a counting of Text 1 and 2 *together* as one text), one has a concise outline of the basic events of the myth: Bali overcomes the Devas—establishes his kingdom—Viṣṇu is born of Kaśyapa and Aditi as a Dwarf—Bali sacrifices—the Dwarf goes to the sacrifice—he begs three strides—Bali grants three strides—Viṣṇu strides—Kingship is returned to Indra.

Of the five stages of the general pattern for *avatāra*-myths outlined above (p. oo), only (1), (4), and (5) are represented here. The approach of the Devas to Viṣṇu (3) occurs only in *Rām*. In many of the later versions of the myth it occurs with extensive variations, and Hacker's suggestion (38) that these form a typically Puranic devotional pattern seems correct. Motif (2) is also absent, and the fact that it was not developed at this stage may have left the way open later for a considerable elaboration on the benevolent conditions of Bali's kingdom. Nevertheless, the suggestion that things are not right when an Asura takes over the control of the worlds is there in the texts, though it is presented in different ways. In Text 1 the focus is so much on Indra's loss of his kingdom and on the subsequent restoration of the kingdom to Indra along with the return of the Devas to their places that the decisive action of Viṣṇu is clearly a result of the threat to the supremacy of Devas. In Texts 2 and 3, the key phrases are "for the welfare of the world (*lokahitāya*)" (line 64) and "intent on the welfare of all creatures (*sarvabhūtahite*)" (v. 10), the former referring to Viṣṇu's birth, the latter related to his striding. The logical implication is that the victory of Bali was not conducive to the welfare of all creatures.

Text 4 does not develop this opposition but rather allows the event to stand as a grand theophany. Just as *BhG* could be seen as culminating in a manifestation by Kṛṣṇa of himself as Lord of the

universe, so could this version (vs. 82–83). Also, as in the *BhG* theophany, there is an emphasis on the brilliance of this manifestation (vs. 79–80). As well as giving depth to the reference in Texts 2
and 3 to Viṣṇu's *tejas,* this latter takes up quite effectively Viṣṇu's
solar associations which appear in earlier materials.

As this survey shows, these texts provide us readily with what
becomes the accepted basic account of Bali and the Dwarf. But
they give no indication of how it might have originated. However,
scattered through *MBh,* there are enough references to Bali to
suggest another, more primitive scenario. While there are some
fairly typical references to Bali and the Dwarf (3.100.21, 2.299.12,
5.10.8), and also some stray references (3.29.1–5, 5.32.23) significant in their import to Myth B (see Chapter 3 below), the largest
number of references is to a fierce battle between Bali and Indra.
Thus:

> Then that one of great *tejas,* Jarāsaṃdha, the tamer of his foes,
> stormed at Bhīmasena as the Asura Bali once stormed at
> Indra. (2.21.8)

> People crowded together and watched that most terrifying
> duel between Śālva and the champion of the Vṛṣṇis which was
> like that between Bali and Vāsava. (3.18.11)

> The battle of the two became fearsome and hair-raising, this
> battle of Bhīṣma and the Pārtha, like that of Bali and Vāsava.
> (4.59.10)

Two other references are from a description by Arjuna of his
riding in Indra's chariot. In one section, Indra's charioteer Mātali
says (3.168.19–20):

> There once was a mighty war between the Devas and the
> Asuras for the sake of the Elixir, Pārtha, and I witnessed it, O
> faultless one. At the killing of Śambara there was a fierce
> battle, and then too I drove the chariot for the king of the gods.
> Likewise I drove the horses when Indra slew Vṛtra and I saw
> the grisly battle of Vairocana. All these gruesome wars I have
> witnessed, but never before did I lose my wits, Pāṇḍava.

The suggestion is that in all of these battles Indra was the winner, including that against Vairocana, which is another name for Bali, the son of Virocana. This is confirmed in a statement of Arjuna (3.165.15):

> Thereupon I set out on that sparkling chariot on which the Lord of the Gods once vanquished Bali Vairocani.

Related to this is another list of those vanquished by Indra (3.165.19). Again Śambara and Vṛtra are included, along with other famous demons, Namuci, Vala, Prahlāda, and Naraka.

Like Vṛtra Śambara has been pictured as an opponent of Indra from *RV* on. What appears to have happened is that Indra's conflicts against Vṛtra were expanded into numerous conflicts with Daityas and Dānavas, and a developing list of Daitya and Dānava "principals" became the basis for the specifics of Indra's victories. Bali would thus seem to have been introduced as a great opponent of Indra who was vanquished by him. Indeed, from the frequent use of the battle between Indra and Bali in similes (a parallel to the uses of Indra v. Vṛtra) it appears that Bali may have begun to rival Vṛtra as Indra's greatest opponent, and chief of the Asuras.

Should this be the case, as seems likely, then this and the fact that, unlike Vṛtra, Bali had no great heritage in Vedic literature, would constitute a plausible explanation of why Bali should have been co-opted as a great opponent of Viṣṇu (such co-opting, of course, being quite in keeping with the incorporation of other myths into the Vaiṣṇava corpus.) *MBh* 5.10.7f ("You have fetched the Elixir, Viṣṇu, and killed the Daityas in battle. Having smitten the great Daitya Bali, you have made Śakra the overlord of the Devas") suggests that one version of the Viṣṇu-Bali story may have been a conventional battle-scene, as was also the winning of *amṛta* by the Devas). At any rate, drawing on the Vedic accounts of Viṣṇu, an amalgam was developed utilizing the picture of Viṣṇu as Dwarf (*Śata* 1.2.5.1–7) and the recurring motif of the three strides.

The ending of Text 2 contains an unusual feature that may indicate a tradition earlier than the others; namely that it is the earth that is taken with three strides and then given to Indra. As Hacker has indicated, this suggests a stage in which the three strides are conceived as being taken horizontally over the earth. Such would be consistent with the account of the Dwarf in *Śata,* where Viṣṇu the Dwarf wins the earth. However, the reference to Viṣṇu's highest step in *RV* 164 indicates that the idea of a vertical striding is not a late one, so that the picture of horizontal strides may well be a later variant, being perhaps an attempt to bring the striding into line with *Śata.*

Another uncharacteristic feature of Text 2 invites some discussion: "The Devas thereby became manifest and the universe was called 'Vaiṣṇava.'" (line 82). The combination of these two ideas suggests that previously the universe was not Viṣṇu's and the Devas were not manifest. It is impossible to determine precisely what this means but it suggests a number of ideas:

(1) There is a suggestion in the Ṛgvedic account of Indra and Vṛtra that until Indra won the battle, the universe was Vṛtra's. Such a view could easily be interpreted more generally to say that the universe was formerly under the control of the Asuras.

(2) Such a picture would not be inconsistent with the accounts in the Brāhmaṇas, even though, as we have noted, the emphasis is on the triumph of the Devas.

(3) It would also correlate quite well with a portrayal in the Brāhmaṇas of the Asuras as the elder brothers of the Devas. There are obviously variant speculations about the relations between the two groups. One, we have seen, has them both arising from the body of Prajāpati. By the time of our texts 1–4, it is established that the group of Devas called Ādityas and the group of Asuras called Daityas are step-brothers, both groups the children of the great Ṛṣi Kaśyapa, the Daityas by his senior wife Diti, the Ādityas by his junior wife Aditi. This picture, not found in the Brāhmaṇas, appears to be an attempt to fill in the details of the "elder brother" tradition.

The elder brother idea is interesting from another perspective. One can see both in ancient Mesopotamia (Frankfort, 182–98) and in ancient Greece (Hesiod, *Theogony,* 455–506) a portrayal of the gods of the present age as the latest generation of gods, this portrayal resting upon important accounts of the displacement of the parent deities by their children. A similar process of evolution may have been mediated via a slightly different family relationship, that is, the displacement of elder brother(s) by younger brother(s), a motif also seen in Jewish mythology in the well-known story of Jacob and Esau (Genesis 25–35) and possibly that of Cain and Abel (Genesis 4).

(4) Whether one should thereby infer that the elder group of deities was once worshipped, perhaps being the deities of an earlier group of inhabitants, is a question that has been raised in relation to all three areas, Mesopotamia, Greece, and India. In India the situation is exceedingly complex. Still, some clear statements can be made: (a) The term Asura was associated in *RV* with a class of quite positive divine beings, including Varuṇa. (b) This class appears to have been displaced from a position of supremacy by the Devas. (c) Varuṇa, one of the original Asuras, became a Deva, and remained a positive, if rather minor, figure. The word Asura came to be used exclusively for a group set in opposition to the Devas. (d) No doubt from the military context of the life of the Aryans, there is a tendency to assimilate the Dasyus (the indigenous peoples encountered by the invading Aryans) and the Mleccas (those who speak unintelligible languages) with the Asuras. Whether one can go further and infer that the significant figures of the developing families of the Asuras — Bali, for example, — were originally deities of the pre-Aryan inhabitants of India is a question that becomes more insistent as we move through this study of Bali. At this stage it is sufficient to say that there is no direct evidence within Sanskrit materials up to the time of the Epics that this was the case.

(5) Staying within the context of the Sanskrit materials, it seems possible to infer that the passage being discussed means that the Asuras under Bali were formerly in control of the universe; but now a new age has begun — the Devas are in control and the universe is Viṣṇu's. (In keeping with this interpretation stands the fact that in Text 2 there is no reference to Indra's former control of the universe, no suggestion that Bali took it from him.)

(6) If this is an accurate interpretation of the verse, then another scenario becomes possible, that at an earlier stage of the developments of this myth, the lordship of the universe was at first Bali's and then Bali lost this "*indra*"-ship to Indra or Devendra, the lord of the Devas.

It is this scenario that stands at the base of the second myth of Bali, to which we now turn.

3

Myth B

In *MBh* 12.216–18 and 220–21, there are two versions of an encounter between Bali and Indra. The first is presented in full (Text 6). Since the pattern of the second is very similar to the first, as also are many of the ideas, I present it in summary form with some direct citations where these are deemed appropriate.

Text 6
[*MBh* 12.216–218]

Yudhiṣṭhira said:

1   Tell me, grandfather, by what wisdom a monarch, stripped of prosperity and crushed by Time's club, should live on earth.

Bhīṣma said:

On that, they tell this ancient story of a discussion between Vāsava and Virocana's son, Bali. Having conquered all the Asuras, Vāsava approached the Grandfather Brahmā and bowing to him with joined hands inquired thus about Bali:
"Although continually giving away his riches
Bali was never in want.

But now I do not see that Bali—
I cannot find him, Brahmā.

He, indeed was the setting sun,
he illuminated the four quarters.
He unwearied, caused the rains
to fall at the proper season.
But now I do not see that Bali—
I cannot find him, Brahmā.

He was Vāyu and he was Varuṇa.
He was the Sun and the Moon.
He was the fire which warms all creatures
and he was indeed the Earth.
But now I do not see that Bali—
I cannot find him, Brahmā."

Brahmā replied:

7   "It is not becoming that you inquire thus about Bali. But one who is questioned by another should not tell a lie; therefore I will tell you about Bali. He is perchance about to be born in an empty house as the most excellent among camels or cattle or asses or horses, O Lord of Śaci."

Indra said:

"If I come across him in the empty house, tell me, Brahmā, should I slay him or not?"

Brahmā said:

"Do not injure Bali, Śakra. Bali is not deserving of death. Rather you should request such instruction as you desire."

Bhīṣma said:

Thus addressed by the Blessed One, the great Indra then wandered the earth. He was seated on the back of Airāvata and he was attended by the marks of his prosperity. Then he saw Bali, clothed in the form of an ass, and living in an empty house, as Brahmā had said.

Śakra said:

13   "You have arrived at birth as an ass! Here you are a chaff-eater, Dānava! This birth of yours is certainly lowly! Are you vexed about it or not? I am astonished to see what has never been before—you under the sway of your enemies, bereft of

prosperity, abandoned by friends, and your heroism and prowess gone. You moved around, surrounded by a thousand chariots and by your kinsmen, scorching all the worlds and disregarding us; the Daityas had you as their leader, were under your sway, and at your command the Earth bore crops without being ploughed. But today you are overtaken by this calamity. Are you vexed about it or not?

17   "When you stood brilliant on the eastern shore of the ocean, sharing your wealth among your kinsmen, what was then your state of mind? You sported many, many years, rendered splendid by prosperity as thousands of divine women danced. All wore lotus garlands, all were in appearance like gold. What was then your state of mind, O lord of the Dānavas? You had an enormous umbrella made of gold and adorned with jewels, and forty-two thousand Gandharvas used to dance before you. When you sacrificed, you had an enormous sacrificial post, entirely gold, and then you made gifts of ten thousand times ten thousand cows. Engaged in sacrificing, you traversed the whole earth, according to the rule of the hurling of the *samyā* What was then in your heart? I do not see now your golden jar, nor your umbrella nor your fan. And I don't see the garland given you by Brahmā, O king of Asuras."

Bali said:

"You do not see the golden jar, nor the umbrella nor the fan. And you do not see, Vāsava, the garland given to me by Brahmā. You ask about my jewels: they are hidden in a cave. But my time will come, and then you will see them.

"This conduct of yours is not appropriate to your fame or your family: You are prosperous and you desire to mock me who am in adversity. Those who have acquired wisdom, those who are contented in knowledge, the calm, the virtuous, the learned — these neither grieve in times of adversity nor rejoice in times of prosperity. On account of your materialistic mindset you are vaunting yourself, Purandara. When you are as I am, then you will not talk like this!"

[12.217]

Then Indra, intent on prolonging the discussion, laughingly said to Bali who was sighing like a snake, "You journeyed around, surrounded by a thousand chariots and by your kinsmen, scorching all the worlds and disregarding us. But now, observing your exceedingly wretched condition, and having been deserted by your relatives and friends, O Bali, do you grieve or not? Formerly unequalled joy was yours and the worlds were under your control. About this fall, do you now grieve or not?"

Bali said:

5 "Considering all this to be transitory, subject to the course of time, O Śakra, I do not grieve. For everything has an end. These creaturely bodies, king of immortals, are transitory. Therefore, O Śakra, I do not grieve. Nor is this form due to any fault of mine. Having departed, the life-principle and the body are born together. They grow together, they perish together. Entirely free, I have attained to this birth. Since I know this, what worry can there be for me? Death is the end of creatures as the ocean is for rivers. The persons who know this well are not infatuated, O wielder of the thunderbolt.

10 "Those who, overwhelmed by passion and infatuation, do not know this, and those whose judgment has been destroyed, sink under the weight of calamity.

"A person who acquires understanding destroys every fault. Freed from sin, he acquires goodness; established in goodness, he becomes serene. But those who turn away from goodness are born again and again; urged on by misfortunes, these wretched ones are in anguish. Success and misfortune, life and death, which result in happiness and suffering—these I neither spurn nor desire. For neither of these is the conqueror, neither the one who slays nor the slain. O Maghavan, anyone who, having slain or conquered, brags of his manliness, should know he is not the actor—but that there is another actor who acts. Who performs for them the destruction and creation of the world? It has been performed by that which has been performed; and the real actor is another. Earth, wind, space, water, and light—these elements are the origin. So what's the use of lamentations?

"One possessed of great learning, and one of little learning, the powerful and the powerless, the beautiful and the ugly, the fortunate and the unfortunate—Time carries off all of these, inscrutible in its energy [*tejas*]. If I have come under the sway of Time, what is the use of anguish at my defeat? A person burns only what has been burnt, and he slays what has been slain, he destroys what has been destroyed before, he takes what is ready to be taken.

"In this ocean there is no island. And where is the other shore? And this side cannot be seen. Contemplating this divine ordinance, I do not perceive its end. If I did not see that Time destroys all beings, there might be for me joy and pride and anger, O lord of Śacī. You are lording it over me, having ascertained that I have assumed the form of an ass, and knowing that I am subsisting on chaff and am living in a house completely devoid of people. But even now, if I wish, I can project several terrifying forms of myself—and if you saw them, you would certainly flee! Time gives everything and Time receives everything again. All is ordained by Time. Do not brag about your heroism, Śakra. Formerly, Purandara, when I was angry everything was agitated. But I know the eternal *dharma* of this world. And now that you also have observed it, do not let yourself be overawed by it. Power and its origin are not at all under one's control.

28 "Your mind is indeed juvenile. It is still now as it was formerly. Concentrate on understanding, Maghavan—find what is constant. Devas, men, ancestors, Gandharvas, snakes and Rākṣasas were all under my control—this you know, O Vāsava. Infatuated by ignorance, creatures used to seek refuge in me saying, 'Honour to that region where Virocana's son Bali is staying.' O husband of Śacī, I do not grieve for the loss of honour, I am not sorry for my fall. My understanding is firm in this respect. I abide under the sway of the Ordainer.

32 "One can observe sometimes that someone born in a good family, handsome, of great prowess lives along with his friends in sorrow. For that is what was destined to happen. Similarly, someone born in a low family, ignorant, of sinful birth, O Śakra, is observed living happily with his friends: for that is what was destined to happen! An auspicious and beautiful woman, Śakra, turns out to be a shrew, and a woman with neither auspicious marks nor beauty is seen to be happy. This condition we've arrived at is not our doing, Śakra, nor is yours

achieved by you, O Wielder of the thunderbolt. It is not something done by you nor something not done by me from which our respective conditions arise. Prosperity and the lack of it come in regular succession. I see you in splendor, established as king of the Devas, prosperous, brilliant and roaring at me. It would not be thus except that Time has attacked me and is standing by; if it were not so, I should have felled you with my fist, even though you are armed with the thunderbolt. But this is not the time for heroism; the time for forbearance has come. Time establishes everything and Time brings things to fruition. If Time approaches me, the powerful Lord of the Dānavas, he will not bring me to roaring and burning with energy or anything else like that. The combined *tejas* of all the twelve illustrious Ādityas, including yourself, O king of the Devas, was assumed by me, single-handed. It was I who lifted up the waters and sent them forth as rain, O Vāsava, and it was I who provided the triple world with heat and light. I protected and I destroyed, I gave and I received. The powerful lord in the worlds, I used to bind and unbind. But today that power of mine is ended, O lord of immortals. All of these no longer surround me in splendor, now that I have been attacked by the armies of Time! I am not the actor, and neither are you, nor is anyone else the actor, O lord of Śacī. The worlds are consumed by the regular movement of Time. People who are well-versed in the Vedas say that Time has as its body months and half-months, is clothed with day and night, has the seasons as its sense-organs and the year as its mouth.

47   "Some people, on account of their understanding, say that this entire universe should be thought of as Time. But from contemplation I am convinced that it is five and fivefold. Brahman is deep and mysterious, like a vast ocean of water. It is said to be without beginning or end, indestructible and supreme. Although it is itself without a distinguishing attribute, it is with attributes when it enters into elements. Those people who discern the truth regard it as unchangeable. One thinks concerning the death of someone, 'He has gone!' But he is not such that you can talk of his going, nor is he other than *prakṛti*. Not having gone the way of all beings, whither will you go? All the five sense organs cannot perceive him who kills not those

who flee, who standing still is not slain. Some call him Agni, and others call him Prajāpati; some call him the seasons, month and half-month, some the days and moments. And others the morning, the afternoon, noon, and also an instant. Thus people speak differently of him who is one. Know that this is Time, under whose sway is the entire universe.

54 "Many thousands of Indras have passed away, O Indra, all endowed with strength and prowess. So also you will pass away, O lord of Śacī. When your hour has come, heroic Time will cause you also to disappear—you who are the exceedingly powerful Śakra, the king of the Devas, drunk with power. This Time takes away the entire universe. Therefore, Śakra, be firm. Time cannot be overcome by you or me or those who have preceded us. That royal Prosperity [Śrī] that you have attained and of which you think, incorrectly, 'She has been possessed by me!'—she does not stay in one place. For she has dwelt in thousands of Indras, all superior to you. This fickle one has left me and gone to you, O lord of the Devas. Do not be overbearing again, Śakra. You should become calm. Having come to you this way she will soon abandon you and go to another."

[12.218]

Then he of the hundred sacrifices saw Śrī, in her own brilliant form, go out from the body of Bali. Then seeing her shining with radiance, the blessed chastiser of Pāka, Indra, his eyes expanded in wonder, asked Bali, "O Bali, who is this one who was stationed in you but has left you? She is radiant, decked with plumes, her upper arms adorned with bracelets, and blazing with her own *tejas*."

Bali replied: "I do not know whether this golden one is an Asura woman or a divine or a human one. You ask her. Or do as you wish, Vāsava."

Śakra said, "O you who have issued from Bali, radiant, adorned with plumes—who are you? I do not know who you are. Please tell me your name, O you of sweet smiles. You who stand here like Māyā herself, blazing with your own *tejas,* having deserted the lord of the Daityas—who are you? O beautiful woman, tell me truly who you are."

Śrī said: "Virocana did not know me, and Virocana's son Bali knew me not. The learned call me Duḥsahā and Vidhitsā. And they also call me Bhūti, Lakṣmī and Śrī. You do not know me, Śakra. None of the Devas knows me."

Śakra said: "O Duḥsahā, is it on account of what has been done by me or what has been done by Bali that you are now leaving Bali after dwelling in him for a long time?"

Śrī said: "Neither the Creator nor the Ordainer commanded me in any way. It is Time, Śakra, that moves me from one place to another. Do not, O Śakra, scorn Bali."

Śakra said: "How is it that Bali has been deserted by you? What is the reason, O goddess adorned with plumes. Why is it that you are not abandoning me? Tell me, O lady of sweet smiles."

Śrī said: "I abide in truth, in gifts, in vows, in *tapas*, in prowess and in *dharma*. Bali has turned aside from them. He was always devoted to Brāhmans, truthful and controlled his passions. But he became jealous of Brāhmans, and though impure he touched what was possessed by them. Formerly he was engaged in sacrifices; but then, with his mind infatuated and harassed by Time, he told the whole world, 'Sacrifice to me.' Having been discarded by him, I will dwell with you, O Śakra. I should be borne with vigilance, with *tapas* and with prowess."

16 Śakra said: "O you who abide amid lotuses, there is not one person among Devas, humans and all other creatures, who is able to endure you."

Śrī said: "O Purandara, certainly there is not even one Deva or Gandharva or Asura or Rākṣasa who is able to endure me."

Śakra said: "Tell me, auspicious one, what I should do so that you may abide in me forever. Tell me the truth."

Śrī said: "O chief of Devas, learn how I may be able to abide in you forever. Divide me fourfold according to the ordinances laid down in the Vedas."

Śakra said: "I will assign you according to power and strength. May there be never any offence of mine, O Lakṣmī, when I am near you. Among humans, it is Bhūmi, the origin of all, who is the upholder. She will be a fourth part of yourself. In my opinion, she is suitable."

Śrī said: "This quarter of myself has been yielded up and established in Bhūmi. Thcrefore, Śakra, make a proper place for my second quarter."

Śakra said: "Among humans, the waters flowing along are beneficial. Let the waters bear a quarter of you. The waters are sufficiently enduring."

Śri said: "This quarter of myself has been yielded up and established in the waters. Therefore, Śakra, make a proper place for my third quarter."

25   Śakra said: "The Devas, the sacrificers, the Vedas, are established in Agni. Agni will uphold your third quarter when it has been duly placed in it."

Śrī said: "This quarter of myself has been yielded up and established in Agni. Therefore, Śakra, make a proper place for my fourth quarter."

Śakra said: "Among humans there are those who are good, devoted to Brahmā, speaking the truth. Let them bear a quarter of you. The good are sufficiently enduring."

Śrī said: "This quarter of myself has been yielded up and established in the good. Protect me, O Śakra, having been deposited in creatures."

Śakra said: "I have deposited you in different creatures. Any who offend you will be chastised by me. Thus let my words be heard."

30   Then the king of the Daityas, Bali, who had been deserted by Śrī, said: "As much as the sun shines in the east, that much it also shines in the south and the west and the north. But when the sun stands still at midday, then there will be again a battle between the Devas and Asuras, and I will then be your conqueror. When the sun, standing fixedly in one place, burns up all the worlds, then in the battle between the Devas and Asuras, I will conquer you, O Śatakratu."

33   Śakra said: "I was given directions by Brahmā that you should not be killed. It is only on account of that, Bali, that I do not hurl my thunderbolt at your head. Go wherever you wish, O lord of the Daityas. Peace to you, O great Asura. There will never be a time when the sun standing in mid-heaven will burn up the worlds. The course of the sun was formerly established by Svayaṃbhū. He moves perpetually according to

this rule and warms creatures. For six months the sun goes on its northern course; for six months on its southern, by this means creating heat and cold for the worlds."

37   Thus addressed by Indra, Bali the chief of the Daityas proceeded towards the south, while Purandara went towards the north. The thousand-eyed Indra, having heard that speech spoken by Bali, which was characterized by freedom from egotism, ascended to heaven.

Text 7
[*MBh* 12.220–221]

In this version there is a subtle difference from Text 6 in Bhīṣma's first statement to Yudhiṣṭhira [220.3.5]:

"For one who has been deprived of sons and wives and pleasures and wealth, and has been immersed in terrible calamity, fortitude is the best attitude. The body of one possessed of fortitude is not emaciated: on account of that health of body he again acquires prosperity. That king whose people are established in *sāttvik* conduct, dear child, for him there is in all actions firmness, patience and perseverence."

There then follows an introduction to the conversation between Indra and Bali in which the reason for Bali's loss of the worlds is indicated in terms that fit those we have seen for Myth A, Phase I, in the context of a battle between Devas and Asuras [7–9]:

After the battle took place between the Devas and Asuras, in which [many] Daityas and Dānavas perished, after the worlds had been traversed by Viṣṇu and Śatakratu was king of the Devas, and after the deities had been offered sacrifices and the four-fold order of men was re-established, the three worlds increased in prosperity and Brahmā was filled with pleasure.

When Indra comes upon Bali, the latter is in a mountain cave on the seashore. When he sees Indra in all his splendour and surrounded by hosts of Devas, Bali neither grieves nor trembles, but stands unperturbed and fearless. When Indra, surprised at this, asks Bali why, he replies, as in 217.19–22, that all is destroyed by Time. But then in a piece reminiscent of Śrī's speech in 218.10.12–13, Bali also says that the Asuras were devoted to *dharma*, devoted to the Vedas and to Vedic rites, intent on keeping vows, possessors of great learning, free of pride, generous, and they behaved properly. But again he returns to Time, and indicates that the wise neither rejoice at prosperity nor lament in times of adversity. Indra concurs, praising him for his wisdom. Observing that Bali is bound by the bonds of Varuṇa — earlier, Bali has indicated that he is bound by Time's cords — he predicts that these bonds will be loosened in the course of time in consequence of human misconduct (220.111–14):

> When the daughter-in-law compels the aged mother-in-law to work; when the son, through delusion, commands the father to work for him; when Śūdras have their feet washed by Brāhmans and have sexual relations fearlessly with wives of Brāhmans; when men discharge their semen into forbidden wombs; when the refuse of houses begins to be carried upon plates and vessels made of white brass; and when sacrificial offerings are borne upon forbidden vessels; when the four *varṇa*s transgress every restraint — then these bonds of yours will begin one by one, to loosen.

At this point in the first account Indra sees a female form leave Bali, learns that it is Śrī and then receives a teaching by Śrī. In the second version there is a break in which Yudhiṣṭhira asks what are indications of future greatness and future fall (221.1) and Bhīṣma introduces the "old story of the discourse between Śrī and Śakra." The setting is different — Nārada and Indra, standing on the banks of the Ganges worshipping the rising sun, see another luminous object approaching them from the west and this turns out to be Śrī.

After a description of her magnificence and some indications of her characteristic qualities, she tells of her residing with the Asuras (221.25–26):

> I also reside for ever with persons that are firmly attached to virtue, that are endued with great intelligence, that are

devoted to Brahman, that are truthful in speech, that are possessed of humility, and that are liberal. Formerly I dwelt with
the Asuras since I am bound to truth and *dharma*. But when I
learnt that the Asuras had reversed their natures, I resolved to
dwell in you!

When Indra asks for further details, an extended account is provided of the virtues of the Dānavas. It concludes with a statement
that is of special interest since it indicates the prosperity of the
Dānavas over many *yuga*s, and gives a specific and quite different
interpretation of the influence of Time (221.48–51):

Since the Dānavas were distinguished for these good qualities,
I dwelt with them from the beginning of the creation through
many *yuga*s. But then Time changed, and there was a change
in the qualities of the Dānavas. I saw that *dharma* deserted
them and that they came under the sway of desire and anger.
Those inferior in qualities resented those superior in all ways,
and when the elders sat in the assemblies and related stories
which told of truth, they ridiculed them. When the elders approached, the younger ones, seated at their ease, refused to
honour them, as they had done formerly, by rising up and
greeting them with respect.

Again there follows a detailed account of their base conduct
(*ādīnācārān*), the reversal of their former nature (*viparyaye*) [221.79]
and the dwelling of Śrī with Indra. (See a similar explanation for
Śrī's desertion of Bali in *MBh* 12.90.24–26.)
The conditions that attended the presence of Śrī are given in
some detail (221.89–92):

The sky became luminous and showered *amṛta* upon the region
of the self-born Grandfather. The celestial kettledrums began
to sound without being struck, and all the directions, becoming clear, were ablaze with splendour. Indra poured the necessary rain upon the crops and no one strayed from the path of
dharma. The Earth became adorned with many mines filled
with jewels, and various melodious sounds hailed the triumph
of the Devas. Eminent human beings, taking pleasure in
virtue, all adhered to the auspicious path that is trod by the

righteous. Humans and Immortals, Kinnaras and Yakṣas and Rākṣasas, all were renowned for their prosperity and cheerfulness. Not a flower, much less fruit, dropped untimely from a tree, even if the wind shook it. All cows began to yield sweet milk whenever desired, and not a harsh word was uttered by anyone at all.

Bali: Indra's Wise Teacher

The two versions are so clearly variants of the one event that the relation between them deserves study. Hiltebeitel, in his discussion of these passages (156–66), allows the two to stand as variants which, taken together, reveal important features of the nature of the goddess Śrī. While it seems legitimate for Hiltebeitel to do this, given the context in which he is working (a generalized understanding of Śrī's relationship to rulers), for our understanding of the development of the character of Bali it is important to analyse the relationship between the two texts.

Help towards such analysis is afforded by the context of the texts. As Bali is Indra's teacher in 216–17 and in 220, so is Prahlāda in 215 and Namuci in 219. In each case the setting is similar to what it is in the Bali versions: Indra finds Prahlāda dwelling in an empty chamber (215.5: *śūnyāgāra niveśanam*), Namuci sitting devoid of propersity (219.3: *śriyā vihīni*). Prahlāda is pictured (215.4–6) as free from stupefaction (*astambham*) and pride (*ahaṃkāram*), firm in goodness (*sattvastham*), devoted to vows (*samaye ratam*), accepting praise and censure equally (*tulyanindāstutim*), restrained (*dāntam*), neither being angry (*akrudhyantam*) nor rejoicing (*ahṛṣyantam*), and regarding equally gold (*kāñcane*) and a clump of earth (*loṣṭe*). Namuci (219.2) is conversant with the birth and death of all creatures, unperturbed like the ocean (*akṣobhyam iva sāgaram*).

Indra's question is virtually the same each time: he observes that they are fallen from their position, bound with cords, under the sway of foes, divested of prosperity (215.11; 219.3). He asks Prahlāda why he is not grieving (*śocitavye na śocasi*); he asks Namuci whether he is sad or cheerful (*śocasyaho na śocasi*).

Prahlāda replies that he who knows the origin and destruction of created objects is never stupefied; that he who regards himself as the doer of acts is wrong—it is nature (*svabhavataḥ*). And he concludes by arguing that one should live "without attachments, without pride, without desire, free from bondage" (215.29: *nirmamo nirahaṃkāro nirīho muktabandhanaḥ*).

Namuci similarly stresses that the one who knows the Ātman and the non-Ātman does not fear calamities, and neither languishes in sorrow nor rejoices in happiness. The wise are not stupefied when affliction comes, but are contented under both happiness and sorrow (219.16).

Two themes not found in Prahlāda but found in the first version of Bali are those of the ordainer (*śastā*) and Time (*kāla*). These are linked in the Namuci version. One obtains what is ordained. Pleasure and pain are the result of Time (219.16).

A point worth noting is that many of the same themes recur in these different stories but in different contexts. Prahlāda does not expound on the Ātman, but Indra acknowledges his knowledge: "You know the Ātman (215.10: *ātmānaṃ manyamānaḥ*)." Similarly, Namuci is not described in these terms, but he expounds on knowing the higher and lower (*parāvarājñas*).

In general terms, one can see a common message being presented by Prahlāda (215), Bali (216–17), and Namuci (219) — either ·via their direct teaching or in the way things are portrayed. They uphold an awareness that all is transitory. The person who is thus aware is unaffected by the dualities of happiness and sorrow, prosperity and adversity, or praise and censure. He is unattached, and unperturbed, not stupefied. More positively, he is constant, firm, and restrained.

The basis of such awareness and detachment is given a fairly unified form in such concepts: the power of Time; the control of a supreme Actor or Ordainer; and the significance of another dimension other than that of this world characterized by birth and death, creation and destruction, that is, — Brahman, Ātman.

The question of how we are to understand these teachings is brought nicely to focus if we consider a verse found in another part of the epic (5.32.23):

> King Bali examined the fruits of acts,
> Non-being and being, the present and transient,
> And failing to find the farther shore,
> Concluded that nothing but Time was the cause.

The conclusion that Bali's reference to Time (*kāla*) is related to his not finding "the farther shore" (*pāram avindamāno*) is open to the interpretation that the teaching of Bali here is wrong, that perhaps he is a member of one of the unorthodox sects. If one looks in detail at the three presentations in 12.215–19, Namuci comes closest to the Ājīvika view (12.219.10–11):

> Whatever is to be obtained by this fellow,
> that is what he gets. Whatever is to be,
> that is the way it is. One dwells in whatever
> womb one has been placed in, not wherever
> he himself desires to be.

Yet neither Prahlāda's nor Namuci's teaching is negativized in 12.215–19, nor is Bali's directly, though there are, as we shall see, problems in relation to Śrī's statements. Certainly it is not true to say that Bali does not find the farther shore, though he does ask, "And where is the other shore?" (217.21). But he refers to Brahman (217.48–53), as the Prahlāda and Namuci discussions refer to Ātman. Again, if one notes how important in *BhG* and some of the later Upaniṣads are the themes noted above, one has to conclude that Prahlāda, Bali, and Namuci are made to stand together as wise teachers of Indra and thence of Yudhiṣṭhira. Thus in the *BhG*, for example, the early sections, where the problem of killing one's kinsmen is discussed, attempt to establish that the true self does not act, and also that the things of this world are transitory. And as the argument progresses, the central emphases are upon living a life unattached to the fruits of one's actions, freedom from desire and anger, and the ability to regard equally pleasure and pain, or good fortune and misfortune.

A confirmation of this interpretation of these sections is found in *MBh* 12.173.3: "It was through wisdom that Bali, Prahlāda, Namuci and Maṅki succeeded in attaining their goal when they lost their prosperity. What is there that is superior to wisdom?"

If these Asuras are being shown as able to teach Indra something significant, then the question of how that is possible is also raised. What suggests itself is this: the Asuras are regularly portrayed in the Brāhmaṇas — and the portrayal is carried through into the Epic in a military rather than a ritual context — as those who, having been in the ascendency, lost to the Devas. They are thus in a fine position to present wisdom about how one should act when one has lost one's kingdom, about how one should respond to adversity. The context of the discussions is one that pervades a great deal of the literature of the late Upaniṣads and of the early Buddhists: the painfulness of existence (such ubiquitous themes as *duḥkha* and *saṃsāra*), the transitoriness of everything, and the importance of non-attachment.

The developing portrayal of the special rivalry between Bali and Indra, of which we have seen evidence above, makes it likely for Bali to receive special attention. One can see this rivalry throughout 216, for it is only at the beginning of 217 that the conversation between Indra and Bali gets to the crucial questions. (In the Prahlāda and Namuci accounts things move much more quickly to this point.) Chapter 216 is a rather forceful setting of the scene, a highly graphic portrayal of the former prosperity and magnificence of Bali and his kingdom.

That setting also underscores the contrast between Bali's present condition and that of Indra, which is now as Bali's used to be. Bali utilizes precisely this contrast to make the point at the end of his wise discussion that there will be many thousands of Indras. Indra, therefore, he says, should not be insolent; he should know that Prosperity is fickle.

This mention of Prosperity (Śrī) becomes the occasion for a concrete, personified demonstration of what Bali has said. Indra sees a female form leave Bali[1] and learns that it is Śrī. Indra asks why she has left Bali, and is given an answer that corresponds to that of Bali himself. The answer is, Time. When Indra questions her further, however, her answer strikingly differs from what Bali had said. Śrī indicates that she abides "in truth, in gifts, in vows, in *tapas*, in prowess and in *dharma*" (218.12); Bali has turned aside from these. She has deserted Bali (or alternatively, she has been discarded by Bali) because Bali has ceased to be good. Clearly, it is not only the inexorable process of time but self-chosen moral qualities as well that determine the duration of prosperity.

After some discussion about how Indra may retain Śrī permanently—such a possibility is in marked contrast to all that has been said in the first part of the account—Bali returns and predicts that when the sun stands fixed in one place and burns up the worlds he will conquer Indra; Indra says that this will never happen.

The clear discrepancy between Śrī's first reply to Bali and the later linking of prosperity and virtue suggests a reworking in such a way as to attempt a radical shift in the impact of the total story. The shift is not an unexpected one, given the resurgence of emphasis in India upon *dharma* in the period following one that was characterized by interest in such concepts as *saṃsāra* and detachment.[2]

But this reworking of the account is really not very successful. The second account of Myth B (Text 7) appears to be a further reworking of the story so that Bali and Śrī agree: once the Asuras were good; Śrī goes to those who live in accord with *dharma*. Śrī herself makes the point at great length when she contrasts the way the Dānavas were and what they later became (221.24–26; 49–79).

As Bali in the first part of this second version continues to speak of Time, so also does Śrī, but in such a way as to rob the word of the connotations it has in the first version and in the first few lines of Bali's reply to Indra in this version. Time is brought within the context of the linking of *dharma* and prosperity. The lesson propounded is that the Asuras lost their prosperity because in the course of time they left the path of *dharma*.

The overall message that comes through the second version is thus *not*, "Endure the vicissitudes of time with patience, calmness, firmness, detachment," but, "Do that which is right, dharmic." The brief discussion of Time in the old vein by Bali becomes something of a *pūrva-pakṣa*:[3] Bali, having appropriately described the situation in keeping with the rest of this version goes off into a discussion about Time, but his interpretation of events clearly misses the point. Śrī is then introduced and she thoroughly explains the interconnection of *dharma* and prosperity.

This is all in keeping with the milieu of Texts 1–5. Not surprisingly, the introductory context is that of Viṣṇu's three strides. Also the felicities attendant upon Śrī's presence (see p.107 above) are similar to those associated with the birth of the Dwarf or the reign of Rāma (p. 77). Yet the milieu is somewhat different from Milieu 1, for there is now a *clear* indication that the Asuras are not inevitably negative figures. It is admitted that once upon a time they were good, and when they were good they were prosperous.

It should be noted how different this critique of the Prahlāda-Namuci-Bali view of adversity is from that suggested in the citation (p. 72 above) from *MBh* 5.32.23. The point is not that Bali fails to find "the farther shore," something beyond the ocean of *saṃsāra* (that is, *mokṣa* or *nirvāṇa*, or a transcendent reality such as Brahman). Instead, the critique is directed within the context of life in the world, and is solidly based on the *karma*-complex, that is, on the idea that good deeds have good effects. Thus, prosperity attends goodness, and when *dharma* is ignored or forgotten, prosperity is lost. The loss of Śrī by Bali is a demonstration of this teaching in the most concrete and direct form possible.

The doctrine of *karma*, related as it is to the ongoing experience of being reborn, is usually more complex than this presentation, in that it does not normally correlate present prosperity and present goodness. Rather, in the classic statement in *Chāndogya* (5.10.7) these are related sequentially on a time line: present goodness ——→ future good conditions. In his teaching of Yudiṣṭhira in *MBh* 12.220.3–5, Bhīṣma introduces something of that complexity when he says that if one who has lost prosperity is established in fortitude and *sāttvik* conduct, he will transcend calamity and again acquire prosperity.

Two further observations are relevant to our discussions. The first has to do with the idea of the binding of Bali. There is no reference to this in our first version, though both Prahlāda and Namuci are described as bound with cords. It is introduced in the second version where, as we have noted, Indra predicts that Time's cords will be loosened in consequence of human misconduct. The milieu being that of *dharma*, the inference seems to be that one day things will be so bad at the human level that Bali, an Asura, and therefore (in accordance with what we have seen of Myth A in its first phase) a symbol of *adharma*, will be released.

The second observation is that with the reversal that transforms Asuras into wise teachers, the way is opened up for such a presentation to continue. Although I have not considered the text significant enough to warrant a major discussion, I think it should be noted that in the *Yogavasiṣṭha* Prahlāda and Bali are again vehicles for the teachings of the wise, similar in many respects to their functioning in Text 6. The pattern is also similar in that

Vasiṣṭha utilizes stories of the past to teach Rāma, as Bhīṣma does to teach Yudhiṣṭhira (5.3.3–14):

> There is in this massive universe, in a certain cavernous part, a world situated below the earth called Pātāla. In that abode of a great multitude of Asuras the son of Virocana, Bali, was the Dānava king. Having as decoration the wide expanse of earth which he had with ease completely conquered, he accomplished a rule by the Daityas for ten crores of years. Then as numberless *yuga*s went by, and as multitudes of Devas and Asuras rose and fell, and as the pleasures of the three worlds were constantly enjoyed by him, Bali the leader of the Dānavas became agitated. Standing one day on the roof of his palace, he began to reflect as follows:
>
> "What is the benefit of this great reign, exercised wonderfully in the three worlds and bringing me great enjoyment— what is the good for me in this they call pleasant, when the full measure of enjoyment is a momentary sweetness that inevitably passes away? A beautiful woman is embraced again and again enjoyed: this spirit of the youthful makes the great ashamed. Why are the intelligent not ashamed when they have performed again and again, day after day, a mass of actions, the pain of which has been experienced? Day and night come round again, and again there is an endless succession of actions. I consider that the continual deception of the intelligent. Among actions continually performed or that should have been performed what action is there that cannot be analysed? What is there other than experience that does not pass away?"

Bali is then given instruction by his *guru* Śukrācārya (of whom much more later) about *jñāna*. He eventually begins meditating and enters *samādhi*. The description of the result is reminiscent of the picture of Bali in *MBh* 12.216–17 (5.3.65–68):

> Then those Dānava servants of Bali together quickly climbed to the top of that crystalline palace. After spending a long time in *nirvikalpa samādhi*, the noble-minded Bali woke up there in their presence. Then the son of Virocana performed there all

his royal duties, with his mind freed from thoughts of "I" and "mine". And he perceived with equal eye adversity and prosperity. And that wisdom about the nature of happiness and suffering neither disappeared nor appeared.

There is a major point of difference between the *Yogavasistha* picture of the wise Bali and these *MBh* accounts. In *MBh*, Bali's wisdom is set thoroughly against the background of the loss of his kingdom. In the *Yogavasistha*, however, Bali, like the Buddha, becomes profoundly dissatisfied although he is surrounded by everything that this world affords. This scenario suggest that it is not just those who, like Yudhisthara, have lost all, but also those who are still enjoying worldly pleasures, who may be led by Bali's example to find a deeper wisdom.

But it is important to note that as well as introducing the picture of the wise Asura later reproduced in *Yogavāsistha*, *MBh* 12.215ff. also opens up the possibility of the Asuras as devotees. If by virtue of their defeat the Asuras acquire wisdom that the Devas do not possess, it may be that they can also know something of devotion that is beyond the Devas.

4

Myth A, Phase 2

In Phase 2 of Myth A there are five texts for consideration (texts 8–12). Text 8 (*Agni* 4.5–11) has already been introduced (pp. 20–21). Of the others, Text 9 (*Harivaṃśa App.* 42B), Text 10 (*Matsya* 244–46), and Text 11 (*Vāmana* 48–52; 62–68) are so similar that I have elected to reproduce only the *Matsya* text *in toto*, especially because the texts are too extensive to be reproduced individually. Discussion of the central issues will, of course, require citation of significant sections of texts 9 and 11.

Text 12 (*Kūrma* 1.16) is reproduced here in full. It is a relatively short piece but important because one might think of it as a transitional text that could be placed with ample reason in Phase 3, which we shall analyse in Chapter V. The evidence is mixed because the issues dealt with in this text are almost entirely those in the other texts of Phase 2 but the milieu is occasionally closer to what we generally find in Phase 3.

There is another version, Text 5, which might be thought to belong to Phase 2. It is virtually identical with lines 2855–2914 of Text 9. Is it then a brief excerpt from Text 9 representing its central event? Or is it the original statement of that event, which Text 9 used later, word for word, as its own core while building up the rest of the account from other diverse sources?

These questions are impossible to answer definitively. Hacker (556–60) and Tripathi (239) draw different conclusions from the evidence. The editors of *Hariv.* relegate Text 9 to the Appendix of that work while retaining Text 5 as part of the critically accepted text of *Hariv.* But this does not clarify the issue as well as one might hope, for the method used in determining the critical text seems unduly stringent.

My reason for deciding to include Text 5 in Phase I, dissimilar as it is to the other texts from this phase, was that the general milieu seemed to me to be the same. To take the most striking elements in particular, the battle between the Devas and the Asuras, though not found in Texts 1–4, appears in other short pieces from this phase, especially in the brief *MBh* passages. In addition, we may consider the extensive listing of Asuras (vs. 70–77). While this might suggest a later stage of development of the myth, it is certainly not out of place in the earlier, basically Epic, period. In Text 5, as characteristically in the short texts from this phase, generally such a list first occurs in the early part of an account, rather than towards the end, as in Text 9 where, given the very extensive treatment of the war between Devas and Asuras occurring much earlier in the account, such a list is redundant.

Text 10
[*Matsya* 244–46]

1   The Ṛṣis said:

You have related to us in detail the *dharma* of a king and also marvellous omens and the meaning of dreams. Now you should describe to us again the greatness of Viṣṇu—how, having become a dwarf he bound the Dānava Bali, and how there occurred that form of Hari stepping over the three worlds.

Suta said:

The ascetic Śaunaka was formerly asked that question in Kurukṣetra at Vāmanāyatana by Arjuna when he was on a pilgrimage. When Arjuna broke his promise about living with Draupadī, he went on a pilgrimage. In the field of *dharma*,

Kurukṣetra, at Vāmanāyatana, an image of Vāmana had
been installed. When Arjuna saw the image of Vāmana he
asked, "Why is this Deva worshipped, who assumed the form
of a dwarf? How did the Blessed One in boar form come to be
worshipped in former times? And how did this field come to be
dear to Vāmana?" Śaunaka's reply was as follows:

8   Without overly much detail I shall relate to you further the
glory of Vāmana and of the wise Varāha, O joy of the Kurus.
Formerly when Indra was banished and the Devas were conquered, the one who had given birth to the Devas contem-
plated their return. And Aditi performed a supremely difficult
and powerful *tapas* for a thousand years, O King: seeing her
sons expelled by the Daityas, O joy of the Kurus, she worshipped Kṛṣṇa in silence, and subsisting on air. And in des-
peration thinking, "In vain have I given birth to sons!" she
gave reverence to Hari with loving words. Awaking to her
highest end she worshipped Hṛṣīkeśa, Deva of Devas, Hari,
the omnipotent one. And she said:

12   "Praise to the destroyer of all pain,
       Praise to the one who wears a lotus garland,
       Praise to the highest source of prosperity,
       Praise to the primal creator.
       Praise to the one of lotus eyes,
       Praise to the lotus-navelled one,
       to the husband of Śrī, to the tranquil one,
       to the one of peaceful splendour
       the one bearing the discus.
       Honour to the origin of the one sprung from the lotus,
       Honour to the source of the Self.
       Honour to the bearer of conch and sword
       Honour to the one whose seed is gold.
       To the one who is knowledge of the Self,
       discrimination, to be considered as the *yogin*,
       the *ātmayogin*.
       To Hari, in the form of Brahman,
       free from qualities and distinctions,
       in whom the universe is established
       but who is not perceived by the world.
       Honour to that Deva, having forms

both subtle and gross, and bearing the conch;
whom humans do not see,
even though they see the universe entire. . . .

The hymn continues in a similar style of praising Viṣṇu by calling to mind his various forms and attributes.

33   In this Lord of all is all the truth
        I have spoken.
        There is no falsehood in him.
        I adore that unborn, undecaying Viṣṇu.
        If Janārdana is that truth
        which I have described — and more besides —
        by that truth may all my wishes
        be fulfilled."

Thus adored, the Blessed Lord Vāsudeva, invisible to all creatures, manifested himself to Aditi and said to her:

"O Aditi, your wishes will without a doubt be fulfilled — by my grace, O virtuous one. Hear me, O eminently fortunate one. What wish you bear in your heart, that desire of yours will soon come to fruition. For a vision of me will never go fruitless."

Aditi replied:

38   "If you, O Lord, affectionate toward your devotees, are pleased with my devotion, let my son Indra be lord of the threefold world. By the great Asuras he has been deprived of his kingdom and his share of sacrificial offerings. If you who grant wishes are pleased, let him receive these. That my son's kingdom was taken away is not the cause of my distress, O Keśava. That through enmity he has lost his share is the cause of my heart's sorrow."

The Blessed One said, "My grace is given to you, O goddess, in accordance with your desire. With a portion of myself I will be conceived in your womb from Kaśyapa. When I have been born from your womb I will slay the enemies of the Devas. Go, and be happy."

43   Aditi said: "Have mercy, O Lord of Lords; honour to you, O origin of all: I shall not be able to bear you in my womb, O Keśava. In you everything is established; you are yourself the

Lord, everything: I shall not be able to bear such a heavy burden as you in my womb!" The Blessed One replied: "That is true, O highly fortunate one. All this world is upheld by me. The Devas along with Indra are not able to bear me. Indeed I support the whole universe, with Devas and Asuras and men, all things mobile, immobile, and also you, Devī, also with Kaśyapa. Blessed are you. Do not be anxious. There will be neither fatigue nor pain for you when I am in your womb. O Aditi, my grace, which is very difficult for others to obtain, I give to you. When I am in your womb I shall by my *tejas* cause the decline of any who is an enemy of your sons. Do not be afraid."

49 Having spoken thus, the Lord thereupon immediately disappeared, and in time he entered her womb. Then when Krṣṇa was in her womb, the entire world shook, the great mountains trembled and the oceans heaved. Wherever Aditi went, placing her beautiful foot, there the earth bowed down from fatigue, O king. And, as had been predicted by the Supreme One, the decline of all the Daityas' *tejas* set in when Madhusudana was in her womb.

[245]

Then the lord of Asuras, Bali, seeing the Asuras bereft of *tejas* asked his own grandfather Prahlāda: "Sir, how is it that the Daityas are now suddenly devoid of *tejas* like a fire that has gone out; as though they have been struck by Brahmā's rod. Is it the bad luck of the Daityas? Or has an instrument of destruction been built by their enemies so that the Asuras, having been deprived of their *tejas*, may be destroyed?"

Thus questioned by his grandson, the wise lord of the Daityas meditated for a long time, and then said to Bali the king of the Asuras, "The mountains tremble, the earth is bereft of its natural firmness, all the oceans have been churned, the Daityas have been rendered devoid of *tejas*. The planets do not move, as formerly, in concert with the movement of the sun, and the supreme Lakṣmī is subject to the desires of the Devas. The calamity is great, not insignificant, O Lord of the Dānavas. This is what you should realize, O tormentor of the Devas."

8 Having thus addressed the Dānava lord, that best of Asu-

ras, Prahlāda, the perfect devotee, concentrated his mind on Hari, the Lord of the Devas. Then Prahlāda, engaging in the pleasing discipline of concentration, travelled to where the Deva Janārdana was. Prahlāda saw him as a dwarf-form in the womb of Aditi—bearing within him, along with the primordial Prajāpati, the seven worlds, the Vasus, the Rudras, the Aśvins, the Maruts, the Sādhyas, the Viśvadevas, the Ādityas, Gandharvas, Uragas, Rākṣasas; and Virocana and his son Bali, the leader of the Asuras, and Jambha, Kujambha, Naraka, Bāṇa, and other Asuras, along with Prahlāda himself, the earth, the sky, wind, water, fire, oceans, trees, rivers and lakes, domestic and wild animals, all kinds of birds and humans and snakes; Brahmā the creator of all the worlds, and Bhava; and also planets, stars, Nāgas, and Dakṣa and the other Prajāpatis. And Prahlāda, seeing this, was amazed; but returning in a minute to his senses, he said to Bali Vairocana, the king of the Daityas:

16   "My boy, I now know the reason why these demons have been deprived of their *tejas*. Listen as I tell it in detail. The Deva of Devas, the origin of the universe, the one without birth, the primal creator of the universe, eternal, supreme, best of all, the boon-granting Hari, the highest of all, supreme over all, authority of authorities, the *guru* of the one who is the seven worlds' *guru*, the lord of lords, the highest of the high, the Blessed One who is without beginning, middle or end, the Lord of the triple world, the great-souled Viṣṇu has descended by means of a portion of himself to be born of Aditi. That Vāsudeva, whose true nature neither Rudra, nor Brahmā, nor Indra know—nor the preeminent ones Sūrya, Indu, Marīci—has descended by means of a part of himself.

21   Formerly by means of a particle of himself the Lord in the form of Nṛsiṃha slew my father. That Vāsudeva who indwells the mind of the Lord of all *yogi*s has descended by means of a part of himself. . . .

28   I salute that Deva by whom, when he had descended by means of a portion of himself into the womb of Aditi, were stolen the splendours of the great Asuras—that Deva who is the infinite Lord, the axe for chopping down the entire tree of *saṃsāra*. This exalted Deva, the origin of the universe has

entered, by means of a sixteenth part of himself, the womb of
the mother of the Devas, and on account of his power, O great
Asura Lord, the bounties of the Asuras have been lost."

30   Bali replied, "Who is this Hari who has caused us terror?
There are Daityas by the hundreds more powerful than
Vāsudeva: Vipracitti, Śibi, Śaṅku Ayas, Śaṅku, Ayaḥśiras,
Aśvaśiras, Bhaṅgakārin, Mahāhanu; Pratāpa, Praghasa,
Śumbha, Kukura; these and others of my Daityas and
Dānavas are quite invincible. These heroes of great power are
capable of raising and holding up the earth. Kṛṣṇa is not half
as powerful as any one of them."

Hearing these words of his grandson, Prahlāda, that most
distinguished of Daityas, said to Bali who was thus abusing
Vaikuṇṭha: "Shame, shame!"

35   Then Prahlāda said, "In my opinion, having a king such as
you, evil-minded and lacking discrimination, the Daityas and
Dānavas will arrive at destruction. Who other than you is of
such evil intent that he would speak thus of the Deva of Devas,
the illustrious Vāsudeva, the unborn Lord. All the Daityas
and Dānavas mentioned by you—and all the Devas, along
with Brahmā and Prajāpati, and the worlds immobile and
endless, and you and I, this world with its mountains, trees,
rivers and streams, the worlds with their oceans and continents—all these are not the equal of Vāsudeva. This entire
world is sustained with one part of himself by that highly
adored, all-pervading supreme person. Who would speak thus
of him except you alone, who are headed for destruction,
lacking in discrimination, of evil mind, with the self uncon-
trolled, unheedful of the teaching of the wise. I am to be pitied
—that in my house was born your wretched father, who has a
son like you, a scorner of the Deva of Devas. Devotion to Kṛṣṇa
remains the destroyer of all sins arising from rebirths. Why am
I not so much as commended by you? None is dearer to me
than Kṛṣṇa, not even my body. This world understands it, but
not you, O wicked Daitya! Even though you know that Hari is
dearer to me than my life, you revile him. You do not show
respect for me. Bali, Virocana is your *guru* and I am his *guru*.
And my *guru* Nārāyaṇa is the *guru* of the world's *guru*. Since
you are reviling Kṛṣṇa who is the *guru* of your *guru*'s *guru*, be-

fore long you shall lose your kingdom. My Deva Janārdana, Bali, is the lord of the universe [Jagannātha]. I have abandoned you and he, my *guru*, is pleased. Since, in disregard of this, you have reviled the world's *guru*, I am placing a curse on you. Since the words spoken by you, reviler of Acyuta, are more serious than the severance of my head, may you lose your kingdom and position. As there is no protection in this ocean of *samsāra* other than Krṣṇa, so may you see before long the loss of your kingdom."

51   The Daitya king, having heard those unpleasant words of his *guru*, bowed down repeatedly to him, attempting to propitiate him. And Bali said: "O sir, be gracious. Do not be angry with me. These words were uttered by me when I was crazed with power and pride. My intellect was clouded by delusion. I am a sinner, O best of Daityas. You have done well in cursing me in my wickedness. I am not as dejected by the fact that I shall lose my kingdom and wealth as that I have been disrespectful to you, sir. It is not very difficult to win sovereignty over the realm of the three worlds or anything else like that, but in this world of flux *guru*s like you are hard to find. So be gracious; do not be angry with me, Daitya-lord. I am distressed, sir, by your angry appearance. Do not curse me."

Prahlāda said:

57   "My child, I have been deluded by anger. That is why you have been cursed by me. My discrimination was carried away by delusion. If my wisdom had not been obscured by delusion, O great Asura, how could I utter a curse, knowing Hari to be omnipresent? O bull among Asuras, the curse with which I cursed you will surely take effect. But do not despair. From today you will be devoted to the lord of the Devas, the imperishable Lord Hari. He will be your protector. On account of my curse, O hero, you will think of me. As I am called to mind by you so I will endeavour to do whatever you consider best."

62   Having spoken thus Prahlāda held his peace. Then the blessed lord Govinda was born in the form of a dwarf. When the lord of the world and lord of all immortals had descended, the Devas were freed from grief as also was Aditi the mother of the Devas. Balmy breezes blew, the sky was free from dust and

there was born in all creatures an inclination towards *dharma*. There was no fear there among kings or Asuras—among all creatures living in the earth, the mid-region or the heavens. And having seen him when he was born, the blessed lord Brahmā, the world's grandfather, performed the *jātakarma* and other ceremonies and praised the Lord of Lords in the hearing of the Ṛṣis. And Brahmā said:

67 Glory to you, eternal Lord; hail, O invincible one;
    Hail, O Self of all selves; hail, you who are free from
        birth and old age.
    Hail, O Infinite one; hail, Immutable.
    Victory to you, Invincible; to you, destroyer of all.
        Hail, O you indwelling the material world.
    You are the supreme Deva, O Omniscient,
        Essence of knowledge and known. . . ."

A long traditional hymn continues.

81   Thus praised, Hṛṣīkeśa in the form of a dwarf smiled and spoke seriously to him who was born from the lotus. "I have been hymned by you, and before that by Indra and the other Devas and by Kaśyapa, and I have promised the three worlds to Indra. I have been praised by Aditi and to her it was promised that I would give to Śakra the triple world freed from all foes. I shall so act that the thousand-eyed Indra will become lord of the world: this I tell you truly."

85   Then Brahmā gave Hṛṣīkeśa a black deer skin, Bṛhaspati gave him the sacred thread, Marīci the son of Brahmā gave him an *aṣāḍha* staff, Vasiṣṭha gave a *kamaṇḍalu*, Aṅgiras gave him *kuśa* grass and the Vedas, Pulaha the *akṣasūtra*, and Pulastya gave him white cloth. And the Vedas adorned with OM and the accents, all the *śāstra*s, and the Sāṃkhya and Yoga systems all worshipped him. And the Dwarf, with matted locks, bearing a staff, umbrella and *kamaṇḍalu*, and comprising all the Devas, O king, went to the sacrifice of Bali. And wherever the Dwarf place his face on a part of the earth, there the earth, hard-pressed, was marked by depression. And although the Dwarf walked slowly he shook the earth with its mountains, oceans and continents.

[246]

Seeing the earth agitated, together with its mountains and forests, Bali bowed down with folded hands and asked Uśanas Śukra: "O teacher, why is the earth with its oceans and mountains and forests trembling? And why does the fire not accept the offerings made by the Asuras?"

3   Thus questioned by Bali, the highly intelligent Śukra, the foremost of Vedic scholars, after meditating for a long time said to the lord of the Daityas: "Hari, the origin of the world, the eternal Self of the World, has descended in the house of Kaśyapa, in the form of a dwarf. He is coming to your sacrifice, O bull of the Dānavas. This earth is trembling on account of its being disturbed by the placing of his feet. The mountains are quaking, the oceans are surging. The earth is not able to bear the weight of the lord of creatures. Devas, Asuras, Gandharvas, Yakṣas, Rākṣasas and Kinnaras, earth, water, fire, wind and sky are all sustained by him. And this Deva sustains all Manus, etc. That is the inscrutable *māyā* of Kṛṣṇa, the cause of the world. By that which is the sustainer and sustained, the world is oppressed. It is on account of his presence that the Asuras are not allowed their share, O best of Asuras, and these fires do not consume the offerings of the Asuras."

10   Bali said: "Blessed am I, and my good deeds have come to fruition, that the Lord of the sacrifice has himself come to my sacrifice. O Brāhman, what other person is more blessed than I? The imperishable supreme Self, whom *yogi*s, ever disciplined, long to see — that lord of Devas will come to my sacrifice. This Hotṛ, the granter of shares whom Udgatṛs hymn — who other than I will approach him, that Viṣṇu, Lord of the sacrifice? Advise me, Śukra, what I should do when Kṛṣṇa, the Lord of all Lords, comes to my sacrifice?"

14   Śukra said: "O Asura, on the authority of the Vedas, the Devas are entitled to enjoy portions of the sacrificial oblations. But by you, O Daitya, the Dānavas have been made enjoyers of those portions. This excellent Deva sustains and protects, and that Lord himself devours creatures at the end of creation. But just now Lord Viṣṇu is engaged in sustaining the creation, and knowing this, illustrious one, you should be on your

guard. O lord of Asuras, you should by no means make any promise regarding even a trifling matter. You should speak words that are gentle and, at the same time, bear no fruit. You should say, 'I am not able to give you anything, O Deva.'—for, O great Asura, Kṛṣṇa is coming here for the welfare of the Devas."

19 Bali said: "O, Brāhman, how can I say no to anyone who makes a request? How can I do so when requested by that Deva who is dispeller of the ills of *saṃsāra*? Lord Hari Govinda, who is pleased by vows and fasts of various kinds, shall himself say 'Give!' Can I ask for anything more? The lord of Devas, for whose sake sacrifices are undertaken by those endowed with *tapas*, purity, and good qualities, will say to me 'Give!' That is indeed a noble, virtuous act, and virtuous is my *tapas* that Hari, the Lord of Lords, will himself receive what is given by me. If I say 'No! No!' to the Lord who has approached me, I will surely receive the fruit of the birth resulting from such action. If in this sacrifice the lord of the sacrifice, Janārdana, asks me for my own head, I will give it to him without fail. How shall I say 'No!' to him when he asks, since I have not said it to any others who have made requests. To say no is not my custom. It is said to be laudable if one arrives at adversity through generosity. And that munificence in which there is a flaw is regarded as inauspicious.

27 "There are in my kingdom none who are unhappy, poor, suffering, unadorned, grieved, nor any devoid of garlands, etc. All my people, O illustrious one, are happy, content, virtuous, satisfied, full of every kind of happiness. Moreover, I am always happy! By your favour, O tiger of the Bhṛgus, I have learnt that this eminently worthy person is the fruit grown from the seed of my generosity. If I sow the seed of my generosity in the great soil of Janārdana, O guru, what will there not be obtained by me? If the Devas prosper by virtue of my gift, even then I shall enjoy a tenfold benefit. This gift will be my most laudable act. Hari, ever ready to do me a favour, has indeed been worshipped with a sacrifice. Thus, without a doubt he is approaching to grant me the favour of a *darśana*.

33 "If, however, the Lord is in anger coming to kill me because I have stopped the sacrificial offering to the Devas, that

destruction at the hands of the Imperishable one would be most laudable. That Hari — by whom this universe is not to be won since it comprises of him — is coming to make a request of me, is surely the result of his grace. He, the true Self, creates everything and annihilates it at his pleasure. How would that Hṛṣīkeśa make the effort to slay me? Knowing this, O guru, you should not, when the lord of the universe Govinda has arrived, oppose my making a gift."

37 Then the Lord of the universe, comprising all the Devas, the incomprehensible, bearing through *māyā* the form of a dwarf approached Bali who was speaking in this manner. Having seen him enter the sacrificial enclosure, the Asuras seated in the hall were agitated and became lustreless on account of his *tejas*. And all the *muni*s who had come there to the great sacrifice began to mutter prayers. And Bali considered his own birth entirely fruitful. Then those who were full of agitation said nothing to anyone and they each worshipped in their minds the Lord of the Devas.

41 Then Viṣṇu, the witness, the Lord of the Deva of the Devas, who had assumed the dwarf-form, saw the lord of the Asuras submissive, along with those great *muni*s. And he was pleased with the sacrificial fire, the sacrificer, the Ṛtviks, the assistants in the sacrificial activity, and the wealth of materials. Then immediately the heroic Bali said "Good! Good!" to the Dwarf who was standing, thoroughly delighted, in the sacrificial enclosure. And Bali, his hair standing on end, and with the *argha* offering in his hand, honoured Govinda. And the great Asura said this:

45 "A mass of gold and jewels, all elephants and horses, women, clothes, ornaments, splendid villages, the entire earth or whatever is desired by you — that I will give you. You are a darling Dwarf. Choose whatever takes your fancy."

When the Daitya lord said these words with much affection, the Blessed One in the form of a dwarf spoke in a smiling but serious manner: "For a fire-sanctuary, O king, grant me land covered in three steps. Let gold, villages, and jewels be given to those who desire them."

Bali said, "What can you do with three steps of land? Choose a hundred times a hundred thousand steps!"

50   The Dwarf said: "With an understanding of *dharma*, O Daitya lord, I am content with this much land. To other seekers you may donate your wealth as they desire it."

Having heard the words of the illustrious Dwarf the powerful Bali granted to him three steps. When water had fallen on his hand, the Dwarf was no dwarf, and instantly he revealed his form comprising all the Devas. The moon and the sun were his eyes, the sky his head and earth his feet. His toes were the Pisācas, his fingers were the Guhyakas. The Viśvadevas stood in his knees, the Sādhyas, those pre-eminent deities, were in his ankles, Yakṣas in his fingernails, and the Apsarases were the lines. His eyes were all the constellations, the solar rays his hair, the meteors his pores, the great Ṛṣis his body hairs. His arms were the intermediate directions, in the ears of the celebrated one were the quarters; in the ears were also the Aśvins, and in his nose Vāyu. The moon god was his kindness, *dharma* was his mind, truth was in his speech, the goddess Sarasvatī was in his tongue. The mother of the Devas, Aditi, was in his neck, knowledge in his wrists. . . .

65   The exceedingly powerful Daitya lords saw Viṣṇu's form composed of Devas and they rushed at him like moths at a fire. And the Lord routed all the Asuras with the palms of his hands and the soles of his feet. Assuming this vast form he quickly took back the earth. As he was striding over the earth the Sun and Moon were in his chest. When he was striding in the middle stride these two were situated in his thigh. When he took his final stride, they were at the bottom of the knee of this Viṣṇu who, O king, was engaged in protecting the Devas. Having won the entire three worlds and having slain the chiefs of the Asuras, the wide-striding Viṣṇu gave the triple world to Indra, and the region called Sutala, situated below the earth, was given to Bali by the powerful Lord Viṣṇu.

71   Then Viṣṇu, the Lord of all lords, said to the lord of the Daityas: "The water given by you was received by me in my hand. Therefore you shall live for a *kalpa*. When the Vaivasvata Manvantara is past and the Sāvarṇa Manvantara has arrived, you shall be Indra. The entire triple world has been given by me to the king of the Devas and seventy-one more four-*yuga* periods must pass. Since formerly, Bali, I was wor-

shipped by you with the highest devotion, all who oppress you will be destroyed by me. Go to the charming nether region called Sutala, at my behest, O Asura and dwell there, protecting yourself accordingly; in a region provided with excellent forests and full of a hundred palaces—with lakes covered by full-blown lotuses, with the finest fountains and clear streams, enchanting with songs and dances. You will be decorated with fragrant perfume, garlands, clothes, and fine ornaments, delighted by garlands and sandalwood, etc. and surrounded by a hundred women. Stay there now at my command and enjoy these various pleasures. You will enjoy these great fortunes as long as you do not make a quarrel with the Devas and Brāhmans. When you do make a quarrel with the Devas and Brāhmans, the bonds of Varuṇa will undoubtedly entangle you. Knowing this, O best of Daityas, as I have indicated, no hostility should be entertained towards them."

82   Thus addressed by the powerful Deva Viṣṇu, Bali bowed down and full of joy said: "O Lord, how shall there be a gift bringing me enjoyment while I dwell in Pātāla at your command?"

The Blessed One said: "Gifts not given according to rule, *śrāddha*s performed without the help of Brāhmans, ablutions without faith—these shall provide your reward. So also sacrifices without fees, deeds done without following the rules, studies without vows—these shall provide your reward."

Having thus given that boon to Bali and the three realms to Śakra by means of that all-pervading form, Hari disappeared. Indra ruled as before, honoured by the triple world, and Bali in Pātāla realised his highest wishes.

Text 12
[*Kūrma* 1.16]

12   His [Virocana's] son, the great Asura named Bali, intelligent, versed in the knowledge of Brahman, and virtuous, defeated Indra. After engaging in the great battle with Bali, and being completely routed, Indra went for refuge to the undecaying Lord Viṣṇu. Thereupon also the goddess Aditi was exceedingly distressed, and with the thought, "May I have a son who will destroy the lord of the Daityas," undertook a most severe

tapas. And she sought shelter with Viṣṇu the Unmanifest, with Hari the Refuge, and in the lotus of her heart concentrated on the inexpressible highest goal, Vāsudeva, the one without beginning or end, Bliss, the pure sky.

Pleased, the Blessed Lord Viṣṇu, holding conch, discus and club, Hari the essence of *yoga*, appeared before the mother of the Devas. Seeing that Viṣṇu had come to her, Aditi, full of devotion, reckoned herself to have achieved her goal, and she praised Keśava.

Aditi said:

19 "Glory to thee, the sole cause of destruction of all suffering;
Glory to thee, the one well versed in *yoga* and of endless
    greatness.
Glory to thee, who are without beginning, middle or end,
    the embodiment of wisdom.
Glory to thee, who are both space and time and pure bliss
    incarnate.

Honour to Viṣṇu, to thee, Kālarūpa,
Honour to thee as Narasiṃha and Śeṣa.
Honour to Kālarudra, the annihilator,
Honour to Vāsudeva — honour to thee!

Honour to thee, the controller of *māyā*,
Honour to thee, obtainable through *yoga*, to thee the Truth.
Honour to thee, devoted to *dharma* and wisdom
Honour to thee as Varāha — and again, honour to thee!

Honour to thee, having a form like a thousand suns and
    moons,
Honour to thee, approachable through knowledge of the
    Vedas, through *dharma*.
Honour to thee, Deva of Devas, first among the first of the
    Devas.
And to thee, O Lord, origin of the universe — again, honour
    to thee!

Honour to thee, Śambhu, intent on truth.
Honour to thee, the cause, Viśvarūpa,
Honour to thee, stationed within the Yogapīṭha,

Honour to thee, Śiva of unique form—again, honour to thee!"

24 Then the blessed Viṣṇu, omnipresent, delighted with the mother of the Devas, smilingly persuaded her to ask for a boon. Bowing with her head to the ground she chose that most excellent boon: "I pray that you will be my son for the welfare of the Devas."

Then the Blessed One, who is loving towards those who seek him, said, "So be it." The Immeasurable one, having granted her wishes, disappeared.

After a long time, the mother of the Devas carried in her womb the blessed Janārdana, Nārāyaṇa himself. When Hṛṣīkeśa entered the womb of the mother of the Devas, terrible calamities occurred in the city of Bali, Virocana's son. Seeing all these portents, the Daitya Lord, beside himself with fear, approached his grandfather, the aged Asura, Prahlāda, and bowing down to him said, "O supremely wise grandfather, why are calamities causing havoc in our city? What shall we do about them?"

31 Hearing his words, the great Asura meditated for a long time and then, having honoured Hṛṣīkeśa, uttered these words: "Viṣṇu is worshipped with sacrifices; to him belongs this entire universe! For the destruction of the Asuras, the mother of the Devas has conceived him in her womb. Vāsudeva, from whom everything is non-different but who is distinct from all else, has entered the body of the mother of the Devas. That Viṣṇu whose nature the Devas do not truly comprehend, has of his own accord entered the body of Aditi. That great *yogi*, the ancient Puruṣa Hari, from whom all creatures arise and whither they go to be destroyed, has undertaken a descent. That Viṣṇu who is not known by distinctions of name or birth, who is Sat alone, who is the Ātman—he is taking birth through a portion of himself. Janārdana, whose *māyā* is the blessed Lakṣmī, the mother of the worlds, Śakti, the one who upholds his *dharma,* has undertaken a descent. He, whose tamasic form is Śaṅkara and whose rajasic form is Brahmā, in his sattvic form as Viṣṇu is taking birth by means of a portion of himself. Contemplating Govinda in this way, with a mind reverent with devotion, seek refuge in him. Thereby you will arrive at bliss."

Then, following the advice of Prahlāda, Bali, the son of
Virocana, sought refuge in Hari, and ruled all with *dharma*.

40   When her time had arrived, Aditi the mother of the Devas
gave birth to great Viṣṇu—Kaśyapa being his father. And
Viṣṇu increased the happiness of the Devas. He was possessed
of four arms, large eyes, with the Śrīvatsa mark on his chest,
resembling the blue clouds, resplendant and surrounded by a
halo. There came before Upendra all the Devas and Siddhas,
Sādhyas and Cāraṇas led by Indra—and also Brahmā
surrounded by the Ṛsis.

The blessed Hari, having received initiation, studied the
Vedas and rules of good conduct from Bharadvāja as an
example for the triple world. Thus does the Lord reveal the
path for life in the world. What he renders authoritative, that
the people follow.

46   Then after some time, the wise Bali, the son of Virocana,
himself worshipped with sacrifices the omnipresent Viṣṇu, the
lord of the sacrifice. He worshipped the Brāhmans giving
them great quantities of riches. And the Brahman-Ṛsis came
to the sacrificial enclosure of that noble one. When he learned
of this the blessed Viṣṇu assumed a dwarf-form at the instigation of Bharadvāja, and came to the place of the sacrifice.
Wearing a black-coloured deer skin and sacred thread, and
holding a rod, the Brāhman, with matted hair and besmeared
with ashes, recited the Vedas. Coming into the presence of the
Asura king, the mendicant Hari requested of Bali a piece of
land measured out with three of his steps. Bali, filled with
affection, washed the feet of Viṣṇu, and caused him to sip
water. Then he took the golden waterpot and thinking, "I will
give to you this land covered in three steps—may the undecaying Lord Hari be pleased," he poured cool water on the
finger-tips of the Lord.

53   Then the primal Deva strode over earth, mid-region and
sky, desirous of rendering free from attachment the Lord of
the Daityas who had sought refuge in him. Having traversed
the triple world, the foot of the Lord went from Prajāpati-
world to the world of Brahmā. The Siddhas who dwell in that
world bowed down to that foot shining like a thousand suns.
And the blessed Grandfather, who is eternal, approached and
glorified Viṣṇu. The foot, having broken through the top of

the shell of the world-egg went further to the divine coverings. Then on account of the breaking of the egg, there fell cool and glorious water, which is enjoyed by the virtuous. And that stream, called "Gaṅgā" then by Brahmā, flowed through the sky.

57 Having gone to *mahat, prakṛti,* and *pradhāna,* and thence to Brahmā, the self-originated, sole Puruṣa, the foot of the Lord stopped. Seeing that imperishable foot, the Devas there sang praises. Beholding that Puruṣa, Viṣṇu, the body of the universe, the great Bali bowed down with devotion to that singular imperishable Nārāyaṇa whom the Devas devotedly adore. Then the Blessed Vāsudeva, the primordial creator, having become a dwarf again, said to Bali, "This triple world now is mine, O Daitya king, since you have given it with devotion to me."

60 Bowing down his head, the Daitya again poured water on the dwarf's fingers, saying, "I give myself to you, the Ātman of infinite splendour, the one of three strides, the one of unbounded valour."

Having accepted the offering of Prahlāda's grandson, the conch-bearing Lord who is the inner Self of the world spoke again to the Daitya: "Enter into the region of Pātāla. Dwell there perpetually, enjoying pleasures unobtainable even by the gods. Constantly meditate on me with devotion. Thus you will again enter into me at the time of dissolution."

63 When he had said this to the Daitya king, Viṣṇu, the possessor of true valour and wide strides, gave the triple world to Indra. And Siddhas, divine Ṛṣis, Kinnaras, Brahmā and the blessed Indra, and the hosts of Rudras, Ādityas and Maruts all praised that great achievement. Having accomplished that marvelous deed, Viṣṇu, who had manifest himself in the form of a dwarf, then disappeared before the eyes of all. The celebrated Daitya, devotee of Viṣṇu, along with Prahlāda and other Asura princes went to Pātāla as directed by Viṣṇu. Bali questioned Prahlāda about the greatness of Viṣṇu, about the supreme path of *bhakti,* and about the performance of *pūjā;* and he did what Prahlāda advised. Having applied himself to the discipline of action, he followed the discipline of devotion, going for refuge to that Immeasurable Lord who bears discus, sword and conch and has lotus eyes.

69   Thus has been narrated to you, O Brāhmans, the prowess
        of the Dwarf. That supreme person always performs deeds for
        the Devas.

A. Of Conventional and Substantive Elaborations

That a new phase begins with Texts 8–12 is indicated by an
array of materials not found in Texts 1–5. At first one might attribute these accretions to the length of the accounts, for all except
the *Agni* version are several times longer than any of Texts 1
through 5. However, the expansions are due not merely to the
conventional elaborations that inflate the original narrative but to
additions of substantive material. Texts 9–12 have many conventional elaborations. A very common example is the hymn of
praise, which occurs frequently in these texts as in numerous Puranic accounts of myths. In general, these hymns do not affect the
myth in any substantive way.[1] The major points at which such
hymns are introduced are:
(a) The request by the Devas that Viṣṇu restore the kingdom of
the three worlds to Indra, as in:

Hariv. App. 42B lines 2619–31:	Brief hymn by Kaśyapa, Aditi, Devas
Matsya 244.12–34:	Aditi
Vāmana 50.33–35:	Aditi
Kurma 1.17.19–23:	Aditi
(*Brahma* 73.9–17:	Devas
Bhāgavata 8.17.8–10:	Aditi
Padma 6.236.14–24:	Kaśyapa)[2]

(b) The birth of the Lord as a Dwarf:

Matsya 245.67–80:	Brahmā
Vāmana 62.36–41	Brahmā (+ Mahārṣis)
Kūrma 1.17.43:	Praise of Devas and others mentioned

In addition, we find this kind of elaboration celebrating the restoration of the worlds to Indra in *Bhāgavata* 8.23.26, even though the
theme receives only passing mention there.

    Conventional elaborations other than hymns are found as well
in the texts. These occur as details embroidered into such elements
as:

1. *The approach of the Devas to Viṣṇu.*

There is considerable variation in the details of the approach to Viṣṇu for help. The variations appear to result from two major concerns—an interest in divine hierarchies, and the portrayal of a special relationship between Aditi and the Lord, since he is eventually born from her. Thus, the patterns vary as follows:

Hariv. App. 42B lines 2463–2650
        Indra ——→ Aditi (Mount Meru);
        Indra + Devas + Aditi ——→ Kaśyapa;
    I + D + A + Kaśyapa ——→ Brahmā (Brahmaloka);
    D + K + A ——→ Viṣṇu (northern bank of milk ocean -
                          called "Amṛta").
Matsya 244.8–48:   Aditi—*tapas* for 1000 years - hymn;
                    Vāsudeva manifested himself.
Vāmana 50.1–40: Indra + Devas——→Brahmā (+ Ṛṣis
                              + Kaśyapa);
   Indra—earth (——→ a sacred place) —*tapas*—
      Viṣṇu appeared;
   Indra ——→ Aditi;
   Aditi—fasting, etc.—sought refuge in the lord of the gods
        appearing in the form of the rising sun (Hymn);
        Bhānu (the sun god) appeared.
Kūrma 1.17.13–26:
   Indra - sought refuge in Viṣṇu;
   Aditi - severe *tapas* - sought refuge with Viṣṇu;
   Viṣṇu manifested himself to Aditi - hymn by Aditi.
(*Bhāgavata* 8.16.1–8.17.4: Aditi sad ——→ Kaśyapa
          Kaśyapa advised *payovrata*
            Aditi *payovrata* 12 days
              Viṣṇu appeared.
Brahma 73.8–18:
   Devas - *mantras* ——→ Viṣṇu;
   Hymn by Devas—Viṣṇu spoke to them.
Padma 6.236.8–30:
   Kaśyapa + Aditi—*tapas* + *payovrata*—worrshipped Lord
             (1000 years)
   Hari (+ Devī) appeared—hymn by Kaśyapa.)

2. *The Portrayal of the Dwarf and His Ritual Paraphernalia.*

The first text to give a portrayal of the Dwarf and to indicate what he carries is Text *MBh* 3 *App*.I.27 lines 67–69 (see above p. 00–00). Subsequent texts continue to utilize elements of this description, in particular his carrying of the staff *(daṇḍa)* and waterpot *(kamaṇḍalu)*, and his wearing of the sacred thread *(yajñopavīta)*. *Matsya* and *Vāmana* expand this by describing the initiation of the Dwarf and the various articles presented to him (see *Matsya* 245.85ff.; p. 00f. above). Later (in Phase 3) *Bhāgavata* adds a further detailed description of the Lord at his birth (8.18.1–3), retaining as well the description of the initiation (8.18.14–19). *Padma* 267.1ff. compresses both sets into a description of the newborn Lord. (For a discussion of two significant pieces of the Dwarf's paraphernalia — the umbrella and the sandals — see G.S. Rai.)

3. *The Manifestation of the Lord in his Cosmic (Viśvarūpa) Form:*

> *Hariv. App.* 42B, lines 2329–2852 (called *sarvadevamayaṃ rupaṃ*)
> *Matsya* 246.53–63
> *Vāmana* 65.19–28
> *Bhāgavata* 8.20.21–29

Included in such large scale conventional elaboration there are also numerous small details encountered sometimes in one text, sometimes in a number of texts. Not infrequently, what is a small detail in one text may become the starting point for an expanded section in a later text. Alternatively, what is a formalistic expansion in a number of texts may be represented in another merely by a formalistic detail. For example, the manifestation of the Lord in his *sarvadevamayaṃ rūpaṃ* is given in great detail in Texts 9–11, but in *Kūrma* it is suggested merely by the word *ādideva*.

4. *Bali's Sacrifice*

Another example of elaboration is the description of the sacrifice. In Phase 1 there are references to Bali's sacrifice *(yajña, yaj)*. In *Harivaṃśa* App. 42B, line 2763, there is a reference to Bali's sacrificing with a horse sacrifice (*kratunā vājimedhena*) and later a eulogy of the horse sacrifice by the Dwarf (lines 2776–96). In *Vāmana* this has been imaginatively expanded (62.32):

A white-coloured horse, endowed with auspicious
markings was released by Śukra in the month of
Madhu to roam the earth, and Tārakākṣa
followed it.

In *Bhāgavata* 8.15.33–35 the sacrifice is not only expanded but greatly exaggerated:

> The Devas having thus disappeared, Virocana's son Bali resided in Indra's city and brought the three worlds under his control. And the descendents of Bhṛgu, fond of their student, made their all-victorious disciple, Bali, perform in due order, a hundred horse sacrifices. Thence, by virtue of the splendour thus obtained, he shone like the moon, spreading abroad in all directions his glory renowned through the three worlds.

In addition to conventional expansions there are also what I would call "substantive elaborations"—sections which add substantively to the ideas being expressed in the myth. One has to beware, of course, of too easily relegating material to the formalistic rather than the substantive genre. A clearly conventional expansion of the horse sacrifice in *Vāmana* appears to be at least potentially substantive in the *Bhāgavata* in that it is part of the latter's poetic portrayal of the glory of Bali's rule.

The major substantive themes among the new materials of Phase 2 may best be summarized as follows:

(1) A war between Devas and Asuras in which the Devas are defeated.

(2) The Devas seek the help of Viṣṇu.

(3) Bali's virtue; the good conditions of his kingdom.

(4) Śrī goes to Bali, then to the Devas.

(5) Portents at the birth of Vāmana; and as he approaches Bali's sacrifice.

(6) The Gurus—Prahlāda and Śukra.

(7) The uses of water.

(8) The binding of Bali.

Of these the first two are less important in terms of what they contribute to the distinctive milieu of this phase of the myth. The first sets the stage for the central acts of the story in more graphic terms than in Phase 1. Although it is mentioned in all of Phase 2 texts, it is only the *Hariv. App.* and *Vāmana* accounts of this war that are expansive. The emphases are quite different. In *Hariv. App.* the context is a see-sawing of the fortunes of Devas and Asuras. The account opens with the death of Hiraṇyakaśipu at the hands of the Man-lion, and the setting up of Bali as king of the Daityas, with a strong portrayal of Bali's majesty (lines 45–59):

And the Dānavas raised the cry of "Glory!" for the anointed Bali, when he, incomparable in heroism, had ascended the lion throne. So all the Dānavas made the most powerful Bali their king, and then, having fallen with their heads at his feet they informed him: "It is well known, Daitya lord, that the entire triple world, mobile and immobile, is yours as it was Hiraṇyakaśipu's. When he had slain your grandfather, O slayer of the Devas, and had taken the triple world, Śakra was anointed by the Devas. You yourself, along with us, should assume again this imperishable triple world, the kingdom of your grandfather. Win back — blessed be thou, O lord — win back your ancestral kingdom. Surrounded by thousands of Asuras along with youthful Asuras, rout the troops of Devas in their own region, heaven. You are of unlimited power and prowess, O king. With your good qualities you excel even your grandfather."

Hearing what they said, the wise and powerful Bali replied to the crores of Daityas, "Let us win the entire triple world."

The effect of the strong portrayal given here and in the defeat of the Devas is brought to focus in the statment by Aditi when she is approached by Indra after his defeat (lines 2469–74):

Virocana's son Bali cannot be slain by you or even by all the troops of the Maruts. The Asura is able to be slain only by the thousand-headed one — by him, O you of a thousand eyes, and no other, Śatakratu. I shall ask your father, the truthful

Kaśyapa, how the conquest of the noble Daitya Bali may be achieved.

This effectively establishes Viṣṇu, "the thousand-headed," as the supremely powerful one. His power is the better magnified in contrast with Indra's defeat. Should one ask how Indra could at all be defeated, the answer is available in Brahmā's declaration that Indra is "eating the fruit of what he has done" (50.5) in that he had forcibly torn an embryo from the womb of Diti, the mother of the Daityas. Although Diti was impure, as Indra maintains in defense of his action, Indra is still guilty of the sin of slaying an embryo. This seems a clear variation on the theme of Indra's sin in slaying Vṛtra, a Brāhman.[3] No such sin taints Viṣṇu, whose power thus remains undiminished; that he is the mainstay of the Devas is unequivocally suggested in *Vāmana,* where the defeat of the Devas is correlated with Viṣṇu's withdrawal from the battle on realizing that Bali is invincible (48. 2–3). The extended portrayals of the Devas seeking help from Viṣṇu has, therefore, a conceptual significance and achieves a dual thrust.

(1) On the one hand they continue to maintain what is clear in Phase I, that Viṣṇu, the greatest of the Devas, is solidly on the side of the Devas and upholds the order of values, of rightness that lends them authority. A complication is introduced into this by the fact that the kingdom of Bali is, as we shall see, marked by goodness and prosperity, and that Bali himself is portrayed as good. It is precisely because this motif is counterpointed with the special relation between Viṣṇu and the Devas that the myth becomes at this stage an exploration of the question of the relationship between goodness and legitimate power: If one is good, does that confer on one a right to rule? Even if one's kingdom is good does that make it legitimate, if in the given order of things, kingship is not one's right?

(2) On the other hand, the Devas' approach to Viṣṇu effectively teaches the path of devotion. The hymns of praise almost inevitably incorporated into this material; the varying practices of *tapas* and vows; the lengthy approach to various significant deities, culminating in the approach to Viṣṇu—all these present accepted styles of devotional activity and an impetus towards diligence and persistence in one's approach to the Lord.

That the Devas can be examples to be imitated raises the point that although the myth is often presented as an account of Vāmana, the Dwarf form of Lord Viṣṇu, the variations of the myth have more to say about how life should be lived than about the Lord *per se*. Throughout the entire corpus of the myth the character and activity of the Dwarf remains essentially the same. The character and activity of Bali, on the other hand, is modified, explored, and continually related to new motifs. And it is significant that it is Bali, much more than the Devas, who receives the attention from those retelling the myths. Perhaps because of the natural relationship between the Devas and Viṣṇu, there is a certain artificiality about the Devas' devotion. In a sense they cannot be anything else than devotees of their powerful younger brother. For Bali, the choice is much more real, more like the condition of humans.

That Bali receives so much creative attention supports my contention that in its vicissitudes this myth is as much Bali's (or even more Bali's) as Vāmana's. Indeed the last verse of the *Kūrma* account (1.16.69), cited above, proclaiming the prowess of the Dwarf and his relation to the Devas as the subject-matter of the narrative, strikes one as highly artificial.

The other six additional substantive motifs have all to do essentially with Bali. And what one reads through them all is centrally a presentation of Bali as a good Asura and a devotee of Viṣṇu. Bali functions in the myth no longer as merely a threat to *dharma*. This second phase of the myth comes from a milieu different from that of Phase 1. This I shall call Milieu 2.

The only text that stands as an exception to the last statement is *Agni* 4.5-11. This text most clearly demonstrates the need to distinguish between phase and milieu. From Appendix B one can see that *Agni* shares with other Phase 2 texts a number of motifs that are not found in Phase 1 texts. These are:

	Motif	Other Phase 2 texts with same motif
3,12	War between Devas and Asuras — Devas lose	All
35	Praise of Viṣṇu (by Aditi & Kaśyapa)	All (specific reference, *Hariv. App.*)

85	Place of sacrifice	*Vāmana*
92	The Dwarf recites the Vedas	*Kūrma*
97	Śukra's warning	*Matsya, Vāmana*
119	Bali pours water on Dwarf's hand	*Matsya, Vāmana, Kūrma*
124	Dwarf no longer a dwarf	*Matsya*
151	Bali to Sutāla (specific)	All except *Kūrma*
158	Indra and Devas praise Hari	*Kūrma*

Such a large number of shared motifs in so short a text makes it imperative that we regard it as part of Phase 2. That it shares two motifs only with *Kūrma* (and also with some later Phase 3 texts) suggests that it is late in this period; perhaps it should be in Phase 3. The milieu, however, is clearly that of Milieu 1. Although motifs 35 and 92 are among those that in the other Phase 2 texts combine to produce or reflect a new milieu, in this text they function merely as formalistic details. Evidently, a writer may share many details of a more advanced phase of the myth, but he may not participate at all in a shared new milieu developing around those details. On the contrary, he may even actively reject the new milieu.

Apart from *Agni,* however, all the texts of Phase 2 are grounded in this new milieu. Not that they use the new motifs in identical ways. But from the variations we can, I think, come to a firm opinion about both the development of this new milieu and the significant issues explored.

B. *Substantive Themes of the New Milieu*

1. *Virtuous Bali and the Movements of Śrī*

It seems appropriate in our discussion to treat themes 3 and 4 (see above, p. 100) together since they are so closely related.

In *Hariv. App.* there are three places where one or other of these motifs is treated. These passages show, first, that it is largely because of Bali's good qualities that he is installed by the Daityas (and by Brahmā) as their king (lines 35–39):

> They saw Bali, intent on *dharma,* ever speaking the truth, his senses conquered, full of valour and learning, and proficient

in all knowledge; he had grasped the meaning of things far and
near, understood the *tattva*s, was immutable; and was, like
Hiraṇyakaśipu, a glorious enemy of the gods.

Later, when the battle against the Devas has been won, a virtuous order is established in the world and *dharma* is sustained
(lines 2430–40):

> All the directions were clear, acts of *dharma* flourished, and the
> sun went on its way in the heaven; all the quarters were
> guarded by Prahlāda, Śambara, Maya and Anuhlāda; the sky
> was protected by the Daityas. The Devas were showing the
> splendours of sacrifice for the sake of heaven. The world estab-
> lished in *prakṛti* was moving on a good course. There was an
> absence of all sin, and good conduct was firm. The Siddhas
> practised *tapas* for the protection of the *āśrama*s everywhere.
> *Dharma* stood on four feet, *adharma* on a part of a foot. Kings
> moved around, engaged in the protection of their subjects,
> and all those following the *āśrama*s were committed to per-
> forming their own *dharma*.

This is immediately followed by the approach of Lakṣmī who,
indicating her pleasure at Bali's victory, enters into Bali (2454).

Thus the scene is set in such a way that everything else that happens in the story goes on against the background of the goodness of
Bali and of his rule, and of the presence of Śrī within Bali.

In *Matsya* these two motifs are both present, but integrated into
the story quite differently. From the time of the Lord's conception,
the Asuras begin to lose their characteristic *tejas*. The statement by
Prahlāda shortly after, that Lakṣmī is subject to the desires of the
Devas (245.6), along with his mention of various cosmic disloca-
tions, suggests a set of oppositions:

If one allows "Śrī with Devas" to be interpreted in a more
abstract way ("There was a shift of good fortune from Asuras to
Devas"), then a logical chain is set up (indicated by ⟶). The

whole boils down to the assertion that when Viṣṇu begins to act, the prosperity of the Asuras is lost.

The significance of virtue is again observed when Bali refers to the good conditions of his kingdom (246.27–28). And he links these good conditions—about which he is happy—to his further good fortune in being able to make a gift to Viṣṇu. Thus a subtle link is made between goodness and the devotional aspects of Bali's character which we shall see are being developed in these texts.

In dealing with Bali's ascendancy, *Vāmana* is much closer to *Hariv. App.* than to *Matsya*, but has its own distinctive features. One is the temporal setting of the war in which Bali became Indra. This is identified as the beginning of the fifth Kaliyuga (48.15). After winning the battle, Bali received counsel from Prahlāda (see below p. III) and as a result, "Bali protected the triple world, ever committed to *dharma.*" (49.1). Thereupon Kali(yuga) complains to Brahmā that his essential nature (*svabhāva*) has been destroyed by Bali. Kali leaves for the forest of Vibhitika. Hence (49.10–13):

> On account of the destruction of Kali, Kṛta [*yuga*] arose in the three worlds and the four-footed *dharma* was active among the four *varṇa*s. Tapas, ahiṃsā, truth, purity, control of the senses, compassion, generosity, kindness, service and sacrifice—these were established and they spread throughout the entire universe. And the powerful Kali was transformed into Kṛta by Bali. The *varṇa*s practiced their own *dharma,* the twice-born entered the *āśrama*s, and kings were ever firm in the *dharma* of protecting their subjects.

As a result of this manifest virtue, Lakṣmī approaches Bali (49.14) and, after some instruction in which, among other things, she indicates (v. 17) that she has come to him because Viṣṇu has abandoned Indra, she (also called Jayaśrī) enters into Bali (49.47–48). Other entities also unite with Bali, such as, Wisdom, Patience, Fame, Splendour, etc. (The list follows *Hariv. App.* very closely.) Finally, a link is made between the virtue of Bali and the ideal conditions of the kingdom (49.51–52):

> This chief of the Dānavas, Bali, was endowed with these qualities, was great-souled, of good judgment, devoted to the Self, a sacrificer, an ascetic, sweet-spoken, truthful and gener-

ous, the supporter and guardian of his people. And while the lord of the Dānavas was ruling over the triple world, there was none afflicted by hunger, or sinful, or unhappy. Humankind also remained ever resplendent, devoted to *dharma*, controlled, and enjoying what they desired.

Despite its thematic similarity to *Hariv. App.*, *Vāmana* has additional ramifications. The most important are two. First, Viṣṇu's withdrawal from Indra is correlated with Jayaśrī's approach to Bali. Secondly, Bali's virtuous reign is incorporated into the system of the four *yugas*.[4] *Vāyu* had placed Bali's rule in the seventh Tretā Yuga (p. 27 above), but that does not correlate well with the perfection of *dharma* under Bali; *Vāmana* attempts a more appropriate placing. There is a suggestion in this that what Bali has achieved is not natural, not in order. The nature of Kaliyuga is destroyed, and *Brahmā* links that with the fact that the Devas have been displaced (49.6). No further mention is made of this, and it plays no significant part in the movement of the narrative, but it initiates an idea capable of further exploration, that while at one level good order is being upheld, at another—that at which we observe the position of the Devas, and of the regular movement of the universe through its phases of ascent and decline—it is being disturbed.

The *Kūrma* deals with these themes in one verse (1.16.40). Śrī does not appear in this account and *dharma* is linked with Bali's devotion to Viṣṇu, which has been engendered in him by Prahlāda. Bali's virtuous rule appears to be a simple consequence of his devotion.

One can see, then, in what varied ways these interrelated motifs can be used. Again a tabulation:

Hariv. App. Bali good ⟶ made king—war—Bali defeats Devas
            world good ⟶ Lakṣmī to Bali
             Indra goes to Viṣṇu for help.

Matsya   Viṣṇu conceived ⟶ Asuras lose *tejas*
            ⟶ cosmic dislocations   Lakṣmī to Devas
         Bali pleased—world free from pain
            —he can make offering to Viṣṇu.

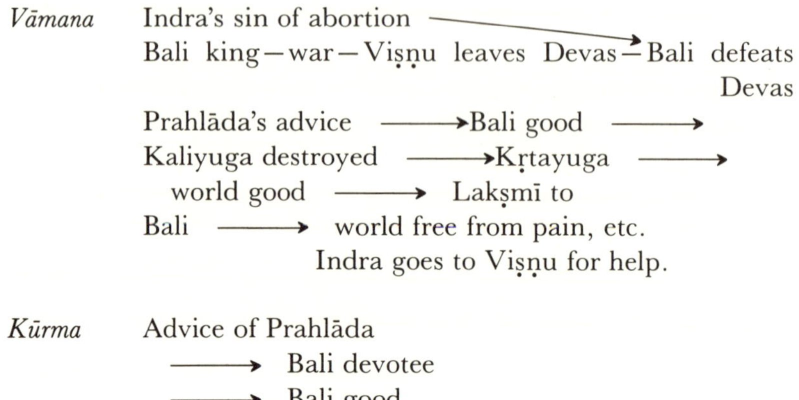

2. *Between Prahlāda and Śukra*

The theme of the portents, theme 5 on p. 100, is integrated with the sixth, that of Bali receiving advice from two gurus. Prahlāda, his grandfather, is presented in all these texts except *Hariv. App.* as a great devotee of Viṣṇu. In *Hariv. App.* 42B. Prahlāda does not appear. The Dutt translation of *Hariv.* does have a section relating to Prahlāda (pp. 934–35), but in the critical edition it is omitted from *App.* 42B and is classified as insert 196 (vol. 2, p. 759). This version is the only one from this phase in which Prahlāda is not portrayed as a devotee of Viṣṇu. He aligns himself with the Asuras and his advice is a repetition of the warning of Śukra, following which it is inserted. But in every other text Prahlāda seizes every opportunity to preach devotion to Viṣṇu. In *Matsya, Vāmana,* and *Kūrma,* for instance, the portents at the time of the conception of the Dwarf become the basis of a conversation in which Prahlāda urges Bali to be a devotee.

Prahlāda's devotion in Viṣṇu is counterbalanced by the hostility of Śukra, the traditional guru of the Asuras (see Goldman, 124–27). Other portents in *Matsya* and *Vāmana,* the shaking of the earth when the Dwarf walks, and the presence of the Dwarf at the sacrifice in *Hariv. App.,* become the basis for counter-advice from Śukra, who warns Bali that the Dwarf is really Viṣṇu and he should not grant him a thing, not even "the tip of a thorn" (*Vāmana* 64.14: *tṛṇagrām*).

Bali is thus very effectively placed in a position of choice. As we mentioned above, the Devas are devotees more or less automati-

cally. When they need help they turn to the Lord for he is from
their class of beings, the greatest of them. But Bali is much more in
the position of humanity; the Asura, like us, has to make a choice.

And the choice is a difficult one. It is a choice between partisan
interest in the mundane prosperity of the Asuras and the tran-
scendence of that partisan spirit in the interests of devotion and
generosity. (In the *Kūrma* version, Śukra is absent and the portrayal of Bali is so thoroughly that of the devotee that the tension of
the choice is reduced. Prahlāda advises him to become a devotee
and he does as advised.)

In the two versions where both encounters are explored (*Matsya*
and *Vāmana*—which are very similar in their treatment of these
motifs), Bali at first represents the partisan position and scorns
Viṣṇu. He later repents and Prahlāda advises him to seek shelter
in the Supreme Person. As a result of Bali's insolent statement,
however, he is cursed by Prahlāda to "lose his kingdom and fall
down" (*rājyabhraṣṭas tathā pata*: *Matsya* 245.49, *Vāmana* 51.36). In
spite of Bali's repentance, the curse remains in force and in *Matsya*
this curse becomes an explanation of why Bali loses his kingdom.

Vāmana pushes further into the implications of the loss of the
kingdom (51.46–48, 50):

> Therefore, O powerful one, you should not be feverish about
> the kingdom. Certainly, things which are destined to happen
> never disappear. A wise man is not despairing with respect to
> the arrivals and departures of sons or friends or wives, plea-
> sures of the kingdom or wealth. As much happiness and suf-
> fering come to one, ordained by past deeds, that a man should
> endure, O Lord of Daityas. The best of men are not disturbed
> at the loss of wealth, nor do they rejoice at the acquisition of
> wealth. They are serene on all occasions.

This is a message which comes to be, we shall see, more and more
profoundly central to the myth.

Despite the fact that Prahlāda has encouraged Bali to become a
devotee, in the second encounter, that is, in the conversation with
Śukra, Bali is not established clearly as a devotee. The point of
dispute in this encounter is whether Bali should act on behalf of
the Asuras or be a good sacrificer who gives to those who make a

request. But the texts treat the question somewhat differently; we should look at them in detail, including also *Hariv. App.*, where the discussion with Śukra appears in what seems its most primitive form.

In *Hariv. App.*, the conversation occurs after the Dwarf has made his request for land. Śukra warns Bali that it is Lord Hari who has assumed the form of a Dwarf "due to a desire for the welfare of the gods" (*śakrapriyahitepsayā*: line 2809), that "he has come to cheat you" (*tvām vañcayitum āyāto*: line 2810), and that therefore Bali should not give him anything. Bali asserts, however, that he desires to please none worthier than Viṣṇu (*kim ataḥ pātram iṣyate*: line 2812), and prepares to make his gift. Śukra warns him again, and Bali replies (2819–21):

"How is it that this Lord Viṣṇu has himself come to my sacrifice? I shall give to the Deva of Devas whatever that powerful one desires. For what other recipient than Viṣṇu might there be who is more worthy than he?"

In this Bali is shown to acknowledge the greatness of Viṣṇu. Even though his devotion is not explicit, it may be inferred, at least as an incipient attitude.

The *Matsya* version follows the same pattern of two speeches, one each by Śukra and Bali. Śukra at first, however, comments on the shaking of the earth, indicating that Viṣṇu is coming to Bali's sacrifice. Bali intimates that he regards himself as highly blessed. It is then implied by Śukra that because Bali has given the sacrificial offerings to Asuras and not to Devas, Viṣṇu will try to restore matters to the conditions authorized in the Vedas. Bali should therefore be on his guard and should promise Viṣṇu nothing. But proclaiming his constancy in being generous, Bali affirms that he would give even his own head to Viṣṇu. The style in which he makes this declaration is unambiguously devotional (see below, pp. 148 ff.).

In *Vāmana*, the *Matsya* version is followed closely, though there are additional complications. The portent of the shaking of the earth is explained by Śukra as the refusal of the fires to accept the sacrificial portions. Bali, after explaining (as in *Matsya* 246.24) that the present event is related to past actions, proceeds to tell a story illustrating karmic links over many births. Since it goes no further, the *Vāmana* version here constricts the *Matsya* devotional vision, accounting for Bali's gift to the Dwarf by his constancy to his custom of giving open-handedly.

Why *Vāmana* does this may be discovered by looking at a wider context. As well as the two conversations shared by other texts (one with Prahlāda and the other with Śukra), *Vāmana* also records two more, both between Bali and Prahlāda. If the four conversations are followed through in order, one discovers that the first shows Prahlāda instructing Bali in *dharma*, the second has him cursing Bali and then instructing him about non-attachment to things that come and go, and the third, that between Bali and Śukra, ends with Bali as the one who is bound by his past to the practice of giving generously. The fourth conversation occurs after Bali has been sent off to Rasātala; there is an extended exposition by Prahlāda on acts of *bhakti*. These acts consist in honouring Brāhmans, using auspicious flowers and grains, constructing temples, and, most importantly, giving generously. To be satisfying, gifts must be appropriate to the different months and must be substantial, such as cows, land, cloth, food, and gold. The fourth conversation culminates in a picture of Prahlāda attaining liberation (*vimuktim ayāyān:* 68.56), and Bali and his wife Vindhyāvali arranging the appropriate worship of God in the temple. Taken in this order then, the four conversations present a thematic sequence which runs from *dharma*, through non-attachment, to a special sacrificial *dharma*, and culminates in an illustration of *bhakti*. Thus, through this thematic movement *Vāmana* gains considerable logical and psychological force.

The difference between *Matsya* and *Vāmana* on the Prahlāda and Śukra sections also demonstrates how subtle changes can add new dimensions to the myth. While *Matsya* shows Bali as a devotee in a fairly straightforward fashion, *Vāmana* incorporates an obvious interest in *karma* as an explanation of events, thereby reiterating the value of *karma* noted earlier vis-à-vis Indra's loss of his kingdom.

The *Kūrma* account simplifies the picture again, presenting only one side of this situation of choice confronting Bali. Śukra is omitted from the account, leaving Prahlāda alone as Bali's mentor. Prahlāda encourages Bali to be a devotee and Bali responds and is portrayed as a devotee throughout the remainder of the account.

Before passing from the conversation between Śukra and Bali,

we must note its consequence, namely, that when the Dwarf
comes to the sacrifice, Bali offers to give him whatever he wishes.
In *Hariv. App.* (42B, 2801-4), the Dwarf replies:

> I have no desire for kingdom, chariots, jewels or women.
> If you are pleased, if your mind is fixed on *dharma*,
> grant me for the sake of my *guru*, three steps of land,
> O Dānava — as a place for a fire-sanctuary [*agniśaraṇa*].

In *Matsya* and *Vāmana*, the account is made more dramatic
through conversations between Bali and the Dwarf. In *Matsya*,
Bali begins by offering gold, jewels, etc. (246.45-46). The Dwarf
responds with a request only for an *agniśaraṇa*, saying that gold,
villages and jewels should be given to those who desire them. Bali
urges him to choose 10,000,000 steps. The Dwarf rejects the offer.
In *Vāmana*, the Dwarf begins with a request for land where his
guru's *guru* may place his fire. After an aside to his wife and son,
Bali urges the Dwarf — whom he knows to be *Viṣṇu* — to ask for
elephants, horses, land, gold, etc. Following up with mild irony he
reminds the Dwarf (65.14):

> O Viṣṇu, you are the suppliant and I, the lord of the world,
> am the donor. Would it not be an embarrassment for both
> donor and suppliant for the gift to be three steps?

The Dwarf replies, as in *Matsya*, that elephants, horses, gold,
etc., should be given to those who request them.

There is an important hidden edge to all of this — the fact that
the Dwarf is a Brāhman. As Bali is being developed as a positive
figure in the devotee mould, a secondary portrayal is of him as one
who gives gifts to Brāhmans. Hazra (249-54) shows that this latter
motif is very important in the Purāṇas of this period. He also notes
that, according to *Kūrma* (2.26.12) one who in devotion gives land
to a Brāhman for his sacred fire achieves liberation.

Clearly, Bali serves in these accounts as a model of devotion,
and also as a model for giving gifts to Brāhmans! The Dwarf, on
the other hand, in his ironic rejection of the abundance of riches
that Bali would pour on him, achieves the dual thrust of suggesting for donors that land for the sacrificial fire is the best gift

and of indicating to Brāhmans that the highest path for them does
not involve a longing for earthly riches.

In the context of this emphasis on giving, we may see with what
significance the name of Bali is charged. In Vedic literature, the
term *bali* is used to cover a wide variety of rituals — the common
element of which is the offering of a gift or an oblation. These gifts
are variously to Devas (Agni, Indra, Brahmā), to Brāhmans, and
indeed to all kinds of beings (see Keith, 359–60; Gonda 1966,
12–13). A key element is that of a mutual and generous sharing
among all beings.

How this term came to refer to this Asura we do not know. But,
given the centrality of the sacrificer in the story, it could well be
that the term was used to indicate this central fact about this
Asura, that is, his sacrificing. As so often happens in the case of
Sanskrit names, the name would thus be in the nature of an epithet.

Once developed as a name, the term "*bali*" could then contribute
further dimensions to the myth. In this phase of the myth, as we
noted on pp. 99–100, it is standard practice to identify Bali's sacrifice as a horse. Since a horse sacrifice is never classified as a *bali*,
the term surely identifies more directly the quality of the
sacrificer's character than the object he happens to sacrifice. The
suggestion here is that everything associated with Bali is invested
with his spirit of boundless giving.

3. *The Uses of Water*

The seventh theme, that of water, is one that is introduced in
this phase. Since developments in this phase (Phase 2) are not very
extensive, we shall have to wait till the next phase to see the realization of the potential of this water symbolism.

The first place in the text where there is mention of water is in
the events related to the Dwarf's coming to Bali's sacrifice. Within
these events there are two different motifs. The first one to develop
—it is the only one in *Hariv. App.* and *Agni*—is the sealing of his
gift of land by Bali, who pours water on to the hand of the Dwarf
(*Hariv. App.* 42B, line 2827, *Agni* 4.10, *Matsya* 246.52, *Vāmana*
65.18, *Kūrma* 1.16.52). This act becomes iconographically central,
for many sculptured images of Trivikrama also present this decisive moment in which *vāmana* becomes *avāmana* , "non-dwarfish"

(a rather delightful compound used in *Agni* 4.10 to portray the cosmic form of Viṣṇu, the form, comprising all Devas, in which he takes the three strides). From the perspective of our look at Bali, it is also crucial as the decisive act of generosity, and potentially as the decisive act of devotion. In these Phase 2 texts, however, the only implication drawn from it is that the promise of Viṣṇu (that Bali will live for a *kalpa* and will be an Indra in the Sāvarṇi Manvantara)[5] is predicated on the fact that Bali gave water to the Dwarf (*Matsya* 246.71 and *Vāmana* 65.51-2). In *Hariv. App.* (42B, lines 2928-29) the promise made by Viṣṇu to Bali is less specific and less original: "The water given by you was received by me in my hand and therefore, Daitya, you have nothing to fear from the Devas."

The other motif in this first section related to water appears to be a concomitant of the portrayal of Bali as a good Asura who lives in accord with *dharma*. He acts as any virtuous person would when visited by an honoured guest—he offers his guest *argha* (*Matsya* 246.44; *Vāmana* 65.4). As part of *argha* or *arghya*, water was offered for the washing of the feet. An ancient ritual, this is described in many of the Gṛhyasutras.[6] In *Hiraṇyakesin Gṛhyasutra*, the following description is given (1.12.18-19; 13.1; Oldenberg, 172-73):

> The host then utters to him the announcement, "The water for washing the feet!"
>
> With that [water] a Śūdra or a Śūdra woman washes his feet; the left foot first for a Brāhman, the right for a person of the two other castes.
>
> With the formula, "The milk of Virāj art thou. May the milk of Padyā Virāj dwell in me!" the guest touches the hands of the person that washes his feet and then he touches himself with the formula, "May in me dwell brilliancy, energy, strength, life, renown, splendour, glory, power!"

Since *pūjā*, the worship of deities, was developed largely on the analogy of paying one's respects to an honoured guest, the offering of water for the feet became a standard part of most *pūjā* rites (T. J. Hopkins, 110). Thus the offering of *arghya* could be interpreted as worship of the Lord by Bali. In the *Matsya* account (but not in *Vāmana*), this is suggested by the use of the verb *pūjayām āsa*. The phrase is forceful precisely because of its ambivalence, since it may signify an act of worship as well as respectful welcome.

Kūrma 1.17.51 replaces the term *argha* with a description of the act of the washing of Viṣṇu's feet by Bali, and his offering of water to be sipped. The epithet describing Bali in this activity (*bhāvasaman-vitaḥ*) strongly suggests an attitude of devotion, as one would expect from the general portrayal of Bali in this version.

The other point in the story where water is important is related to the striding of the Lord. This is the account of the origin of the Ganges, which occurs in *Vāmana* and *Kūrma* but not in *Hariv. App.*, *Agni,* or *Matsya.* The accounts in *Vāmana* and *Kūrma* are quite similar, and both quite different from those of Phase 3 versions (See below pp. 139-42). In these Phase 2 versions, Gaṅgā originates from the cracking or splitting of the shell of the world egg, Brahmāṇḍa. The actual details differ slightly. According to *Kūrma,* the Lord stepped over the earth (*pṛthivī*), the mid-region (*antarikṣa*), and the sky (*diva*). Then the foot of the Lord went from the Prajāpati world to the Brahmā world, split the top of the shell of the world egg and went even further. From the break in the egg issued forth a stream of cold water, which Brahmā called "Gaṅgā."

According to *Vāmana,* in one step the Lord took the universe of moving and stationary things. Then (65.31-34):

> In the second step, with one half of the step he covered the Svar, Mahar, Jana and Tapas worlds; with the other half the Vairāja world, and the sky was filled with the central part. Then, O Brāhman, striking in the sky the interior of the egg of Brahmā with his enormous foot, Viṣṇu reached the place devoid of light. By that foot moving through the universe the cauldron of the universe was powerfully cleft. There a jagged (hole) appeared which was called "Kuṭilā" ("jagged"). It was called "Viṣṇupadī," O *muni.* And the ascetics honoured it as "Suranadī," the river of the gods.

These pictures are quite similar despite the different terms used to denote the *loka*s or worlds beyond the triple world. In earlier versions the three steps are generally correlated with the traditional three worlds: the earth, the mid-region, and the sky. (There is by no means unanimity in the designation of these. Thus in *Ram* (1.28.10) they are not specified; in *Vāyu* (2.36.78) they are *pṛthivī,* *kha* and *div*; in *Hariv. App* (42B lines 2909–11), *bhūmi, nabhas* and *param. Agni* (4.10) uses the ancient syllables [see *Chāndogya* 2.23.2–3] *bhur, bhuvar, svar.*) In *Vāmana* and *Kūrma* this correlation is not adhered to. Rather there is an interest in a more developed cosmology. There are two different accounts of the worlds beyond the triple world. That followed by *Vāmana* is also found in a detailed treatment of the *loka*s in *Visṇu* (2.5,6). The worlds beyond Svarloka are Maharloka, Janaloka, Tapoloka and Satyaloka. *Vāmana* pictures·the second step of Visṇu as passing through these (though Satyaloka is omitted).

Another description of the worlds follows the patterns of *Bṛhadāraṇyaka Upaniṣad* (3.6) in which the worlds of the universe are related to the hierarchy of deities. Thus, in the celebrated discussion of Yājñavalkya and the inquisitive girl, Gārgi, regarding the structure of the universe and the nature of its ruling spirit, the various words — of the atmosphere, the sun, the moon, and the stars — the words are matched against an ascending scale of divine forces (Radhakrishnan and Moore, 84):

> "On what then, pray, are the worlds of the stars woven, warp and woof?"
> "On the worlds of the gods, O Gārgi."
> "On what then, pray, are the worlds of the gods woven, warp and woof?"
> "On the worlds of Indra, O Gārgi."
> "On what then, pray, are the worlds of Indra woven, warp and woof?"
> "On the worlds of Prajāpati, O Gārgi."
> "On what then, pray, are the worlds of Prajāpati woven, warp and woof?"
> "On the worlds of *Brahman*, O Gārgi."
> "On what then, pray, are the worlds of *Brahman* woven, warp and woof?"
> Yājñavalkya said: "Gārgi, do not question too much, lest your head fall off. In truth, you are questioning too much about a divinity about which further questions cannot be asked. Gārgi, do not over-question."

It is difficult to tell whether what is conceived of here is a multi-level arrangement of worlds, but that seems to have been the accepted interpretation in early texts. Later versions moved by various sectarian attitudes placed Vaikuṇṭha (the world of Viṣṇu), Śivaloka, and Goloka, Kṛṣṇa's "world of cows", in varying positions beyond Brahmaloka (see *Brahmavaivarta, Kṛṣṇajanmakhaṇḍa* 4).

The *Kūrma* account follows the arrangement given in *Bṛhadāraṇyaka* by placing Brahmaloka on the highest level in the hierarchy and Prajāpatiloka on the second highest.

It is clear that these two versions, using quite different details, present the second step taken by Viṣṇu as passing through all these upper worlds and finally going so far as to break through the shell of the egg to the cosmic waters on which the egg rests. Again, the cosmology that underpins this image is given in *Viṣṇu* (2.7.22–23; Wilson: 176):

> The world is encompassed on every side and above and below by the shell of the egg of Brahmā, in the same manner as the seed of the wood-apple is invested by its rind. Around the outer surface of the shell flows water, for a space equal to ten times the diameter of the world.

The Ganges is thus pictured as a stream of cosmic waters flowing in through a hole in the shell of the egg of Brahmā—the hole caused by the high-stepping foot of Viṣṇu. The absence of this theme from earlier accounts leads one to postulate an original turn to the story designed to utilize earlier traditions about Viṣṇu and about the Ganges. That the Ganges is known as Viṣṇupadī in the epics (*MBh* 13.26; *Rām* 3.50.26) and early Puranic literature (e.g., *Viṣṇu* 4.4.15, 2.2.31, 2.8.103) suggests that its origin was in heaven, for quite early materials appear to refer to the zenith as Viṣṇupada (Gonda, 1954: 55ff; 1970: 8). The belief in the existence of a cosmic spring of honey (*Ṛgveda* 1.154.5), which Gonda interprets as the nectar of immortality, supplements the faith in Gaṅgā's powers expressed, for instance, in Kapila's promise to Aṃśumān that the latter's grandson, Bhagīratha, would be responsible for bringing Gaṅgā down to earth (*Viṣṇu* 4.4,28–31; Wilson: 302):

> "I have told you," replied Kapila, "that your grandson shall bring down upon earth the Ganges of the gods; and when her waters shall wash the bones and ashes of thy grandfather's

sons, they shall be raised to Svarga. Such is the efficacy of the stream that flows from the toe of Viṣṇu that it confers heaven upon all who bathe in it designedly, or who even become accidentally immersed in it: those even shall obtain Svarga, whose bones, skin, fibres, hair, or any other part, shall be left after death upon the earth which is contiguous to the Ganges."

In this second phase of the myth then, the uses of water symbolism are rather disparate. On the one side, all actions of Bali involving water are added together to portray him as a devotee and sometimes to explain in terms of karmic effects why he escapes being bound. On the other side, the ancient traditions about the origin of the Ganges from the site of Viṣṇu's highest step are linked with the accounts of the striding, by means of a radical modification of the details about the strides. The story is thus connected with what appears to be an increasing obsession of the Puranic writers, namely, the interest in the sacred geography of India, and the underlining of the importance of certain places through stories indicating their relation with certain sets of superhuman beings. One of the great achievements of Phase 3 is a powerful unification of these disparate elements into a grand vision of the symbolism of water.

4. *The Binding of Bali*

In this phase there is considerable originality in the treatment of the theme of the incarceration of Bali in Pātāla. The tradition of the binding of Bali is very old, as the literary evidence from Patañjali (above, p. 25) makes clear. The tradition that Bali is sent to the netherworld is invariably present. That he is sent there bound is mentioned only once in Phase I texts (*Vāyu* 2.36.86). This suggests that it is regarded as a detail bearing no message essentially different from his banishment to the netherworld. Like the banishment, the binding gives assurance that Bali's threat to order is effectively counteracted.

In Phase 2, however, with the portrayal of Bali as a virtuous figure and perhaps a devotee of Viṣṇu (in some texts, *clearly* a devotee), the tradition of his being bound becomes something of a problem. All these texts either attempt to explain why Bali was bound or modify in some way the binding motif.

In *Hariv. App.*, after taking the three worlds with his three steps,

Viṣṇu gives them to Indra and assigns Sutala to Bali. There follow
then a number of conversations: in the first Viṣṇu tells Bali that
because of his gift of water, he will have nothing to fear from the
Devas, that the Devas will respect him, and that he will attain his
desires (lines 2929–35). But he is warned that if he does not honour
Indra, the *nāga*-bonds (*nāgapāśa*) will bind him (line 2940).

Bali then asks Viṣṇu to tell him what will be his "share" in Pātāla
and the reply is very close to that in *Matsya* 246.84–85:

> A *śrāddha* without a Brāhman present, study without vows, a
> sacrifice without the appropriate gifts, an oblation without a
> priest, a gift without faith, and an impure *havis*—when these
> are offered, they belong to you. The virtues of those who bear
> enmity towards men, of those who bear enmity towards my
> devotees, of those attached to buying and selling, and of those
> engaged in the Agnihotra; and the gifts of those who make
> donations and sacrifice without faith—all these will be yours
> by my grace, O Daitya lord. (lines 2948–55).

Although no indication is given that Bali has not heeded Viṣṇu,
he is then nevertheless bound with seven-headed *nāga*s. The great
divine Ṛṣi Nārada later comes to him and seeing him is filled with
compassion (*kṛpayā abhipariplutaḥ*: 2974) and gives him a means of
release (*mokṣopāyam*: 2975). His instruction effects a subtle shift
from the limited view of release from these snake bonds to an
obviously more generalized view of emancipation. In a matching
movement Bali sings a hymn of praise with a regular *pāda* refrain
"*tena satyena mokṣaya*: by that truth release me." The hymn includes
a series of *śloka*s on the mighty acts of God, all used as a basis for
Bali's petition for release (2996–3025). Finally, after the prayer is
finished he is released by Garuḍa. Again, there is mention of Bali's
entitlements—from sacrifices without rites and without Ṛtviks,
etc. The account of the binding of Bali is thus a mere background
in *Hariv. App.* to the presentation of *bhakti* as the way to release
from bondage.

The *Matsya* version is close to *Hariv. App.* except that Bali is not
bound. The warning is there (246.80), but it is not carried
through. *Matsya* has so firmly established Bali as a devotee that it
does not need a further exposition of that fact. This allows the

writer to explore Bali's fate in other terms. That Bali falls from the kingdom is linked with Prahlāda's curse; the promise that he will live for a *kalpa* and will one day be Indra is linked to his gift of water poured on the hands of the Lord. *Matsya* appears quite concerned about the relations between *bhakti* and *karma*, and takes pains to explain why the good Bali, the devotee of Viṣṇu, should be deprived of his kingdom. That Bali is not bound, but is merely warned about the possibility, clearly fits in with such a concern.

In *Vāmana*, we have already noted a strong interest in the karmic aspects of the fortunes of Indra and Bali. This is continued in relation to the binding motif. As in the tradition found in *Matsya*, there are the promises that Bali will live for a *kalpa*, and that he will be Indra (54.51–52)—this reward again related to his gift of water to the Dwarf. A new theme is introduced to account for his being bound. The Lord takes the world in two steps. The third stride is unfulfilled or uncompleted (*asaṃpūrne*: 65.33). The Lord says to Bali (65.35):

> From a debt unpaid arises a binding terrible to behold, O Daitya Lord. Make my step complete, sir, or receive bondage from us.

There follows a discussion between Viṣṇu and Bali's son Bāṇa, in which the latter says (65.44):

> It is no marvel that the world is traversed completely, but your three steps are not now fulfilled. You are able to traverse the universe with a step. This is a *līlā* you have performed, O Lord of the universe.

In his reply, Viṣṇu concurs with this [65.50], saying that the three steps have been made for Bali's welfare (*hitārthāya*) also. After Bali is bound (65.66), there are further details which enlighten this statement. Bali does not appear to be literally in bondage, for he enjoys a beautiful city and palace along with his wife Vindhyāvali. But then Viṣṇu's discus Sudarśana goes to Pātāla, and Bali sings a hymn to the discus, asking it to take away his sins. The discus then renders the Asuras free of *tejas* (*kṛtvā nistejaso 'surān*: 67.19). Then follows the conversation of Bali with Prahlāda and the detailing of Bali's acts of devotion. In this section, *Vāmana* appears to be following the traditions of *Hariv. App.* and modifying them so that the discus becomes the instrument of liberation from sin as Prahlāda guides Bali to *bhakti* as he does in *Matsya*.

In *Kūrma*, Bali is portrayed as a devotee early in the story (after he has received instruction from Prahlāda) and this picture is maintained throughout. There is no binding of Bali; he enjoys pleasures unattainable even by the Devas; and he is instructed by the Lord to meditate with devotion, so that at the time of the *pralaya* (dissolution) he may be given refuge by Viṣṇu.

C. The Significance of Myth B for Phase 2 of Myth A

The range of these developments shows that the crucial input into this second phase comes from the two versions of Myth B and from the adjacent *MBh* account of Prahlāda. Thus, from the first version of Myth B the following are derived:

(1) The good conditions of Bali's kingdom.

(2) The assertion that Bali will one day be Indra.

(3) The idea that one should not be disturbed at the loss of family, friends, kingdom or wealth, and that one should be serene in all vicissitudes (*Vāmana* 51.46–50); or alternatively, that losses and durance free one from attachments (*Kūrma* 1.17.53).

(4) The picture of Bali as devotee appears to derive from that of Bali as wise Asura. In *MBh*, Bali and Prahlāda stand together as wise beings; in most of these texts of Phase 2, by the end of the story they stand together as devotees. It is impossible to say precisely how these developments came about. Since *Viṣṇu* almost certainly precedes in time all of these Phase 2 texts, it would appear that the tradition of Prahlāda as a devotee, clearly established in *Viṣṇu*, took place first. But *Hariv. App.* 42B, which appears to me the most primitive of the Phase 2 texts, does not introduce Prahlāda at all, concentrating on Bali alone as a devotee. So it is possible that the two traditions developed independently in a common milieu. *Matsya* and *Vāmana* bring the two traditions

together in a portrayal of Prahlāda as the wise teacher of his grandson Bali.

The account of the good deeds of Bali may have been derived from either version of Myth B, for both refer to the former good deeds of the Asuras, those deeds having been virtuous enough to have secured Lakṣmī's abode with the Asuras.

The idea that Bali will prosper through actions carried out beyond the pale of *dharma* is found only in the second version of Myth B. When this idea is incorporated into Myth A, an amazing shift occurs. In Myth B, the context is temporal: the age when such non-dharmic acts occur will see Bali as Indra. In this phase of Myth A, the context is locational: it is because such non-dharmic acts do occur that Bali will prosper in Pātāla.

It is, of course, important to emphasize that these materials are not taken over just as they stand. They are worked into the context of Myth A with a variety and originality that leaves one in awe at the ingenuity and flexibility of these Puranic writers.

5

Myth A, Phase 3

The four texts I have included in Phase 3 bear much in common with Phase 2 texts. Yet we shall be justified in seeing them as representatives of a new phase because we find signs of a new milieu in these texts. All except *Bṛhannāradīya* portray Bali as a devotee of Viṣṇu much more forcefully than do the Phase 2 texts. Moreover, there are quite distinctive modifications that derive their force from being set against a background of Phase 2 texts.

Of the four Phase 3 texts, the *Bhāgavata* version (Text 14) is available in a number of translations (Burnhouf, Dutt, Sanyal, A. C. Bhaktivedanta Swami Prabhupada). It is, therefore, not reproduced here. Within the body of the discussion it will be cited at some length on crucial points — and I allow these to stand as they are in order to introduce the distinctive flavour, the *rasa*, of this work. Nor is *Bṛhannāradīya* reproduced here, chiefly because it has little to offer by way of new developments. There are a number of details it shares with other Phase 3 texts — the praise of the Lord by Aditi and Kaśyapa, and the praise of the Lord, when his striding is accomplished, by Devas and other classes of beings. In common with other phase 3 texts *Bṛhannāradīya* emphasizes the praise of the Lord by diverse groups of worshippers, but it does not contribute significantly to the distinctive milieu of Phase 3. It shares with *Kūrma* the picture of the Lord returning to his dwarf-form, and the splitting of the world-egg by the Lord's feet. But it shares with other Phase 3 texts an emphasis on the Ganges as water from the Lord's feet.

The accounts of the myth given in *Brahma* and *Padma* are translated here *in toto*.

Text 13
[*Brahma* 73]

[The narrator is Brahmā] There was a great Daitya, Bali by name, the enemy of the Devas, and invincible. And with respect to *dharma*, fame, protection of creatures, devotion to his *guru*, truth, heroism, power, generosity, and patience there was in the triple world none to compare with him. The Devas, having seen his great magnificence, absorbed in their thoughts, discussed together in secret how they might overcome Bali. When he was ruling his kingdom the triple world was free of vexation. There were no enemies, no physical illnesses nor mental illnesses of any kind. Drought and *adharma,* atheism and wickedness were not in evidence even in dreams, when Bali ruled his kingdom. Routed by his great arrows, their bodies pierced by his glorious sword, their limbs sundered by his authority and power, the Devas found no peace. Then placing jealousy before all else, in distress they approached Viṣṇu with *mantra*s, and their limbs shone with his glory and light.

9   The Devas said, "We are distressed and our *sattva* has gone, O bearer of conch, discus and club. May you ever bear arms for our sake. While you are our Lord, O Lord of the world, this is our sorrow: how can Speech, giving reverence to you, honour the Daitya?

> With mind and deed and voice
> we have come for refuge to you.
> We have your feet as our refuge —
> How can we be subject to the Daitya?

We sacrifice to you with great sacrifices,
We praise you with many words, O Constant One,
We have you as our only refuge —
How can we be subject to the Daitya?

Ever dependent on your heroism,
the Devas with Indra as king
attained to the position granted by you —
How can we be subject to the Daitya?

Having created in the form of Brahmā,
becoming Viṣṇu, you protect the worlds.
You destroy them with the power of Rudra.
How can we be subject to the Daitya?

15   Dominion is our reason for being in the world —
Without dominion what is the point of our existence?
But our dominion has been lost, O Lord of Devas —
How can we be subject to the Daitya?

You are without beginning,
You are Ananta, the upholder of the world,
You are the destroyer of the enemy —
How can we be subject to the Daitya?

Our portion nourished through your dominion,
and conquering the world through your power,
we shall be firm, O Lord of the Devas —
How can we be subject to the Daitya?"

When he heard these words, the destroyer of the Daityas
spoke to all those immortals in order to bring their purpose to
its fulfilment.

19   The Blessed Lord said: "This Daitya Bali is my devotee. He
cannot be slain by Suras or Asuras. As you should be sustained by me, so also should Bali. I shall take away his kingdom in the triple world without a battle, O Devas, and binding Bali by means of a *mantra*, I shall give to you the kingdom."
Saying, "So be it!" the hosts of Devas went off to heaven.

And the Blessed One, the Lord of the Devas, entered the womb of Aditi. When he took birth, festivals were held. He, the Lord of the sacrifice, the sacrificial Puruṣa, was born as a dwarf. In the sacrificial enclosure, Bali, consecrated for the horse sacrifice, was surrounded by the leading Ṛṣis. In that sacrifice Bali was moving about and sacrificing with Śukra, his family priest, an expert in Vedas and Vedāṅgas. And while that chief of Ṛṣis, Śukra, was family priest, none of the share of the sacrifice went to Devas or Gandharvas or Pannagas. And the worship of those who were severally making offerings and eating and performing the sacrifice, came to completion, the worlds also proceeding to fulfilment.

27   Slowly the Dwarf came to that place, chanting the Sāmaveda. Wearing ornamental earrings, the Dwarf approached the sacrificial enclosure. While he was chanting the sacrifice Śukra saw the god Vāmana, the destroyer of the Daityas, bearing the form of a Brāhman. Knowing the donor to be the fruit of sacrifices and asceticism, and the slayer of Rākṣasas, he then quickly spoke to the king of abundant *tejas*. Having shared the wealth with the donor Viṣṇu in accordance with the *dharma* of warriors, the supremely wise Śukra, tiger of the Bhṛgus, spoke to Bali, the best of the powerful ones, who had been consecrated in the sacrifice along with his wife, and who was meditating and presenting the sacrificial oblation to the sacrificial Puruṣa.

32   Śukra said: "This Brāhman who has come to your sacrifice in the form of a dwarf is not just a Brāhman, O Bali. In truth he is the Lord of the sacrifice and bearer of the sacrifice. This child has surely come to make a request of you for the benefit of the Devas. It should be granted then by you, along with me, O lord."

In reply to his family priest, Śukra, Bali, the tamer of his foes, said: "Blessed am I, that the Lord of the sacrifice has come to my house in incarnate form. Having come here, he will receive whatever he requests from the leftovers of the sacrifice."

36   Saying this, Bali, along with his wife and his family priest Śukra, came to the place where the lord of Brāhmans, that

Dwarf, the son of Aditi, was. With folded hands, the Dwarf asked for land measured with three steps. "Grant this, O best of kings. The gift should not be made with anything else. What is the use of wealth?"

Having said, "So be it," and having worshipped him with a stream of water poured from a waterpot decorated with many precious stones, Bali gave the land to the Dwarf. While the leading Ṛṣis were watching along with Śukra, and while the lords of the world were looking on, he gave the land to the Dwarf. As the assembly of the Daityas was watching, and the shout of victory was being raised, slowly the Dwarf said: "Blessed art thou, O king. Be favourable to me. Grant me land measured with three steps." And swiftly he was answered; the Daitya Lord said, "So be it," when he saw the Dwarf. Then the Lord of the sacrifice, the sacrificial Puruṣa, grew—having the form of the strider, so that the sun and moon were in his heart, the Devas in his head. The eternal and immutable Deva strode forth in the form of the strider. And, seeing him, the Daitya king, his wife beside him, full of politeness, spoke these words:

44　"O Viṣṇu, lord of the world, creator of the world by your power, step over as much as was won by me—lord of Devas, you who created all things with their particular natures."

Then immediately Viṣṇu, that one of great power, spoke these words: "O lord of the Daityas, O powerful one, I shall step forth. Watch, Daitya king!" And Bali again and again said to him who had spoken thus, "Step, Viṣṇu."

48　Having placed one foot on the shell of the Tortoise, he placed the other on the sacrifice of Bali. The second step reached the eternal Brahmaloka. "There is no place for the third step, O Lord of Asuras. Where shall I stride? Grant me land." Thus said Hari to Bali.

His wife by his side, Bali smiled, folded his hands and said: "The entire universe was created by you. I am not the creator, O lord of Devas. It's your fault that it is too small. What can I do, O creator? But also since I have never before spoken an untruth, O Keśava, render me one who is truthful still! Place your step on my back!"

52 Then, pleased, the Blessed Lord, in his third form, worshipped by the Devas, said, "Choose a boon, you blessed one. I am pleased with your devotion, O Daitya king." Then Bali said to the Lord of the world, "I ask nothing of you, the Lord of the three strides." And pleased, Viṣṇu himself granted him what he desired in his heart. And Bali went down to Rasātala.

56 Having thus given everything to Bali, Hari installed him, that enemy of the immortals, in Rasātala — and he was accompanied by his wife and son. And Hari gave the sovereignty over the Devas to Indra as it should be. And at that time he there set forth his step worshipped by the Devas. O you of great wisdom, having seen that second step of my father Viṣṇu arrive at my abode, I began to think: "Since the foot of Viṣṇu has come here, what should I do that may be for my welfare? I see my best waterpot full to the brim. The water is that supremely holy water given by Śiva — an excellent gift, the best benefaction, the supreme granter of peace; it is auspiciousness, the giver of auspiciousness, and ever granting enjoyment and liberation; being in its true nature the mother, it is the nectar and medicine of the worlds, O Virtuous One — pure, purifying, worthy of honour, supremely excellent, endowed with all good qualities. Just from the contemplation of it there is the purification of the worlds — what then, from seeing it? Such pure water is fit for offering *argha* to my father." Thinking in that way, I took the water appropriate for *argha*. As I recited *mantra*s, I poured that *argha*-water on the feet of Viṣṇu. That water fell on Meru and came to earth as four streams, in the east, the south, the west and the north. That which fell toward the south, O *muni*, Śaṅkara caught with his locks. That which fell toward the west went again to my waterpot. That water which fell in the north, Viṣṇu caught himself. In the east, the Ṛṣis, Devas, Pitṛs, and Lokopālas caught the auspicious water. Therefore, it is said to be the best. Those waters which went in a southerly direction, they ferry one across the world; those waters sprung from the feet of Viṣṇu are holy, bearing one across the world. From the remembrance of those waters, which were caught in the hair of Maheśvara and which became auspicious through having been born from his matted hair, one obtains all one's desires.

Text 15
[Padma 6.266–67]

1   [The narrator is Śiva] A son was born to Prahlāda, who was called Virocana. His son was the powerful Bali, the resplendent king. He was the best of those versed in *dharma*, he was bound to truth and his sense organs were perfectly controlled; he was Hari's most loved devotee, ever delighting in *dharma*, virtuous. Having conquered all the Devas, including Indra and the hosts of the Maruts, the powerful one placed the three worlds under his control and set up his kingdom. The earth gave forth much grain and fruit, bearing it without having been tilled. The cows gave a rich yield and all the trees flourished with fruit. All people were happy in their own *dharma*, shunned sin; and, all sorrow dispelled, they continually worshipped Hṛṣikeśa. Thus the Daitya Lord, Bali, established his kingdom with *dharma*. And the Devas, Indra and the others, approached Bali as his servants. Assuming power and pride, Bali enjoyed his dominion in the three worlds. Seeing that his son had lost his kingdom, and on account of his desire for the latter's welfare, Kaśyapa, whose essence is *dharma*, together with his wife Aditi, engaged in *tapas* before Hari, and undertook the *payovrata*. And they worshipped the lord of the Devas, Padmanābha Janārdana. When he had been worshipped by Kaśyapa for a thousand years the eternal Hari then appeared along with the Goddess. Then Kaśyapa beheld him — he had eyes like lotuses, carried the conch, discus, and club, was dark blue like a sapphire, was decked out with all kinds of ornaments and was resplendent in shining crown and armlets, necklace and earrings. His chest shone with the gem "Kaustubha" and he was dressed in yellow clothes and seated along with Śrī before that noble leader of the Brāhmans. With his mind filled with joy, Kaśyapa saw the lord of the worlds and, in order to obtain peace, along with his wife, that best of the twice-born made obeisance.

14   Kaśyapa said: "Honour, O honour to you, O Lord of
      Lakṣmī,
omniscient Lord of the world,
self of all, Lord of all Devas,

agent of creation and destruction.
Honour to you, with your body of bliss
which has neither beginning nor end;
who takes all kinds of forms,
whose body consists in the Vedas and Vedāṅgas,
who art the eye of all.
Honour to you, the Self of all
and more minute than the minute,
Honour to the Self, full of auspicious qualities,
the object of yogis' meditation.
Honour to the ever youthful,
the one who is in play the husband of Śrī and Bhū,
ever free, one mass of bliss,
abiding in the highest dwelling place.
O Caturātman, honour to you,
O Caturvyūha, honour to you.
Honour to you, of five forms.
Honour to you the essence of beauty.
Ever are you worshipped by those *yogīs*
who are devoted to the essence of beauty,
and established in the five perfections
for those who know the five goals and the five elements.

20   Poets know that you have your true nature
abiding in the five, that you are ever victorious,
that your Self comprises the four Vedas,
that you are self-fulfilled.
The Brāhmans, your servants, protect the whole world—
those twice-born who comprise the three Vedic groups,
and are devoted to religious duties,
O you who are loving to your devotees.
On account of their regard for compassion,
they are freed from the bonds of existence.
Honour to you, sustainer of the three worlds,
self-sustaining, the Self of all.
Honour to you, creator and sustainer,
the All, present in all.
Honour to Nārāyaṇa, to Kṛṣṇa,
to Vāsudeva, to the Archer,
to Viṣṇu, to the Victorious—
to you endowed with perfect goodness."

25   Being praised in this way with primal hymns by the great
     Ṛṣi, Janārdana was pleased and spoke in these profound
     words: "I am pleased, O best of the twice-born, since I have
     been worshipped by you with devotion. Choose a boon, fortu-
     nate one. I will fulfil your desire."
     Then Kaśyapa, along with his wife, spoke to Hṛṣikeśa. "O
     Lord of Devas, become my son and effect the well-being of the
     Devas, winning back the threefold world won by Bali by virtue
     of his strength. Since you are well-known as Upendra, become
     the younger brother of Indra and conquer Bali by some
     means. With the use of your *māyā,* give the triple world to my
     son, Śakra, for all time to come."

30   Addressed thus by that Brāhman, Janārdana said, "So be
     it." And being praised by the Devas, he disappeared from
     them. And at that time the Lord, the creator of creatures, en-
     tered the womb of Aditi, the wife of the noble Kāsyapa. And
     just then Bali, engaging in severe *tapas,* together with the eight
     great Ṛṣis instigated a sacrifice extending over many days—
     and he was the performer of it.

     [6.267]
     Then at the end of a thousand years Aditi gave birth to the
     great Lord of all the worlds, the unwavering Viṣṇu in the form
     of a dwarf. Hari was in the form of a beautiful child, wore the
     gem Kaustubha on his chest, shone like the full moon, was full
     of beauty—and had eyes like lotuses and a very short body.
     That god who frequents all the Vedāṅgas was clothed in a
     boy's apparel. The Lord was provided with emblems—girdle,
     skin, staff, etc. Seeing him thus, all the Devas led by Indra,
     praised him and along with the great Ṛṣis made obeisance to
     that one of great splendour. Then the Blessed One was
     gratified and spoke to those highest of the Devas: "May the
     best of Devas choose what I should do today."

6   Then, happy, the Devas said to the Supreme Lord: "At this
     time the sacrifice of Bali is being conducted, O crusher of
     Madhu. In terms of time spent and words uttered, the Daitya
     lord's sacrifice is unequalled, O Lord. Having requested the
     three-tiered world you should make an offering there."

8   Thus addressed by all the Devas, Hari came to Bali, who
     was sitting in the place of sacrifice along with the eight Ṛṣis.

When the Daitya king saw the boy who had just arrived, he suddenly stood up and, smiling as he did so, said. "Viṣṇu himself has come." And he worshipped him according to precept, and having halted at the flower seat, he bowed down with folded hands, and said in a stammering voice, "Fortunate am I, contented am I, my life is fulfilled — since I have worshipped you, O lord of the twice-born. What should I do that is pleasing to you? I ask that you speak to me, O best of the twice-born, indicating the reason why you have come here, O best of Veda-knowers."

13   Then with mind overjoyed, the Dwarf said to the king: "Listen, O king of kings, and I shall tell you the reason for my coming. Grant to me, O Lord of the Daityas, earth for a fire-pit. You should grant me earth sufficient for me to take three strides. The gift of earth is the best of gifts. A person who gives land, O king, to any Brāhman, even if it is the size of a thumb, becomes lord of the earth. There is no purifying agent known which is like the gift of land. The one who receives and the one who gives are both considered of holy deeds, controlled, and bound for heaven. Therefore, O Mahārājah, give to me earth measured by three steps. Do not be afraid to give that small piece of land, O king. Through giving the three worlds you will be known as 'lord of earth.'"

20   With a happy countenance, the king said "So be it." That ruler decided to make a gift of land to the dwarf! Then his family priest, Uśanas, observing the king of the Daityas, said: "Land should not be given, O king. This is Viṣṇu, the supreme Lord, Hari, who has been invoked by the Devas. He has come here to deceive you and to take the whole earth from you. Therefore land should not be given to that noble one, O king; ask him, O king, to make another request."

24   Then smiling, the king said calmly: "Every good deed I have done was done to please Vāsudeva. Today I am fortunate in that Viṣṇu himself has come. Life itself and great happiness are his gifts. Therefore I give him the three worlds including the sky."

27   Having spoken thus, the king devoutly washed the Dwarf's feet and duly gave him the desired land, formerly water. And the king, having paid his respects, gave wealth to Viṣṇu and

happy within himself addressed that Brāhman again: "I am fortunate, I am satisfied, in that I have given the earth to you, O twice-born. O Lord of the twice-born, accept this land desired by you."

30 King Viṣṇu said to King Bali, "I will not take the earth with a step now while you are watching." Saying this, he abandoned the boy form; and assuming the form of Trivikrama he took this earth — 500 crores wide, supporting sea and land — with oceans and continents, with Devas and Asuras and humans. Stepping out with one foot, the Puruṣa, the destroyer of Madhu, said immediately to the lord of the Daitya kings: "What am I to do?"

34 Now that Trivikrama form of the Lord, of great energy for the sake of the welfare of Devas and noble Ṛṣis, was not able to be seen by Brahmā or Śaṅkara. That step, having taken possession of all the earth, went a hundred *yojanas* too far. The eternal Janārdana gave the divine eye to the king of the Daityas, and revealed to him his own form. Having seen that Viśvarūpa form of God, Bali, the Lord of the Daityas became unsurpassedly happy, his eyes flowing with tears of bliss. Having beheld God, he honoured him, and praised him with hymns. Then with stammering speech and joyous heart he said: "Fortunate am I, fulfilled am I, since I have beheld you, the supreme Lord. Take the three worlds, O Supreme Lord."

40 Then Viṣṇu, the Lord of all, the Imperishable, extended upwards his second unwavering step to the top of Brahmaloka, endowed with stars and planets, and completely encompassed by Devas. But the step of the Imperishable One was not completed, O thou of beautiful countenance. Then the grandfather [Brahmā] seeing that foot of the Deva of Devas marked with discus, lotus, etc., and with his mind full of joy, said: "Fortunate am I." And taking his own waterpot Brahmā in devotion washed that foot with water standing nearby. The water of the powerful Viṣṇu became imperishable. That sacred, pure water fell on top of Meru, and streamed forth in four directions for the purification of the world — as Sītā, Alakanandā, Cakṣu and Bhadrā, in due order. Thereupon Alakanandā, as it is called, from the south of Meru became threefold, going on three trajectories, in three streams purifying the

worlds. In the upper regions it was called Mandākinī, in the lower Bhogavatī, and in the middle the swift Gaṅgā, auspicious for the purification of humanity. Seeing it flowing from the middle of Meru, O beautiful one, in order to purify myself I bore it on my head. Having supported the beautiful Gaṅgā water for a thousand divine years I became "Śiva," O goddess, worshipped in all worlds. He who bears on his head the waters of the Gaṅgā originating from the foot of Viṣṇu will undoubtedly be honoured by the world. He who says "Gaṅgā, Gaṅgā" for a hundred *yojanas* is freed from all sins. He goes to Viṣṇuloka. Then King Bhagīratha and the great ascetic Gautama, having worshipped me with *tapas,* made a request for Gaṅgā. And pleased, I gave to them, for the welfare of the worlds, that auspicious Gaṅgā, most beautiful of rivers, sprung from Viṣṇu. Since it was brought down by Gautama, it is glorified as "Gautamī;" since it was requested by this king Bhagīratha it is called "Bhāgīrathī." Because of your devotion the birth of Gaṅgā is declared as incomparably the best.

55   Then the glorious Nārāyaṇa, kind to his devotees, gave to the powerful Daitya lord, Bali, the beautiful world of Rasātala. He made Bali king of all the Dānavas and the Nāgas and also the sea-monsters, until the time of the inundation. The smiter of the Daityas, Viṣṇu the son of Kaśyapa, the Immovable, having by means of a disguise as a boy taken the worlds from Bali, happily gave them to Indra. Then the Devas, along with the Gandharvas, and the Ṛṣis, of great glory, were satisfied, and worshipped the Imperishable with divine hymns. And he cast off his great form in order to reveal himself to them; when he had been worshipped by the gods, he disappeared. Protected well in this way by the glorious Viṣṇu, Śakra, the king of the gods, became great lord of the three worlds. All the splendour of Vāmana has been declared to you, O beautiful one.

A. Further Modifications of Milieu 2 Themes
The first thing to notice with these materials from this milieu is that a number of the formalistic and substantive expansions found in Phase 2 texts continue to be important and there are further

expansions and modifications. The formalistic expansions of the pleadings of the Devas for the birth of Viṣṇu are modified by simplification. At the same time, these modifications appear substantive. *Brahma* generalizes again to a picture of the Devas going to make their requests. But now their action is placed firmly against the background of the felicitious state of Bali's kingdom and the Devas' defeat at his hands. We realize that it is envy (*mātsarya*) (73.8) which leads them to approach Viṣṇu. There is no attempt to explain the reasons for, and the ramifications of, the virtuous conduct of an Asura such as Bali and the prosperity of his kingdom. These are accepted without question, as is the painting of Bali as a devotee. So Bali and the Devas are now on the same level in terms of potential, Bali actually appearing superior to the Devas. Certainly, Bali is now far from representing *adharma;* he is incomparable in his commitment to *dharma,* truth, heroism, generosity, etc.

In *Bhāgavata,* the request to Viṣṇu to appear as an *avatāra* finds a locus in the mother of the Devas, Aditi. This is in keeping with the characteristic feminization of the devotee in this text. In its most extensive form, this feminization is seen in the picture of the *gopīs,* the colourful pastoral women whose relation to the young Kṛṣṇa is explored so imaginatively in the tenth *skandha* of *Bhāgavata.* That this portrayal of the peak of *bhakti* — in the feminine mode — should be prefigured in a portrayal of Aditi as a great devotee is not surprising.

Nevertheless, Kaśyapa has quite an important place within the text. He gives instruction to Aditi, at first chiding her for her worry about her children being deprived of their prosperity and position, and for her prayer that they might regain the supremacy, prosperity, fame and position of which they had been robbed (8.16.16: *eśvaryaṃ śrīr yaśaḥ sthānaṃ hṛtāni*). Kaśyapa tells her that preoccupation with such matters is the result of Viṣṇu's power of illusive energy (8.16.18: *māyābalaṃ viṣṇoḥ*) and of infatuation (8.16.19: *moha*).

He exhorts her to be devoted to the Lord and then gives detailed instructions (which he had received from Brahmā) about the manner of worshipping the Lord. His counsel includes a hymn of praise (8.16.29–37) and an extended passage on the worship of the Lord in image form, reproduced below in part (8.16.38–43):

Having honoured Hṛṣīkeśa by invoking him
with these *mantras*
one should with faith worship him
by washing his feet with water and so on.
And worshipping him with sweet-smelling garlands
one should bathe the Lord with milk.
And one should worship him by offering
clothes, the sacred thread, and ornaments,
and by washing his feet with water,
with perfume and incense,
and with the twelve-syllabled *mantra*.
If one is prosperous, one should give an offering
of *śāli* rice cooked in milk
along with butter and molasses,
and one should perform *homa* with a root-*mantra*.
And having yourself eaten of the offering
you should give it to the devotees.
And one should worship the Lord
with water to rinse the mouth;
one should make an offering of betelnut.
And having praised the Lord with hymns
one should chant the *mantra*
one hundred and eight times.
Having circumambulated him,
one should happily bow to him
lying prostrate on the earth.
And placing the remnants of the offering
on one's head
one should wait upon the Lord.

This worship also includes a style of devotion typical of *Bhāgavata*
(8.16.47):

With dance and music and songs, with hymns of praise and
benedictory sayings, and also with stories, one should perform *pūjā* to the Blessed Lord every day.

The whole is called by Kaśyapa "*payovrata*," and Aditi follows this
regimen for twelve days.

    Padma appears to be a response to the *Bhāgavata* picture. It shares with *Bhāgavata* a portrayal of the action of Aditi as including the vow called *payovrata* (*Bhāgavata* 8.16.29–8.17.3; *Padma* 6.266.8). But it carries the picture one step further by focussing the activity on Kaśyapa; it is his hymn to Viṣṇu that is recorded (6.266.14–26). *Padma* seems thus to be countering the *Bhāgavata* feminization of *bhakti*.

In addition to such substantive modifications of the conventional elaborations of Phase 2, there are further modifications to Phase 2 substantive elaborations.

1. *Virtue and Prosperity in Bali's Kingdom*

We have noticed how Phase 2 texts correlate the advent of Śrī to reside within Bali with his virtue and with his kingdom's righteous character. In the Phase 3 texts this correlation is no longer evident. Śrī is not even mentioned in the context of the virtuous character of Bali and his kingdom. Rather in each case these good conditions form the backdrop for the discontents of the Devas.

The most important new feature is that in both *Brahma* and *Padma*, there are further distinctive details of the good conditions. In *Brahma*, it is the absence of any kind of illness or drought (73.5–6). In *Padma* 266.4, the prosperity is portrayed in agricultural and pastoral terms—setting forth the abundance of grain and fruit and milk—with the additional picture of the earth as having become bountiful without being tilled. The absence of the frequent privations of human existence, and the contrastingly glorious bounty of the earth become, as we shall see, important ingredients in later developments and ramifications of the myth.

2. *Between Prahlāda and Śukra*

The Phase 2 placing of Bali in a position of tension between Prahlāda and Śukra has the effect of portraying a gradual development of Bali to the point at which he becomes a devotee. In the Phase 3 texts that tension is reduced by different kinds of modifications. Prahlāda does not appear in *Brahma* or *Padma*. And in *Bhāgavata* his appearance is radically shifted in the text: he comes in at a very late stage in the narrative to give specific and significantly *Bhāgavata* teaching, as we shall see in our examination of the context and contents of the quite distinctive *Bhāgavata* account of the myth.

The most interesting shift in characterization is that of Śukra in

Brahma. Śukra is now also portrayed as a devotee. The warning in earlier texts that the Dwarf is most likely Viṣṇu becomes here a positive proclamation. In the light of the shift, one can see more clearly that Śukra appears in Phase 2 texts as the great representative of demonic interests, and Bali, in rejecting Śukra's advice, breaks out of the type-casting of the demons to become a good demon, that is, a devotee even though he is a demon. In *Brahma,* a further step has been taken. Now not even Śukra functions as the typical representative of the Asuras. As potential and actual devotees the Asuras stand together with the Devas on equal terms in the *bhakti* complex. This still does not mean, however, that it is appropriate for Bali to remain Lord of the three worlds. While the writer depicts the Devas as motivated by jealousy, he also allows that their claim is legitimate. Indra returns to his lordship (73:57), and Viṣṇu takes away the three worlds from Bali. But the fact that Bali is a Viṣṇu-*bhakta* is now used to explain the fact that Bali, unlike other famous Asura or Rākṣasa enemies of the Lord, is not slain by the Lord, nor even involved in a battle with him.

This version thus brings into strong relief the question of the relation between *dharma* and *bhakti* (with material prosperity an important side issue), as well as the question of how the Lord is related to these two systems. The thematic centrality of these questions is of course maintained throughout the texts of Phases 2 and 3. But *Brahma* indicates in the strongest possible fashion that the system of *bhakti* does not disturb the system of *dharma,* that is, the given order of things. Bali and Śukra may appear as more attractive figures than the Devas, but that is no justification for a revolution or an overthrow of the cosmic order. While hierarchies are irrelevant in the context of *bhakti,* and all beings including the demons are seen as potential devotees, within the ongoing movement of the universe, however, the hierarchies are maintained. And through virtually all the ramifications that this myth is able to take on—and there is much still to come—this conviction is retained.

Bhāgavata also presents the Asura as a devotee in the strongest possible fashion. Nevertheless, the earlier picture of Śukra is retained. Thus the tension of Bali's choice is retained as well as the negative aspect of the characterization of Asuras. The latter aspect is utilized in a highly creative fashion by the writer of *Bhāgavata.*

3. *The uses of water*

In Phase 2 texts there are three points in the story where the use
of water is significant: (1) Bali as a good host offers *arghya* water to
the Dwarf; (2) Bali seals his donation of land by pouring water on
the Dwarf's hands; (3) when Trivikrama strides, his foot goes too
far, piercing the membrane of the cosmic egg, and this allows the
cosmic waters to enter the world, these waters becoming the
Ganges.

As we have indicated, in Phase 2 texts the implications drawn
from these are rather disparate. In the Phase 3 texts there is a radical unification of the use of water as a devotional motif. Although
the details differ somewhat in the three accounts, the effect is the
same in all. Thus, in respect to Bali's encounter with the Dwarf,
both *Brahma* and *Padma* conflate the *arghya*-offering and the sealing
of the donation into an act of worship, a concrete act of devotion,
Brahma utilizing the motif of water poured, and *Padma* that of
washing the Dwarf's feet (*Brahma* 73.39; *Padma* 267.27).

Bhāgavata does not conflate the two but unifies the two acts, so
that they become mere variants of one act of devotion. Thus,
when the Dwarf arrives at the sacrifice (*Bhāgavata* 8.18.27–28):

Then, having greeted him with words of welcome,
Bali washed the feet of the Blessed One
and worshipped that charming one
through whom fetters are released.
And the virtuous Bali placed on his head
that water so auspicious,
purified by the Lord's feet,
capable of removing the sins of mankind.
That water is also borne on his head,
with profound *bhakti*
by the Deva of Devas, Girīśa,
who wears the moon as a diadem.

Later, when the boon has been granted [8.20.16–18]:

Having first worshipped him, touching water,
Bali granted to the Dwarf the land.
Then Vindhyāvali his wife came, wreathed with ornaments,

and she brought a golden jar filled with water.
Honouring with joy the two beautiful feet of the Dwarf,
Bali himself washed them.
Then he placed on his head that water
capable of purifying the entire universe.

An important additional element is included in both cases: Bali's placing of the ablutionary water on his own head. We shall see that this carries enormous symbolic power in the context of the *Bhāgavata* vision of *bhakti*.

The other event, that of the origin of the Ganges, is also presented in an entirely original style shared by these three versions. After the second step has been taken, Brahmā pours water upon the upraised foot of Viṣṇu and the water falls to the earth as the Ganges.

In *Brahma*, the action is tied back to the earlier terminology, *argha* (73.63), the water being called *arghavāri* (73.64). According to *Padma*, Brahmā washes the Lord's feet with *bhakti* (267.43: *bhaktyā prakṣālayām asa*), and in *Bhāgavata* too (7.21.3) *bhakti* is mentioned.

In these texts, a further step is taken to integrate the Ganges into the story. The origin of the Ganges is not, as in some Phase 2 accounts, a chance happening. It is itself the result of an act of devotion on the part of Brahmā. The great holiness of the stream is thus a result of this devotional act.

There are, of course, variations in the treatment, giving the story different ramifications. In *Brahma*, the story of the Dwarf and Bali is introduced via the legend of the Ganges and it culminates in an extended explanation of the origin of the Ganges. One gets the impression that the real point of the account is the glorification of the river. Much is made of the purifying qualities of the water used. There is no suggestion that the water is purified by contact with the feet of Viṣṇu; it is already pure—inherently so, it appears. Also, the water is already associated with Śiva, having been given by him to Brahmā.

The modifications in the uses of water are quite radical in that the use of water in the *arghya* is transferred from Bali to Brahmā, making the entire *arghya* event trace the origin of the Ganges to Brahmā's devotional act. Brahmā's extended description of his act

(*Brahma* 73:58–69) suggests that his use of the water in an act of respectful hospitality towards his father Viṣṇu is evidence of its excellent qualities; hence the importance of the Ganges as a sacred stream. This importance is highlighted without belittling the devotion of Bali. The potent *arghya* act is transferred to Brahmā so that it becomes the climax of the story, but Bali is still presented as a devotee. Devas and Asuras, Brahmā and Bali — all are devotees in the *Brahma* version.

According to the *Bhāgavata,* the Lord covered the entire universe with two steps and his foot reached Satyaloka with his second stride. There Brahmā proceeded to offer water to wash the upraised foot of Viṣṇu (*Bhāgavata* 8.21.4):

> And being purified by washing the foot
> of the Wide-Strider,
> the water from Brahma's water-pot
> became the celestial river.
> And that glory of the Blessed One
> falling onto the sky-world
> purifies the three worlds.

This is set in a context of worship of Viṣṇu by Brahmā. The latter offers praise and with the other Lokapālas brings objects appropriate for offering *pūjā* to the Lord. Brahmā's act of offering water can thus be seen as a central part of an act of devotion, and a parallel to those acts already performed by Bali.

The artistry of the *Bhāgavata* accounts is striking. There is no reference to the fall of the Ganges on to the head of Śiva at this point in this story; but an oblique reference has already been made (see above p. 139), for the water Bali uses to wash the feet of the Dwarf is identified by a reference to Śiva (8.18.28). That this action of Bali occurs before the Ganges comes to be and that the water used by Bali is not from the Ganges but apparently from the Narmadā [8.18.21] do not appear to trouble the *Bhāgavata* poet. The events of the story are set in a mythical past in which time sequences and geographical distinctions can easily be overlooked in the interests of a powerful message. And thus, allowing as a presupposition the story of Śiva and the Ganges, Bali can be seen washing the feet of thc Lord with the water which is caught by Śiva in his hair and which is poured by Brahmā on the Lord's feet (whence it acquires its purity). This doubling of the image of washing the Lord's feet (along with the attendant focus on the symbolism of water) reinforces the importance for the devotee of such devotional acts.

In *Padma,* the water becomes imperishable (*akṣayya*) and is called pure (*vimala*) and sacred (*tīrtha*) after it has been used by Brahmā to wash the feet of Viṣṇu. Thus *Padma* appears to follow the *Bhāgavata* usage rather than *Brahma.* But Śiva is used in a new and more direct way. It is he who is recounting the story and he tells of his part in the descent of the Ganges in such a way as to show himself receiving his beauty (*śubha*) and his auspiciousness (*śivatva* = Śiva-ness) because he has held on his head that water from Viṣṇu's feet—which seems to emphasize, in a style similar to that of *Bhāgavata,* that he is a devotee of Viṣṇu. In addition, he reiterates (267.50) the promise of the *Bhāgavata* that whoever bears on his head the water from the feet of Viṣṇu (that is, the Ganges) will be honoured by the world.

The vitality of the water symbolism is evident in these texts. Yet the full force of the image of placing on one's head the water from the Lord's feet—particularly in its *Bhāgavata* setting—is not realized until one examines in detail the treatments in *Brahma* and *Bhāgavata* of the Lord's third step.

B. The Lord's Third Step

The single most important change in the story in Phase 3 is that concerning the Lord's third step. It is a change of which the symbolic force is quite stupendous. In *Hariv. App., Matsya, Vāmana,* and *Kūrma,* the suggestion that Bali is a devotee does not affect the main thrust of the story: the winning back of the three worlds. In *Bhāgavata* and *Brahma,* however, the picture of Bali as devotee is poignantly incorporated into the account of the three strides: the Lord wins back the worlds with two strides, and in his third step he places his foot on Bali's back (*Brahma*), or on his head (*Bhāgavata*).

In order to grasp the full import of this, particularly in its role in *Bhāgavata,* it is necessary that we look at a range of developments in the treatments of demonic and other opponents of the Lord in his *avatāras* which reach clear definition in the *Bhāgavata* portrayals.

The most notable element marking development in the relationship between the Lord and his enemy is a situation in which the enemy is saved at the time as he/she is killed by the Lord. The original for this appears to be the account of the death of Śiśupāla in the *Mahābhārata*. Kṛṣṇa decapitated Śiśupāla with his discus, and Śiśupāla crashed to earth (2.42.22–24):

> The kings saw a fierce *tejas* issue from the body of the king of Cedi, like the sun from the sky, O great king. And that *tejas* greeted Kṛṣṇa, whose eyes are like lotus petals, and who is honoured by the worlds, and entered him, O lord of men.

The explanation for this has already been given by Bhīṣma (2.41.3): "This great-armed one is surely a portion of the *tejas* of Hari. Thus the widely renowned Hari desires to recover it again." The picture of a being who is the incarnation of part of the power of a deity is fairly common. No implications are drawn from this story, though one should perhaps read here an assertion of the Lordship of Kṛṣṇa even over one who is his greatest enemy. There is no indication in *Mahābhārata* whether we should infer that Śiśupāla is saved. But *Viṣṇu* assumes that Śiśupāla is saved and goes on to explain why. The question is posed, why had Śiśupāla not enjoyed this felicity earlier, that is, in his previous births as Hiraṇyakaśipu, killed by Viṣṇu's Man-lion *avatāra* (as also in *MBh* 1.61.5), and as Rāvaṇa, killed by Rāma. The answer is developed from an idea expressed in *BhG* ("Whoever at the time of death, leaving aside his body, departs remembering me, goes to my own mode of being; of this there is no doubt," 8.5). In the earlier births he had not been aware that his destroyer was Viṣṇu. When he died as Hiraṇyakaśipu his mind was perplexed by the predominance of *rajas*. For this reason he was reborn as the rajasic Rāvaṇa. At the point of his death as Rāvaṇa, he was impressed with the idea that Rāma was a mere mortal, so he was reborn in the human family of the kings of Cedi. As Śiśupāla, however, he was in hatred constantly uttering various names of Kṛṣṇa, and Kṛṣṇa was ever present in his thoughts. Thus meditating on Kṛṣṇa at death, to Kṛṣṇa he went, all his sins being consumed by thoughts of Kṛṣṇa (*Viṣṇu* 4.15.4–12).

The account of Śiśupāla's death in *Bhāgavata* also dwells upon the idea that intense hatred has given rise to a continual meditation upon the Lord (10.74.45–46):

> Then a light arising from the King of Cedi's body
> entered Vāsudeva before the eyes of all creatures
> like a meteor falling to earth from the sky.
> Meditating
> with his mind aroused by an enmity
> that was maintained through three births
> Śiśupāla has gone to be Kṛṣṇa's.

To understand fully the Śiśupāla story in *Bhāgavata,* one has to remember that as in *Viṣṇu,* Śiśupāla has been, in former births, Hiraṇyakaśipu and Rāvaṇa. There is in *Bhāgavata* an addition, a parallel, in which it is said that Hiraṇyākṣa is reborn as Kumbhakarṇa and Dantavakra (10.78.10). A further addition is that Hiraṇyākṣa and Hiraṇyakaśipu were originally Jaya and Vijaya, devotees of Viṣṇu and gatekeepers in Vaikuṇṭha. The mind-born sons of Brahmā went on one occasion to Vaikuṇṭha, and were turned away by these gatekeepers because they were naked: as a result, Jaya and Vijaya were cursed by these Brāhmans to be born as Asuras, with the promise that they would return to Vaikuṇṭha after being born three times (3.15.12–35). Thus, one reason why the *avatāras* of the Boar, the Man-lion, Rāma, and Kṛṣṇa are necessary is that the curse upon these devotees must be fulfilled.

It is clear, then, that the meditation of Śiśupāla that has gone on through three lives is of a higher intensity than the meditation of the gatekeepers of Vaikuṇṭha. That is why Jaya and Vijaya have to pass through three lifetimes. Yet, this qualification is not uniformly held necessary. There are other enemies in *Bhāgavata* who are not depicted as devotees in the way that Jaya and Vijaya are, and yet they are saved by being slain. One of these is Kaṃsa, whose meditation of enmity is also depicted (10.2.23–24):

> Thus, refraining from his most terrible designs
> Kaṃsa the mighty
> keeping alive his enmity towards Hari,
> awaited his birth.
> Sitting, lying, standing, eating or strolling,

he thought of Hṛṣīkeśa
and saw the universe pervaded by him.

This description is given at the time of Kṛṣṇa's birth. Later, when Kaṃsa dies at Kṛṣṇa's hands, there is a similar statement (10.44.39).

A slightly different though related motif can be seen in the story of the great Rākṣasī Pūtanā. The story as told in *Bhāgavata* is basically the same as earlier accounts in *Hariv.* and *Viṣṇu:* Pūtanā comes at night to kill the infant Kṛṣṇa; having placed poison on her breasts she goes to suckle him. She appears in the form of a beautiful young woman and everybody thinks she is Śrī come to visit her husband, so she easily gains access to the baby. When Kṛṣṇa sucks, however, he is unharmed by the poison; moreover he sucks the life out of her.

A new section is added to the story in *Bhāgavata:* Pūtanā's body is cut up and cremated (10.6.34–35):

> From the body of Pūtanā when it was burned
> smoke arose fragrant as sandalwood:
> her sins had been destroyed
> since she had suckled Kṛṣṇa.
> The blood-sucking Rākṣasī, Pūtanā,
> devourer of children and men,
> gave her breast to Kṛṣṇa, intent upon killing him—
> and obtained bliss!

Pūtanā, comes with evil intent, but performs the actions of a mother—and so is saved.

Further light on these events comes from a conversation between Yudhiṣṭhira and Nārada in which the former expresses surprise that Śiśupāla and other enemies of Kṛṣṇa should have attained to oneness with the Lord. In his reply, Nārada says (7.1.29):

> Concentrating their minds on the Lord
> through desire, hatred, fear, affection or devotion,
> and having laid aside evil,
> many have gone to his abode.

This is a generalized reference to various emotions—*kāma, dveṣa, bhaya, sneha,* and *bhakti*—which give rise to intense meditation upon the Lord. Nārada then gives specific examples (7.1.30):

> The *gopīs* through desire have won the victory,
> Kaṃsa through fear,
> the king of Cedi and other kings through hatred;
> the Vṛṣṇis through a blood-relationship,
> you through affection, we by means of devotion.

According to Nārada, anything that binds one to the Lord in one's thoughts, anything that normally characterizes an intense or close relationship between two people, so that they are always in each other's thoughts — whether such a characteristic has a positive or negative tone — is able to bring a person to liberation. There is even the strong suggestion by Nārada that a negative relationship is more effective for the gaining of liberation than a positive one (7.1.26):

> It is my firm opinion
> that a mortal does not so easily attain to
>   unity with God
> through *bhaktiyoga* as through the arising of
>   enmity.

The *Bhāgavata* does not always, however, elevate the negative relationships above the positive ones. At times the negative is used as a contrast to a more acceptable positive relationship, as in the final comment on the Pūtanā story (10.6.36):

> How much more shall he obtain bliss
> who gives with faith and devotion
> his dearest and best to Kṛṣṇa, the soul supreme.
> And what of those attached to him
> like a mother?

If even Pūtanā, an evil creature, can be saved, how much more easily shall the true devotee be saved, the devotee who gives not the evil poisonous breast but the most life-giving nourishment, one who does not merely play the part of a mother but is attached to Kṛṣṇa as is a mother to her child.

The *Bhāgavata* gives an alternative explanation of why Pūtanā is saved (10.6.37):

> His feet abide in the hearts of his devotees,
> his feet are honoured by those honoured among men;
> with those feet he trod on her body
> when he sucked her breast.

Pūtanā, in her act of suckling Kṛṣṇa, is blessed by the touch of Kṛṣṇa's feet.

There are three other conflict-stories in *Bhāgavata* where the touch of the Lord's feet is important. The first is that of the Varāha or Boar *avatāra*. This story is recounted in two parts in *Bhāgavata*. The first (3.13ff) tells of the raising of the earth from Rasātala by the Boar; the second of a battle between the Boar and the Daitya Hiraṇyākṣa that ends in the death of Hiraṇyākṣa. Towards the end of the account, when Hiraṇyākṣa has been killed, the gods led by Brahmā utter these words (3.19.27–28):

> Ah, who can attain to such a death?!
> That one upon whom *yogi*s in *samādhi*
> meditate in solitary places—
> by his feet the Daitya wretch was slain.
> While beholding his face
> the Daitya laid aside his body.

There follows a short hymn to the Lord in which the same themes are reiterated (3.19.30):

> How fortunate is this one
> causing great harm to the worlds,
> to be slain.
> Through devotion to your feet
> we, O Lord, are happy.

There are two major ideas here. The first is that it is a marvellous thing to be killed by the Lord, to be smitten by his feet, and to die beholding him. The second is a suggestion that the Daitya thus slain is really a devotee of the Lord. The power of this suggestion is realized most fully when one remembers that, as we have seen,

Hiraṇyākṣa was a devotee of the Lord while dwelling in Vaikuṇṭha, one who, on being banished from Vaikuṇṭha, prayed that he might not be beset by the infatuation that destroys remembrance of the Blessed Lord (3.16.26).

The second myth in the sequence of the *Bhāgavata* where the touch of the Lord's feet is important relates to Bali, and we will return to it after we have looked at all the related motifs. The third myth utilizing this motif is that of the taming of the great serpent king of the Yamunā, Kāliya.

In *Myths and Symbols in Indian Art and Civilization,* Heinrich Zimmer commented on the well-known story of Kṛṣṇa and Kāliya. He noted that instead of being killed by Kṛṣṇa, Kāliya was sent away from the river, where his presence was injurious to cowherds and cows, and forced to dwell in the ocean; and Zimmer drew this conclusion (1962:87):

> Krishna played the role rather of moderator than of annihilator. He liberated mankind from a threat and a peril, favoring life against the slaying breath of the serpent, and yet recognizing the rights of the destructive power; for the venomous serpent was as much a manifestation of the Supreme Being as were the pious cowherds. It was a manifestation of one of the darker aspects of God's essence, and had appeared out of the all-producing, primary, divine substance. There could be no elimination, once and for all, of this presence which seemed to man wholly negative.

Zimmer goes on to reflect upon the difference between this, which he sees as a typically Indian approach, and the annihilation of serpents by the heroes of Greek mythology. He argues that the differences are typical of a contrast between Western and Indian approaches to evil and to the darker aspects of existence. With respect to Indian thought, a case can certainly be made for what he says. In a speech of Kāliya which Zimmer cites, the point is made that in poisoning the Yamunā, Kāliya is performing his own *dharma,* acting in accord with his own inherent nature; and this seems to be accepted by Kṛṣṇa.

Yet, Indian mythology is not always so kind to dangerous and negative beings as Zimmer suggests. In many an account of a conflict between a hero god or goddess and a demon, the conflict ends

in the death of the demonic power. And the fact that Bali is not
slain appears to have raised questions for some of the Phase 2 and
Phase 3 writers that we have examined.

At any rate, it is clear that in the *Bhāgavata,* the sparing of
Kāliya is integrated with other concerns of the poet. That Kāliya is
not killed is due in part, it appears, to a prayer for forgiveness offered by his wives to Kṛṣṇa. In the process of uttering this, the
wives draw the most unexpected implications concerning the
crashing dance upon Kāliya's head (10.16.36–38):

> Those who find refuge in the dust of your feet
> long not for heaven
> nor to be world emperor, nor to rule in Rasātala.
> Not yogic powers do they desire
> nor even freedom from rebirth.
> This lord of serpents, sprung from *tamas,*
> the embodiment of wrath,
> has obtained that which is so difficult to obtain.
> There is supreme bliss for him now,
> such as he desires — even while he lives
> revolving on the wheel of rebirth.

It is clear that in all these cases it is regarded as a great blessing
for the enemy to have the Lord's feet touch him. In order to understand why this is, we should look briefly at this motif as it is developed in Indian *bhakti* movements and more specifically at its use
in *Bhāgavata.*

The earliest indications of a cult of the Lord's feet appear in
Buddhist sculptures. The feet were one of the signs used to represent the Buddha (Zimmer 1955, 1:6) at a time before the Buddha
image became standard. Some early bas-reliefs — at Bharhut
(Zimmer 1955, 2, Pl.32a) and at Amarāvati (Zimmer 1955, 2: Pls.
87,94,95c) — depict what are almost certainly groups of worshippers bowing in reverence and adoration to the feet of the Buddha.
Much that we find in Indian *bhakti* movements involves a trans-
ferring of actions frequently used in human context to a context of
worshipper and the deity being worshipped (see Thomas Hopkins:
110). It is interesting, therefore, to compare some of the bas-reliefs
of the adoration of the Buddha with the medallion found at Amarāvati (Bussagli/Sivaramamurti: 14) portraying the offering of gifts

to a young king. There is striking similarity in the general arrangement of the scenes and in the actions of those giving gifts and those offering reverence to the Buddha. That a throne was sometimes used to represent the Buddha, and that the feet of the Buddha are sometimes set on a footstool in front of a throne, is evidence that, to some extent, the adoration of the Buddha developed upon the analogy of paying one's respects to a king. Vaiṣṇava *pūjā* extended and deepened this analogy, for the worship of the image was carried out in a style appropriate for the honouring of a respected guest. And in this hospitality ritual, as we have seen, one of the major acts was the washing of the Lord's feet.

In *Bhāgavata,* the feet of the Lord are a central focus for devotion. Clinging to the Lord's feet is continually seen as a way to emancipation from *saṃsāra,* though the relationship between the lotus feet and *saṃsāra* is presented from different perspectives. In one mode, the problem is the evils of *saṃsāra* and the Lord's feet are the antidote; in another, the crucial problem inherent in *saṃsāra* is that mortals cling to the things of the world and so miss the bliss of the feet of the Lord.

The bliss of the touch of Hari's feet is a theme that runs through *Bhāgavata.* Pṛthu, as a typical devotee, says (4.20.24), "I do not desire to be anywhere, O Lord, where there is not the nectar of your lotus feet." Even in Vaikuṇṭha, this is the greatest bliss; and even Śrī, the Lord's wife, undergoes *tapas* out of a desire to be sprinkled with the dust of Kṛṣṇa's feet (10.16.36). The natural beauty of Vṛndāvana, which the authors of both *Hariv.* and *Bhāgavata* delight in describing, is encompassed in a theology of Kṛṣṇa's feet; trees lean down their topmost branches to touch these feet; grass, bushes, and ground are blessed, and Vṛndāvana becomes the glory of the earth (10.15.5–10). The goddess Earth is rendered beautiful by the touch of these feet (10.30.10). In numerous imaginative and poetic flights, *Bhāgavata* suggests that so long as one is drinking the nectar of the Lord's feet, so long as one is a bee at Kṛṣṇa's feet, nothing else matters.

One further point, noted by Philip Rawson (iii; see also Carstairs: 79) is helpful if we are to understand the use of this motif in these conflict stories.

> Indians attribute a clear set of values to different parts of the body. The head is most valuable; the feet the least. To touch someone with one's foot is an insult. But to pay true reverence

to someone, one may set their feet on one's own head, and worship them.

The realization that there is a negative element inherent in this symbolism of the feet is an effective stimulus towards contemplating further the negative mode of *bhakti* in Bhāgavata. It is clear, as we have seen, that *Bhāgavata* did not originate the idea of the enemy who is saved when slain. Rather it continued a tradition, perhaps implicit in *MBh* and clearly explicit in *Viṣṇu*, about the salvation of Śiśupāla. While the tradition that Śiśupāla had formerly been a devotee in Vaikuṇṭha — with the corollary that as an enemy he is a devotee in disguise — appears to act as a rationalization of the salvation of the enemy. The scope widens when Kaṃsa and Pūtanā are added to Śiśupāla, transforming enemies of the Lord to his devotees, albeit in a negative manner. The implication is that negative modes of attachment are as valid as positive ones, that love and hate are two sides of the same coin. The important thing is that one has to be attached to the Lord.

There are many places in *Bhāgavata* where the elements of *bhakti* are described (Gail, *passim*). Frequently what is presented is a formal list of characteristics. There is one section, however, where a distinctive, emotional style of *bhakti* is described (7.7.34–36):

> When a man has heard of the incomparable glories
> and heroic deeds performed by Hari in bodies assumed in
>   play —
> and when, from too much joy,
> the hairs of his body stand on end,
> and with tears in his eyes and uncontrolled speech
> and neck stretched taut
> he sings out loud, shouts and dances —
> When like one possessed he laughs and cries,
> he meditates and pays homage to men,
> often sighing, engaged in introspection, all bashfulness
>   gone;
> and "Hari! Lord of the world! Nārāyana!" he cries —
> then is a man released from all bondage.

The intensity of attachment to the Lord, evidenced here in its emotional concomitants, is characteristic of many of the great devotees portrayed in *Bhāgavata,* the archetype being the *gopī*s who love the baby Kṛṣṇa, laugh at his childish pranks, are amazed at his wonderful heroic acts, sing songs about his *līlā*s, are enchanted by the sound of his flute, and leave everything in order to be with him. The *gopī*s are obsessive in their attention to Kṛṣṇa. But so is Kaṃsa, and though it is the obsession of hate, it bonds him to Kṛṣṇa as surely as the love of the *gopī*s.

If attachment can be in positive or negative modes, so too can the Lord's favour. To some the gracious act consists in punishing, taming, and humbling; indeed, it may be seen as particularly gracious in that the one so treated is liberated from attachment to pride, wealth, and the other infatuating paraphernalia of the world. And again *Bhāgavata* continually encourages an attitude of *vairāgya* or detachment, and is at pains to free the devotee from attachment to or infatuation by *prakṛti*, the senses, body, home, family, and wealth (4.20.6, 4.29.36, 5.9.12, 6.1.56, etc.). This attitude is reinforced by the motif of the Lord's feet, the instrument of humbling. It is a force unto itself, for there is no greater bliss than to have one's head touched by the feet of the Lord.

Having looked at this exceedingly rich context, we can now see how the *Bhāgavata* picture of Bali and the Lord's third step draws on, and at the same time contributes to, the *Bhāgavata* vision.

The background to this shift in the story is to be found in the *Vāmana* account that the Lord took the world in two steps — so that the third step was unfulfilled (*Vāmana* 65.33). According to that narrative, Bali was thus left owing Viṣṇu a debt and hence was bound.

It seems likely to me that the *Brahma* version was the first to develop this shift. I suggest this because the crucial elements of *Brahma* are all there, in disparate form, in *Vāmana*. Thus Viṣṇu's statement in *Brahma* 73.48, that there is no place for his third step, is a mere modification of *Vāmana* 65.33. Bali's statement in 73.50 ("The entire universe was created by you. . . It's your fault that it is too small!"), appears to be a variant on Bāṇa's statement in *Vāmana* 65.44 (see above, p. 120). And the request of Bali that the Lord place his foot on Bali's back recalls another account of the Dwarf in *Vāmana*, that is, his overcoming of the demon Dhundhu (52.82-85):

Seeing that the three strides had been granted by the great lord of Asuras, the illustrious Lord, the one of endless power, assumed the form of Trivikrama to stride over the three-fold world.

Having assumed that form and having slain the Daityas he honoured the Ṛṣis and with his first stride he stole back the earth endowed with jewel-mines and cities, mountains and oceans.

And the Lord, wishing to make the Devas happy, with his second step quickly took the mid-region along with the heaven, the abode of the Devas, that sky adorned with moon, sun and stars.

When his third step was not completed, the Blessed Lord Trivikrama fell on the back of the most excellent Dānava with his body the size of Mount Meru.

By utilizing this motif, *Brahma* is able to show Bali freed from his "debt" (cf. *Vāmana* 65.35) and so there is no account of his being bound. In addition, Bali is able to remain true to the characterization of him in 73.3 as incomparably truthful.

Bhāgavata is less closely related to the *Vāmana* details, and the theme of Bali's truthfulness is treated at greater length than in *Brahma*. The Lord says (8.21.31–34):

The earth has been traversed by me
in one step, the mid-region and the quarters
by my body. And you see for yourself
that the heavenly region has been traversed
by my second step.
You made your promise.
Since you have not kept it you should
dwell in hell. So, with permission from your *guru,*
enter hell.
For indeed, vain is his desire
and heaven is far from him
who, rather than fulfilling his promise
to a Brāhman, cheats him.
Being proud, you have not given
what you promised me.
On account of this untruth,
you must spend some time
in hell.

This appears to be an elaboration of *Brahma* 73.50-51 and, in that light, Bali's request that the Lord place his third step on Bali's *head* (*śīrṣṇi*) seems to be a deliberate modification that brings it into touch with the common *Bhāgavata* motif of the devotee's head at the Lord's feet.

In a style that is common in *Bhāgavata,* there is an excursus upon the event of the Lord's third step. Bali launches into a meditation upon the relation of the Lord to Asuras. He sees the Lord as secretly the Asuras' supreme *guru* who, by punishing them, is able to destroy the Asuras' blindness through intoxication or pride. He also mentions that many Asuras have reached *siddhi* or perfection through an attachment of enmity; although this does not fit too cleanly into Bali's argument, it does effect a connection between this event and those which refer to the salvation of the enemy through hatred.

Further discourses, first by Prahlāda and then by the Lord himself to Brahmā, extend the implications of Bali's defeat. The loss of his wealth is seen as a favour, for it is thus that Bali is freed from infatuation with birth, action, youth, beauty, knowledge, authority, and wealth. In consequence he is set free from the power of *māyā.* And this is, as we have seen, thoroughly in keeping with the *Bhāgavata* view of *vairāgya.* It also reflects the statement in *Vāmana* (51.46-48, 50) about Bali's loss of his kingdom (see above, p. 109).

There is a touch of genius in the *Bhāgavata* development of these conflict stories, for there are important messages for all devotees that these stories are uniquely able to convey. There is a natural intensity of emotion in hatred and anger, an obsessiveness evident in Kaṃsa's uninterrupted vision of the universe pervaded by Kṛṣṇa, which makes the negative mode peculiarly fitted to portray the ideal of intense concentrated attachment to the Lord. This is the ideal to which Bali alludes.

But the strong focus of the Bali story lies in the other perception —that nothing can better tear the devotee away from things that bind and impel him towards the Lord than that vision of the Lord whose chastening frees one from attachment. This is brought to concrete form in a story that reaches its climax in the touch of the Lord's feet, that insult which is bliss.

6

Myth A in *Skanda Purāṇa*

The enormous and encyclopedic *Skanda Purāṇa* contains five versions of the story of Bali and Vāmana. Three of these (Texts 17, 18 and 19) are quite short and contribute little of any substance towards new developments. The other two (Texts 16 and 20) are quite substantial and provide some important features for discussion.

Since we have presented a good number of texts in translation demonstrating the styles of Puranic expansion, it seems appropriate now merely to outline the story in each case. Where the actual details of the text are of significance for the discussion, a translation of the relevant section will be presented in the context of the discussion.

Text 17
[*Skanda* 1.1.17.286–1.1.19]
Bali, eager for a fight, approached Amarāvatī with his army. The Devas fought with the Asuras for some time without defeating them, and then asked Bṛhaspati about the Asuras and were told that the latter were invincible, and that they, the Devas, should leave Amarāvatī. This they did, and assuming diverse bird and

animal forms they went to the *āśrama* of Kaśyapa and sang hymns to Aditi. She approached Kaśyapa and was advised to undertake a vow. Viṣṇu appeared to her in the form of a child at the time of a conjunction of the twelfth day of the month with the constellation Śravaṇa.

Praised by Aditi, the Lord told first his club [*gadā*] to go and slay Bali—and then his discus Sudarśana, and his bow—but these weapons were unable to do so.

Then the Asuras besieged Amarāvatī and, finding it deserted, entered it happily. Bali was anointed king by Śukra and proceeded to set up his kingdom. And he was manifestly generous. Asked why Indra was not generous like Bali, Lomaśa explains that Indra obtained his kingdom in Amarāvatī with a thousand horse sacrifices; the result was that he was poor.

There follows a passage in praise of generosity which is linked with *bhakti* and *mokṣa;* and then an excursus on Bali as formerly Kitava, summarized thus by O'Flaherty (1975, 127–28):

There was an evil man named Kitava ["rogue"], who reviled gods and Brahmins. One day he accidentally spilled on the ground some flowers he was going to give to a whore; they were offered to Śiva, and so when Yama came to take the evil one away, Kitava was released from Yama and even given the throne of Indra. He refused to have any contact with Indrāṇī despite the panderings of Nārada, and he gave Airāvata and Uccaiḥśravas [Indra's elephant and horse] to the sages Agastya and Viśvāmitra, and he gave the wishing-cow to Vasiṣṭha. When Kitava's time was up, Indra regained the city of the gods [Amarāvatī] and blamed Yama, saying, "You gave my throne to Kitava, who did this despicable thing, giving all my treasures away. Get them back for me." Yama said to Kitava, "You evil man, you should not have given away someone else's possessions; on earth, generosity is praised, but in heaven no one should give anything to anyone." Then Yama told Citragupta to throw Kitava down to hell, to punish him, but Citragupta refused, saying, "How can Kitava go to hell when he acted in such a praiseworthy way, giving those treasures to the sages? And his evil acts have been burnt to ashes by the grace of Śiva." Yama told Indra to ask Agastya and the others to give back the treasures, and he did. Then, through the ripening of his deeds, Kitava was reborn as the son of Virocana — as Bali.

The story thus returns to Bali and then goes on to provide another background. Wanting to kill the Daitya king, Indra went to Virocana's place assuming the form of a Brāhman mendicant. He asked for whatever he should take pleasure in. Virocana, saying that to give him the kingdom is too easy, and that Śrī (prosperity) is not adulterous, offered Indra his head. It was after Virocana's death at the hands of Indra that Kitava was born as Bali, Virocana's son, eventually becoming Indra in the city of the Devas.

Meanwhile, Hari, pleased with the vow of Aditi, was born in the form of a boy. He was initiated to studenthood by Brahmā, who gave him the sacred thread while the other Devas gave him staff, belt, antelope skin, etc. Then he went to the sacrificial enclosure of Bali and chanted the Sāmaveda. When Bali saw the Dwarf boy he fell to the ground and honoured the boy with his head (18.178).

After a conversation between Bali and the boy about Bali's ancestors, the request for land was made and Bali granted it (18.198). Bali was warned by his *guru* that he should not give a gift to Viṣṇu, who had assumed the form of a boy, that Viṣṇu should not be worshipped by him; for formerly Rāhu had been slain by Viṣṇu who had assumed the form of Mohinī. But Bali said that he would give to Viṣṇu in the boy-form whatever was asked for, because Viṣṇu is entitled to gifts and is the lord of all the fruits of *karma*. Śukra became angry and began to curse Bali (19.9).

Then Bali worshipped the Dwarf. His wife Vindhyāvali washed the boy's feet and they granted him the earth. Viṣṇu enhanced his form and took the earth with one step, all the heavens with a second. His foot went up to Satyaloka and was washed with water falling from a waterpot. From the water from his foot Gaṅgā was born — and was brought down to earth as the preeminent *tīrtha* of *tīrtha*s. Thus the entire world was taken possession of with two steps.

Then Viṣṇu again assumed the boy form. And he told Garuḍa that *he* should take the third step. And after reviling Bali, Garuḍa did so, and then bound Bali in Vāruṇa bonds.

Vindhyāvali, seeing her husband bound came and asked why. When told that three strides should have been granted, she pointed out that the entire unified triple world had been won; nothing more could be given. Then she asked the Lord to take his three steps—one on her head, a second on her son's head, the third on her husband's.

The Blessed Lord then sent Bali off to Sutala, complimenting him as the best of all givers. He also granted him a boon. Bali replied, "This entire mobile and immobile world was made by you. Therefore I desire nothing except your lotus feet."

Text 18
[*Skanda* 5.1.63.10–270]
There once was a Daitya king, intent on devotion to Viṣṇu, named Prahlāda. He was full of all kinds of virtues. His grandson was Bali, ever virtuous. All his subjects were happy, and his kingdom had no negative qualities.

Bali was in his assembly hall surrounded by many Daityas and other classes of beings when Nārada came to the hall. He reported Indra's angry words about Bali and encouraged Bali to fight Indra. Bali engaged in a battle with the Devas, and conquered and subdued them. The Devas went for refuge to Brahmā who told them to go to the best of *tīrtha*s, Uttaramānasa, (50) to the Viṣṇu-saras *tīrtha*. When asked about devotion to Viṣṇu, Brahmā recounted to them the words of the sage Mārkaṇḍeya, who recited the thousand names of Viṣṇu (included in the text), and then pointed out the benefits of reciting and learning them. (205)

The Devas then praised Viṣṇu and asked him to be born from the womb of Aditi as the younger brother of Indra. Acceding to this plea, Viṣṇu was born as a Dwarf after some time.

Bali sacrificed a hundred horses. Various Ṛṣis [Kaśyapa, Bhṛgu, Atri, Nārada, Vasiṣṭha] were officiants (240). The Dwarf came to the sacrifice and chanting *mantra*s from the four Vedas stood at the door of the sacrificial enclosure. Bali, having worshipped the Dwarf, led him to the middle of the *sabhā,* offered him a seat and also offered to give him whatever he wanted. The Dwarf indicated that he had seen many sacrifices—of Varuṇa, Kubera, Dharma, Prajāpati, Vāyu, and the royal Ṛṣis—but none like

Bali's. Bali reiterated that the Dwarf should request whatever he desired. The Dwarf begged three steps of land for a place to reside in. Bali offered to give much more — elephants, horses, chariots, jewels, male and female slaves, women, and wealth — but then granted the three steps, even though Śukra advised him against it (261).

Then Hari measured out the Brahmāṇḍa (that is, the egg of Brahmā) by his steps and returned Indra's kingdom to him. And the Dwarf made a *tīrtha* in the holy Ṛddhisiddhi *āśrama,* and the *tīrtha* was called "Vāmana pool."

In the month of Bhādra, the conjunction of Śravaṇa with the twelfth day of the bright half is called "Vāmanadvādaśi."

Text 19
[*Skanda* 7.1.114]

When Bali was bound by Viṣṇu, his right step was placed (at Puṣkara) by the Viśvarūpa form of the Lord. His second step landed on Meru's peak, his third in the sky. The Brahmā egg was split by his toe and water rushed out and it fell onto the surface of the earth. It is renowned as "Viṣṇupadī Gaṅgā."

Text 20
[*Skanda* 7.2.14–19]

Bali was very powerful and he made the earth fertile. There was prosperity, goodness, and beauty. Earth was like heaven. People were free from poverty, suffering, and death. Indra was satisfied by Bali with sacrifices. There was no fighting, enmity or strife.

Nārada was wandering through the earth, and in the three worlds he saw no battles. He became distressed: "What need is there for bathing and sacrifices, etc., when there is no strife?"

Nārada went and reported this to Hari. Viṣṇu at first issued a call to battle, but then under the direction of Bṛhaspati he went to Mount Mandāra and instructed the great Ṛṣis to engage in a great sacrifice for Bali, saying that he would come to it.

The Ṛṣis went to Bali's sacrificial enclosure. Bali was pleased and offered gifts to them. Viṣṇu became a dwarf, a Brāhman, and he made pilgrimages to numerous *tīrths.* (An excursus on tīrths and Śivarātri follows.) The Dwarf later engaged in study and yogic exercises. Then the Dwarf saw Nārada descending from the sky and offered reverence (Excursus on the birth of Nārada).

Nārada again complained to the Dwarf against Bali—that the warriors were not fighting and there were no battles between Devas and Dānavas. The Dwarf explained that since Bali sacrificed to him, Bali should not be killed by him.

The Dwarf then went to Bali's sacrifice. He received food and alms and with the other Brāhmans he chanted the Vedas. Bali welcomed the Dwarf and (221) offered him *dakṣiṇā*. Śukra attempted to stop him, but Bali said, "He who composed the Vedas has come as Viṣṇu to me (230). Blessed am I" (235). Bali then brought water to wash the Dwarf's feet and offered *pūjā*. Then Bali granted the Dwarf three strides of earth as a place for a *maṭha* (240).

Śukra again warned that this should not be given to the Dwarf —that the Dwarf was Viṣṇu. He refused to pour water on the hand of the Dwarf. Bali himself poured the water and the Dwarf grew in size, assuming his four-armed form. He was praised by the divine Ṛṣis.

Having taken the entire egg of Brahmā with two steps, Viṣṇu had no place for his third step. His foot reached the top of the egg and the movement of his foot fractured the egg. From that fracture water flowed to the three worlds—Gaṅgā, sprung from the foot of Viṣṇu.

God, having taken the earth, caused Bali to dwell in Pātāla. Bali's son Bāṇa asked why, and was told it was because the *dakṣiṇā* was not completed. Nevertheless, the Lord said Bali would be Indra in the Sāvarṇi Manvantara.

Bali asked how he could receive *darśana* of, and offer *pūjā* to, the Lord's feet. The Lord said, "I will abide forever in your heart."

The Lord also said that at the great festival "Dīpapratipad," kings would worship Bali. And "as your kingdom is now, so will that festival be." And the Lord gave the world to Indra.

Text 21
[*Skanda* 7.4.19]

The Lord told Durvāsas that he was unhappy that he was subject to Bali on account of the latter's *bhakti*. Durvāsas went to Bali and requested that he send God off to subdue the Daityas. Bali said, "How can I abandon Keśava [Viṣṇu] whom I have won by means of many virtuous deeds? He formerly took different forms, and having become a dwarf he asked for three steps. He then became 'Trivikrama' and took away the three worlds. I will not leave the feet honoured by Brahmā, Rudra and Indra."

He held firmly on to the feet. Viṣṇu granted his feet to Bali, and went himself to prosperity [*samṛddham*].

A. Minor Versions

These five *Skanda* versions of the myth reflect quite different milieux. Since Texts 18, 19, and 21 are shorter and less complex, we shall look at them first.

Text 18 contains details found in more developed texts of Phase 2 and Phase 3. Thus, the picture of the great *Ṛṣis* in attendance at Bali's sacrifice is found in *Kūrma* and *Padma*. The suggestion by Bali that the Dwarf should ask for much more than three steps of land is a motif in *Vāmana* (65.14) and *Bhāgavata* (8.18.32). The warning of Śukra is closest to that in *Bhāgavata*.

Despite these indications of a drawing upon details seen only in these later texts, the milieu in which Text 18 moves is virtually the same as Milieu 1. None of the concerns that I have discussed in relation to Milieux 2 and 3 are in evidence here, except the portrayal of Bali's virtue and the good conditions in his kingdom. But the basic thrust is the winning back of the worlds by the Lord, and the return of Indra to his kingdom.

There are, as usual, unique details specific to Text 18. Another *tīrtha* is introduced (Uttaramānasa: 5.1.63.50); and the approach of the Devas to Viṣṇu is linked — as I suppose was inevitable at some time — with the reciting of the thousand names of Viṣṇu. This has the effect of a specific idealization of the devotion of the Devas. The Dwarf's indication to Bali that he has seen many sacrifices, but none like Bali's, underlines a theme that is increasingly stressed in later texts, namely, the massiveness of Bali's sacrifice. Now it is linked to Bali's offer to the Dwarf. But none of these changes the Milieu 1 thrust of the text.

Text 18 shares a couple of details with other *Skanda* texts: the introduction of Nārada into the story as a catalyst of the events that occur (also in Text 20); and, at the end, the linking of the myth with a specific day—"Vāmanadvādaśī" (this is shared with Text 17). Since these motifs are much more significant in the other extensive texts, we shall merely note here that this text draws on elements of a further *Skanda* phase — and leave a detailed discussion of these for our considerations of Text 17 and 20.

Text 19 is quite brief, being part of a *māhātmya* of the *tīrtha* Puṣkara. The assertion that Viṣṇu's second step was placed on Meru is unique to this version. The picture of the splitting of the egg of Brahmā by Viṣṇu's toe and the inrush of water which becomes the Ganges is an important motif from Milieu 2. The text draws on none of the major themes from Milieu 3, and shares none of the significant new *Skanda* motifs.

Text 21 is very brief and the portrayal of the winning of the worlds with three steps is basically from Milieu 1. There is, however, the portrayal, first evident in Milieu 2 texts, of Bali as a devotee of Viṣṇu continuing his devotion after the loss of his kingdom. But a specific Milieu 3 theme, that of the Lord's feet, helps us to see the focus of Bali's devotion. And now there is a peculiar twist to the story. Bali, asked to send Viṣṇu away, is unwilling to do so. He clings to Viṣṇu's feet. Viṣṇu leaves his feet with Bali and goes to join the spirit of prosperity.

This is a strange touch, surely atypical. But it is exceedingly important in terms of the total picture of these texts. I asserted in the introduction that a consideration of the entire corpus, in a structuralist style, was important, as variations on a theme could help us to see some features that might not be otherwise discernible. This minor text offers a major contribution to the total picture. In its peculiarity it sensitizes us to the grand theme explored in all texts after the introduction of elements from Myth B into the various accounts of Myth A — the question of the interrelations between *dharma, bhakti* and prosperity. The entire corpus is an astonishingly varied series of explorations of these interrelations. A further complication is added by virtue of the fact that there is the ancient tradition that Bali will be Indra in the Sāvarṇi Manvantara. This means that when Bali is portrayed as a devotee, the further step that one might expect, his attainment of liberation is unlikely to eventuate since this would do violence to such a long standing tradition.[1] Thus, in *Bhāgavata* the implication of the story appears to go with the picture of Kāliya in the same text — Kāliya also cannot be portrayed as obtaining *mokṣa* due to a similarly ancient tradition about his being sent off by Kṛṣṇa to the ocean — that one who knows the touch of the Lord's feet, that is, the true devotee, does not desire even freedom from rebirth.

Thus, throughout the corpus there are various significant links and disjunctions:

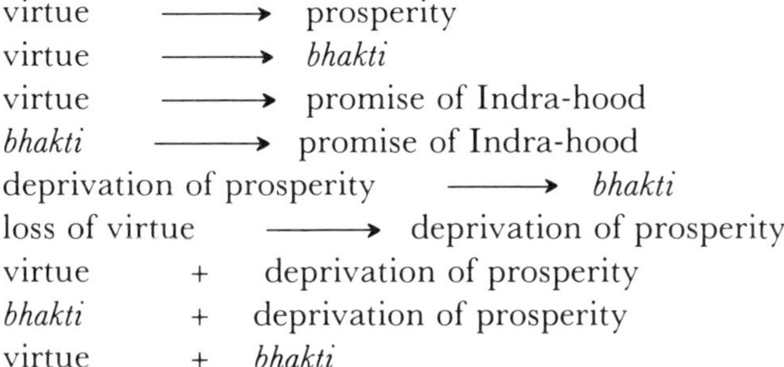

It is difficult to be *absolutely* sure of the implications of Text 21, but it appears to be written from the point of view examining the desirability of prosperity. That examination generates the claim that *bhakti* will not necessarily assure prosperity.

The total picture, then, indicates that the question of the inter-relations of these various positive symbols of Indian culture was much more fully debated and with more diverse positions being expressed than we are aware of from studies based on the better-known texts.

B. Skanda Elaborations: Texts 17 and 20

Text 17 is quite long and significant. Many motifs are shared exclusively, or almost so, with *Bhāgavata:*
   —the conjunction of Śravaṇa with the twelfth
   —Bali honours the Dwarf boy by placing his head at the boy's feet
   —Bali is warned by Śukra that the boy is Viṣṇu
   —Bali along with Vindhyāvali worships Viṣṇu
   —the Dwarf's feet are washed (also *Kūrma, Padma*)
   —the worlds are won back by the Lord in two steps (also *Brahma*)
   —Bali is bound by Garuḍa (also *Hariv. App.*)
   —the Lord's foot reaching up to Satyaloka is washed with water from a *kamaṇḍalu*—the water becomes the Ganges (also *Brahma*)

There are other motifs not found in *Bhāgavata* but shared with other versions:

—gifts are presented to Vāmana by the Ṛṣis (*Matsya*)
—the Dwarf chants the Sāmaveda at Bali's sacrifice
(*Brahma*)
—after taking back the worlds, Viṣṇu re-assumes the boy form (*Kūrma*)

This range of details shared with specific texts suggests that the writer of this version was familiar with a number of earlier versions. The large number of motifs shared with *Bhāgavata* indicates a primary dependence on *Bhāgavata* traditions. And further specific motifs indicate both a continued participation in Milieu 3 and a creative extension of *Bhāgavata* ideas.

1. *Heads and Feet*

There are three different events which draw on the symbolism of placing one's head at the feet of the Lord. The first is rather indirect—Virocana offers his head to Indra, since prosperity cannot be shared. More interesting is the new version of what happens after the Lord has assumed the worlds with two steps. The principal focus of the story shifts to Vindhyāvali who asks why Bali has been bound. The answer given, to the effect that Bali has not fulfilled his promise, leads her to respond that there is nothing to give. But then in an exaggerated form of Bali's offering of his head to the Lord for the third step—the *Bhāgavata* version—Vindhyāvali offers places for the three steps: the heads of herself, her son and her husband.

I find this a delightful imaginative leap. Bali, typically male, thinks of himself—and offers his own head as an act of devotion. Vindhyāvali, however, does not act just for herself. In a style so typical of women—in traditional societies at least—she involves not just herself but also her family in this act of humiliation which is bliss.

The motif of the Lord's feet as a focus for devotion is also seen at the end of the story when Bali is offered a boon. His response is that he wants nothing except the Lord's lotus feet. (It is likely, given the specific form of this, that the portrayal in Text 21 of Bali clinging to Viṣṇu's feet, depends directly on this text.)

2. Śravaṇadvādaśī

As mentioned in relation to Text 18, it is important to consider another issue, that of the various indications of a special day linked to Vāmana, the Dwarf.

In *Vāmana SM* (10.82–84), there is the following link of Vāmana and Dvādaśī:

In the most holy Jyeṣṭha *āśrama* and in Viṣṇupada, those who perform *śrāddha*s, observe vows, and perform rites according to the injunctions or without shall doubtless become inexhaustibly meritorious. By keeping a fast on the Ekādaśī of the bright fortnight of the month of Jyeṣṭha, having a *darśana* of Vāmana on Dvādaśī, bathing in the Viṣṇupada Lake, and making a gift to the best of one's ability, one attains to the highest state.

In *Bhāgavata* (8.18.5):

The Lord was born in Śroṇa on Śravaṇadvādaśī in the Muhūrta of Abhijit.
All *nakṣatras* and stars and the like rendered that birth auspicious.

In *Skanda* (1.1.18.22) (from Text 17):

Delighted with her year-long vow, Janārdana then appeared on the twelfth [*dvādaśī*] in conjunction with Śravaṇa.

In *Skanda* (5.1.63.266–7) (from Text 18):

In the month of Bhādra, the conjunction of Śravaṇa with the twelfth day of the bright half is called "Vāmanadvādaśī," which is able to destroy the effect of a *crore* of murders.

There is no clear indication of the point of this in the context of

Text 18. The other texts cited indicate a linking variously of a *darśana* of Vāmana and the twelfth of the bright half of Jyeṣṭha, the birth of Vāmana at the conjunction of the twelfth and Śravaṇa in Sroṇa (the month of Śrāvaṇa?), and the appearance of Viṣṇu to Aditi at the conjunction of the twelfth and Śravaṇa. In *Skanda* (5.1.63) the month is Bhādrapada.

The purpose in especially noting these details will become clearer in our next chapter. Concerning these materials, two observations are in order: that there appears to have developed some significant relationship between the Dwarf and Śravaṇadvādaśī; and that the actual form of the relationship seems to be in a fluid state.

Discovering what is actually occurring in historical terms in the background of these passing references is complicated by the discrepancies in the portrayal of Śravaṇadvādaśī in other texts. Probably the earliest reference is that in *Vāmana* (53.50–66). The setting of the reference is the story of a wealthy merchant who is attacked by robbers and left destitute. He wanders aimlessly in the forest, and eventually ends up sitting under a *śami* tree. He sleeps and when he wakes he sees a *preta,* a ghost, surrounded by hundreds of other *preta*s. After some discussion, during which the *preta* instructs the merchant that he should not feel sorrow at his loss of wealth, food and water appear and the merchant and the *preta*s all eat.

The merchant inquires about the food and the *preta* tells about his former life and his miserliness. But then he indicates that on one occasion he joined in the festival of Śravaṇadvādaśī (53.50–55):

Then the festival named Śravaṇadvādaśī took place in the month of Bhādrapada. And the people of the city — Brāhmans, Kṣatriyas and others — went to take a bath at the confluence of the Irāvatī and the Naḍvalā.

Along with my neighbours, I also went there. Becoming pure and observing vows on Ekādaśī, I undertook a fast.

Then I donated a strong and new waterpot, filled with water from the confluence. It was covered with a cloth and with it were an umbrella and a pair of shoes.

I also gave an earthen pot filled with sweet curd and boiled rice for a pure, wise, and virtuous Brāhman. In my life of seventy years, that gift alone was given by me, and nothing else, O merchant's son.

After death, the narrator continues, he became a *preta*. But unlike the other *preta*s, he is provided with food — in such quantities that the other *preta*s are also able to eat. All this because of the merit of that day.

When the merchant asks what he should do, the *preta* answers (53.63–66):

> O high-minded one, I will tell you completely what should be done by you for my welfare, what will be best for me.
> Take your bath in the auspicious *tīrtha* of Gayā, and having thus become pure, make an offering of *piṇḍa* balls after indicating my name.
> By the offering of balls of rice to us there, I shall be released from the state of being a *preta,* my friend, and I shall attain to the world of those who have given all.
> So this white and holy Dvādaśī in the month of Bhādrapada, joined with Budha and Śravaṇa is held to make for the very best.

Although it is not clear that the instructions thus presented detail the ritual of Śravaṇadvādaśī, a subsequent description of the merchant's actions clarifies this. It also makes clear that what is indicated is a *śrāddha,* for as well as offering the *piṇḍa* balls to the *preta*s, the merchant offers them also to his own ancestors (*pitṛs*) (v. 70), and to those of his *gotra* (v. 71).

There follow details of subsequent lives of the merchant, indicating the blessings he receives from this action.

This appears to be an extension of the message of *MBh* (13.39.11) that those who perform *śrāddha* on the day the constellation Śravaṇa is in ascendancy will attain to heaven (see Vettam Mani: 735). But there are (in *Vāmana* 53.53) other significant ritual details: a water pot, an umbrella, and a pair of shoes all suggest a relation to the Dwarf, and in other texts this relationship becomes more explicit. In *Agni* 189, 3–7, the following prayer is recorded, to be offered on Śravaṇadvādaśī:

Fasting on the twelfth, I worship a golden image of the Dwarf making use of a pot of water; and then I eat on the thirteenth. I invoke Viṣṇu the Dwarf, who bears discus and conch, who is provided with waterpot, umbrella and a pair of sandals, and is covered over with two pieces of white cloth. I wash with clean water as well as with the *pañcāmṛta,* etc., the image of Viṣṇu who carries a club and an umbrella: "Honour, honour to Vāmana. I offer this *argha* to you, O Lord of the Devas." Ever is he worshipped by persons who are themselves worthy of such *argha.* "Endow me with all kinds of enjoyment, liberation, offspring, and fame — and make me lord of all."

Later another prayer is suggested (189.12–15):

Honour, honour to you, Govinda, to you known as Budha and Śravaṇa. Destroy all my sins and bestow on me all kinds of happiness. O Janārdana, O lord of Devas, may you ever be pleased with me. The Dwarf is the granter of discrimination and he is the donor who abides in wealth. It is the Dwarf who receives from me and makes gifts to me. The Dwarf ever abides in wealth. Glory, glory to Vāmana!

This passage also refers to the practice of bathing at the confluence of two streams (vs. 2, 11) and the importance of giving gifts to Brāhmans (v. 15).

In *Garuḍa* 1.136, there is a similar portrayal of the Śravaṇadvā-daśī *vrata* or vow, with this specific reference to the Dwarf (v. 6):

Gems shall be put in a water pot and the deity Vāmana shall be worshipped. The image is covered with two pieces of white cloth. An umbrella and a pair of sandals also accompany the same.

But it is clear from other texts that the link with Vāmana was not everywhere a part of Śravaṇadvādaśī in Bhādrapada. *Padma* (6.70), while incorporating details for *pūjā* into the account of the day, makes no specific mention of Vāmana or sandals or an umbrella, but relates the *vrata* to the *preta*s in a manner similar to that of *Vāmana* (53). Also in *Bhāgavata* (7.14.19–24), there are instructions about the performance of *śrāddha* by Brahmans for their parents and relations. One of the times mentioned for these *śrāddha*s is *dvādaśīśravaṇa* (v. 20), and there is a further mention of the conjunction of *dvādaśī* with the constellations Anurādhā. Śravaṇa, and the Uttarās (presumably Uttaraśphalgunī, Uttarāṣāḍhā and Uttarabhādrapadā) (v. 23). But then the picture is broadened in v. 25 when it is indicated that actions performed on these days — bathing, muttering of prayers (*japa*), offering of sacrifice (*homa*), a vow (*vrata*), the worship of Devas and Brāhmans (*devadvijārcana*), and gifts to ancestors, Devas, men or *pretas* — all bring their reward. This affirms both the general auspiciousness of the conjunction of Śravaṇa and *dvādaśī* and a special relationship established between these and offerings for the dead.

We have before us, then, an important question about the linking of Vāmana and Śravaṇadvādaśī. But many details from modern Kerala increase the ramifications greatly, and so we must consider the question more fully in a later section.

Text 20 is another major piece. There are many incidental new details. For example, Bali is not to be slain by the Dwarf because he has sacrificed to him; Śukra offers two warnings, on the second occasion refusing to pour water on the Dwarf's hands so that Bali himself has to do it; the Dwarf is portrayed as a *tīrthayātrin,* a pilgrim visiting various holy places; Bali's question of how he may have a view of the Lord's feet and offer worship to them is answered by the Lord with an indication that he abides in the heart. However, there are three sections that I regard as of considerable significance.

1. *Bali's Reign*

The first is the portrayal of the conditions of the earth during Bali's reign. This is much more detailed and extensive than in earlier versions (7.2.14.8–18):

> Later Bali was born, and he was exceedingly powerful. And Bali rendered the earth abundant. The earth was very fertile, well watered, resplendent with grain. Flowers were fragrant, fruits were tasty, and there were coconut trees and an abundance of honey. Brāhmans were all conversant with the four Vedas, Kṣatriyas were skilled in battle; Vaiśyas were devoted

to caring for cows, and Śudras were happy in serving others. The people were always of good conduct and free from illness and calamity. They were all happy and corpulent, ever blissful, ever diligent. Their limbs were anointed with saffron and aloes. They were finely dressed and beautifully adorned. Released from poverty, pain and death the people were long lived. At night the regions of earth were graced by lamps and were as light as the day. And mortals lived on earth like the Devas in heaven: the Asura Bali established his kingdom on the earth which had the appearance of heaven. The sound of festive instruments was constantly enjoyed by the king. The Daitya enjoyed earth as Indra enjoyed himself in heaven. And Indra was ever satisfied with sacrifices performed by Bali.

The Devas and Dānavas did not fight each other. There was one guardian of earth so there was no fighting on earth. There was not even the fighting that is attributed to natural enmity — neither between mongoose and snake nor between cat and mouse. The entire world had become friendly.

Of particular note here is the portrayal of the beauty and abundance of the earth and the emphasis on the absence of all kinds of strife.

2. *Nārada*

The second important motif is the part played by Nārada in the story. Nārada is portrayed as quite unhappy at the lack of strife in Bali's kingdom and the reason he gives for his distress [*pīḍā*] constitutes a significant contribution to Indian views on the necessity of evil (7.2.14.20–23):

I need not perform my ablutions, and what need is there for sacrifices? All my actions can be other than chanting and offering sacrifice, etc.

Bathing occurs where elephants fight with the scraping together of their tusks. Morning and evening prayers occur when adorned with the corpses of those slain, where there are set up elephant heads split by blows from spears.

When carnivorous animals are satisfied there is that sacrifice dear to me — and when those not vulnerable to elephants' heads are slain by warriors in battle. Where there are cries of elephants and the best of men, there is *homa* offered.

Again (vs. 25–26):

> What makes the earth shine is ever the worship of the immortals. What should I do with the Devas in heaven; what with men on earth, and what with the Pannagas in Pātāla who no longer fight one another?

And when he goes off to report to the Devas what he has seen on earth he complains (38–41):

> As long as Bali is king you don't have any use for me. All the planets, the Ādityas and so on, are controlled by the pride of Time. Clouds, when summoned, hover overhead and then in delight pour rain on the earth. There is no disease or death. Yama is not impelled by Dharma. The kings enjoy the fertile earth.

Much later, Nārada complains to the Dwarf that the warriors are not fighting and that there are no wars between Devas and Dānavas (7.16.6–7).

Nārada is often portrayed in Hindu literature as one who stirs up disputes, and this characteristic of his is here directed towards the tradition of Bali's perfect kingdom in such a way as to negativize it. At the same time, his argument becomes a Hindu equivalent of the Christian argument that evil is a necessary possibility for the development of good — that without the possibility of choosing good we would not be fully human; and hence follows the possibility of choosing evil. The line of argument here is that if everything is beautiful and rich and prosperous, and if there is no tension or strife or unhappiness, the impetus towards the good actions of the ritual is lost. Which means, presumably, that when everything is fine, in the final analysis everything is not fine. An interesting sidelight is thrown by the observation that warriors do not fight and Devas and Dānavas do not battle. The natural order of things is disturbed. One might even say, after considering the case of the Kṣatriyas who do not fight, that *dharma* is upset.

We shall see that this is not the last word on Bali's perfect kingdom. It is, however, a cogent counter to the human tendency towards "dreaming of systems so perfect that no one will need to be good" (Eliot, 170).

3. Bali and Dīvālī

The third element of note in Text 20 is the linking of Bali and the festival (*utsava*) of Dīvālī—called here "Dīpapratipad." The relevant section, substantially the same as *Vāmana* (65.58–60), where it is called "Dvarapratipadā," is as follows (7.2.19.22–26):

> Another festival should be celebrated in the great festival of Śakra. This will be a great festival called "Dīpapratipad."[2] At that festival the finest of men, happy and thriving and finely bedecked, will with due care worship you with offerings of flowers and lamps. It will be the most auspicious festival on earth, and known by your name, O Daitya. By means of that festival you will be made happy for the year. Men who are full of a firm devotion will also worship you in accord with prescribed rules. May they have happiness and good fortune. And as your kingdom is now, so will that glorious festival be.

Across most of northern India and in much of the southern peninsula, the central part of the festival of Dīvālī or Dīpāvalī today is the lighting of lamps on the new moon day (*amāvāsya*) of the month of Āśvina (late October or early November) in honour of Lakṣmī or Śrī and in Bengal, of Kālī (Hastings, 5:868; Kane, 5:200). But this is only one part of an extremely complex festival. Dīvālī spreads over a period of some four or five days; that is, there are records of various aspects of the festival being celebrated from the 13th of the dark half of the (lunar) month of Āśvina to the 2nd of the bright half of the month of Kārtika.

The following is a compilation of various features that have been, or still are, part of the festival celebrations as they are related to each of the five days.

(a) *13th of dark half of Āśvina:* This is called in Gujurat and Saurāṣṭra and Uttar Pradesh "Dhanteras;" prior to this day or on the day itself, houses are painted and decorated, courtyards are cleaned, and metal vessels are polished. Frequently the lighting of lamps begins on this day but only a few, or even just one lamp is lit. *Padma* 6.124.4 refers to the practice as "yamadīpa" and suggests that by setting up such a lamp in honour of Yama, the god of death, one avoids sudden or accidental death (see Kane, 5: 195–96).

(b) *14th of the dark half of Āśvina:* A major tradition is that on this day Kṛṣṇa killed Narakāsura, king of Prāgjyotiṣa (see *Viṣṇu* 5.29). Rai Bahadur B.A. Gupte gives the following account (36):

> On this day, all Hindus bathe very early, before sunrise, after anointing their bodies with many perfumed unguents and oils. There are two baths taken one after the other, just as is done on the death of a near relation. After the first bath, a lamp made of rice-flour and an oval piece of the same stuff called *mutke* are waved round each male by some girl or married woman and the fruit of the cucurbitous plant, *chirāt,* is placed in front of him. He then crushes the fruit under his left foot, extinguishes the lamp with the toe of his left leg, and takes the second bath. He wears a new dress and partakes, with his friends and relations, of the numerous dainties prepared for the occasion.

Kane (5:197) identifies the locus of this practice as the Deccan, and also regards the fruit that is crushed under foot as a representation of Narakāsura. Kane also notes that in the *Bhaviṣyottara,* reference to lighting a lamp for Naraka is linked with instructions for *tarpaṇa* to Yama, concluding that this day was originally "called Narakacaturdaśi because Yama was to be propitiated for fear of hell." (5: 1, 197) In addition (Kane, 5:1,198),

> Several works such as the Varṣakriyā-kaumudī and the Dharmasindhu prescribe that on the evenings of the 14th of the dark half and the amāvāsyā of Āśvina men with firebrands in their hands should show the way to their *pitṛs* [deceased ancestors] with the mantra 'May those men in my family who were cremated and those who had no cremation performed for them and those that were burnt only by resplendent fire [without religious rites?], reach the highest state [or goal]; may those [pitṛs] who, leaving the world of Yama, came for the *Mahālaya*

srāddhas [in the dark half of Bhādrapada or Āsvina acc. to pūrnimānta reckoning] find their way by the brilliant light [of the firebrands] and reach [their own worlds].

Kane thus notes that much of the material related to this day has to do with the mythology surrounding death. He therefore concludes that the introduction of the Kṛṣṇa-Narakāsura story is a later development built out of the facts that (1), the names for hell and of this Asura are the same, and (2), there is thus offered the possibility of a glorification of Kṛṣṇa as part of the festival. He notes that today people commemorate only Narakāsura; hardly anyone does Yamatarpaṇa.

Susan Snow Wadley, in her discussion of religion in Karimpur, U.P., says that the day preceding Dīvālī (*choti devālī*) is regarded in that region as extremely inauspicious and all members of the household go to bed with lampblack on their eyes and oil in their ears as protection against the evil spirits who are moving around that night (Wadley, 196).

(c) *Āśvina amāvāsyā (New Moon Day)*: This day, as we have said, is devoted to the worship of Lakṣmi (though in Bengal Kālī takes her place). Understandably, it is a particularly important day for merchants and traders. For those who follow the Vikrama calendar this is the last day of the year, and so accounts are closed on this day. Account books are worshipped, and presents are given to relatives, friends, and subordinates (Thomas, 94). Gupte mentions (36) the popular tradition that Brahmā gave each of the four *varṇas* a specific festival — Rakṣabandhana to Brāhmans, Dasarā to Kṣatriyas, Dīvālī to Vaiśyas, and Holi to Śūdras.

The emphasis on this day is strongly on prosperity and material well-being, of which Lakṣmī is the ruling deity. In some texts it is said that Kubera, the god of wealth, should be worshipped, and this again serves to underline the emphasis on material prosperity.

(d) *1st of the light half of Kārtika:* This day, New Year's Day in the Vikrama calendar, is called "Balipratipadā" in honour of Bali. According to some, Bali was deprived of his kingdom on this day (Thomas, 93). But one of the earliest accounts we have of this part of the Festival, that of Al-Biruni (2.182), says that on this day of the year Bali is released and returns to earth:

1st Kārtika or new moon's day, when the sun marches in Libra is called *Divālī*. Then people bathe, dress festively, make presents to each other of betel leaves and areca nuts; they ride to the temples to give alms and play merrily with each other till noon. In the night they light a great number of lamps in every place so that the air is perfectly clear. The cause of this festival is that *Lakṣmī* the wife of *Vāsudeva* once a year on this day liberates *Bali*, the son of *Virocana*, who is a prisoner in the seventh earth. Therefore the festival is called *Balirājya* i.e. the principality of *Bali*. The Hindus maintain that this time was a time for luck in *Kṛtayuga* and they are happy because the feast day in question resembles that time in the *Kṛtayuga*.

In many parts of North India, this day commemorates not the kingdom of Bali but the kingdom of Rāma, the return of Rāma to Ayodhyā, and his coronation. (Gupte, 37) It is also a day associated with the worship of cattle, and the worship of Mt. Govardhana. For those not living near Govardhana, the building of a Govardhana with cow dung or heaps of cooked food was prescribed, till some time ago. Today *govardhanapūjā* has disappeared except from some rural areas of Uttar Pradesh. Susan Wadley gives the following description of *govardhanapūjā* as performed in Karimpur (128–29):

In the associated ritual, the first step is to construct ritual figures out of cow dung, collected by the women earlier in the day and deposited in a corner of the courtyard. The women use the cow dung to make a rectangular, three-dimensional figure. The figure has a head and often feet, and around the boundaries are a series of mountains [*pahar*]. Within the rectangle, cow-dung images of all the members of the family are placed, along with images of all the family's animals [including the ubiquitous dogs], and other valued agricultural items, such as a plow, the village pond, etc. . . . The basic figure itself is variously identified as a cowherd, or, more specifically, as Krishna. The mountains are there to protect the family which they enclose, an obvious reference to the Krishna legend re-

lated in the associated myth. At some time during the day, one
of the women will worship the figure and the mountains for the
family. Later, when the figure has been destroyed, the cow
dung will be fashioned into cakes which will be preserved until
the Holi bonfire three months later.[3]

Padma 6.124.30–33 gives the following instructions:

> Having in the morning worshipped Govardhana one should
> engage in gambling at night. Refraining from milking the
> cows, which have been decorated, one should say,
> "O Govardhana, O supporter of the earth,
> you who are active in protecting Gokula,
> you who were raised by the arm of Viṣṇu,
> grant us a crore of cows.
> May Lakṣmī, who was provided
> with the form of a cow by the World Protectors,
> bring *ghee* for the sacrifice
> and may my sin be taken away.
> Let cows be before me
> Let cows be behind me
> Let cows be in my heart.
> I dwell in the midst of cows."
> This is the form for the worship of Govardhana.

Here a link is made with Lakṣmī and also with the practice of
gambling, a practice still important on this day. This is legiti-
mated by a story of Śiva's gambling with Pārvati (see *Padma*
6.124.26–27).

In certain areas the construction of Govardhana appears to be a
substitute for the practice of making images of Bali and of various
members of his family. In Maharashtra, women prepare effigies of
Bali either in rice-flour or cow-dung, and repeat the blessing,
"May all evil disappear, and Rajah Bali's empire be restored"
(Thomas, 93; see also Walker, 1:452; and Gupte, 36).

Gupte (39–40) gives further details of the different constructions
of these figures.

> The Chāndraseni Prabhus of Bombay mould their effigies of
> Bali Rāja out of cooked flour, while the *mālis*, or gardeners of

Indore, who are Sudras, use cow-dung. In the houses of the former, the figure of the king and that of his consort are mounted on horseback, followed by a mounted minister, and saluted by four footmen, who stand like a guard of honour, in a row. The whole scene is placed in a silver or brass tray. The Sudras mould a figure on the bare floor, lying flat with its face upwards. The former draw, from the 8th day of the second half of Ashwin to Divāli, a set of symbols in rice-flour or powdered calcspar on the floor of their compounds or verandahs and in front of the main entrance.

F. R. Allchin (121) mentions a custom of the Mahadev Kolīs of Bombay: they drive their cattle over a small bonfire and then make them trample on a cow-dung cone described as a model of Bali. This practice suggests itself as a variant on the one, mentioned above, of crushing underfoot a fruit representing Narakasura. It also seems related to the practice, recorded in the texts but no longer in vogue, of the tying of Mārgapālī ("the protectress of the road"). A rope made from *kuśa* grass was tied between a tree and a tall pole and everybody—including king, Brāhmans, elephants, and cows—was made to pass under it (Kane, 5: 205-6). Kane also refers to the Gāyandānṛ festival of Bihar and Orissa, celebrated on the first of the bright half of Kārtika, in which cows, with their bodies and horns decorated in bright colours, chase and kill a small pig. The parallel here to the custom of the Mahadev Kolīs described above seems self-evident.

A further important feature of this day is that it is, as we have said, New Year's Day in the Vikrama calendar. The historical or quasi-historical basis of this is that King Vikramāditya of Ujjain, a descendent of the Guptas, was crowned on this day and dated his era from the day of his coronation (Thomas, 93; Gupte, 37). There would appear to be some connection between these events and the traditions about Rama's coronation and Bali's reign. What that connection is is not immediately clear. To that question we shall return later.

(e) *2nd of the light half of Kārtika — called Yamadvitīyā*
Kane again cites (5:201) the *Bhaviṣyottara* 14.18-23:

On the 2nd tithi of Kārtika bright half Yama was treated by Yamunā to a dinner in her house; therefore this tithi became declared in the world as Yamadvitīyā; wise men should not take mid-day meal in their own houses but they should take food from the hands of the sister through affection, as doing so increases one's welfare or prosperity. Gifts should be made to sisters; all sisters should be honoured with golden ornaments, clothes, reception, and meals; but if there be no sister, one should honour a woman whom he regards as sister [uncle's or aunt's daughter or a friend's sister].

Far more important today than the prescribed rituals of worship is the custom of sisters feasting brothers, who in turn bring gifts for sisters. Kane thinks that this is an independent festival tacked on the Dīvālī festivities in order to extend the period of enjoyment. It seems a logical extension of the family celebrations of Dīvālī to provide for renewing of the family ties which people have shared in childhood and youth. The drawing on the Ṛgvedic myth of Yama and Yamī — Yamī becoming in the medieval texts Yamunā — may be merely a happy accident. The association of Yama with earlier parts of the festival may be used to validate the practice of a brother visiting his sister as a parallel to the story of Yama and his sister.

Dīvālī is obviously a very complex festival. One naturally wonders whether it may be possible to unravel stages of the developments of such complexity. It is likely that such a festival did not spontaneously appear in all of this complexity, that the complexity represents a development from simpler forms. It is also likely that additional symbolic elements find their way into the total symbolic mix because of their association with symbols that are already part of the festival.

On this basis I indicate below possible lines of association. In most cases, as I have indicated by ⟶ , we have no way of determining which symbol gave rise to which. I have included in brackets beneath each associated pair the basis upon which one might expect one symbol to suggest another.

In a number of cases it is possible that neither of the symbols of an associated pair gave rise to the other, that each developed from an association on the given basis from some other symbol now lost to us. I have indicated a number of places where this seems quite a likely possibility, the projected lost symbol being indicated by ?.

(1) Yama ⟷ ? ⟷ Bali
    (netherworld)

(2) Yama ⟷ Narakāsura
    (death-hell [Naraka])

(3) *pitṛs* ⟷ Yama
    (realm of death)

(4) Bali ⟷ Narakāsura
(Asuras overcome by Viṣṇu's avatars)

(5) 14th Aśvina inauspicious ⟷ *death (pitṛs)*
    (inauspiciousness)

(6) Bali ⟷ Lakṣmī
    (Myth B and its extensions)

(7) Lakṣmī ⟷ account books, merchants
    (material prosperity, wealth)

(8) Lakṣmī ⟷ presents
    (prosperity, wealth)

(9) Bali ⟷ presents
    (generosity)

(10) Lakṣmī ⟷ Kubera
    (property, wealth)

(11) Reign of Bali ⟷ Reign of Rāma
    (ideal conditions)

Coronation of Vikrama
    (kingship)

(12) Lakṣmī ⟷ cattle
    (prosperity, chattels)

(13)   cattle ⟷ Govardhana
              (Kṛṣṇa's cowherding)

(14)   Lakṣmī ⟷ gambling
              (prosperity)

(15) Construction of Govardhana + figures
       —in cow-dung or cooked food

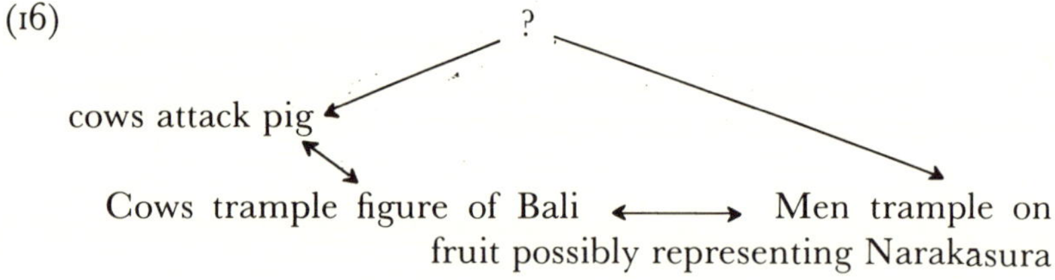

Construction of Bali figures (+ designs)
       —in cow-dung or cooked flour

(construction of decorations, images of significant
   persons, symbols)

(16)

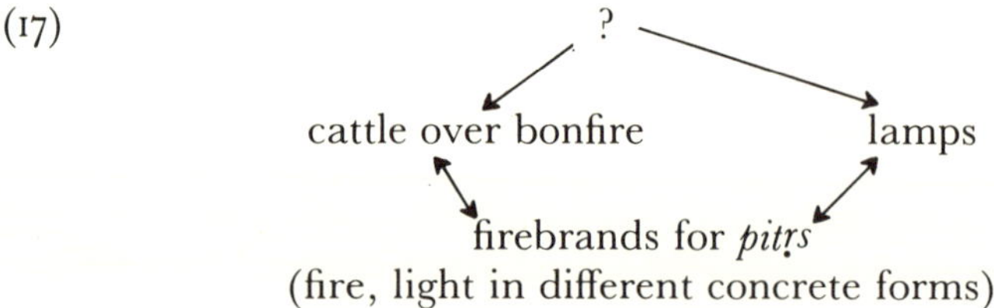

cows attack pig

Cows trample figure of Bali ⟷ Men trample on
                              fruit possibly representing Narakasura

(destruction of inauspicious or adharmic—as Phase 1)

(17)   ?

cattle over bonfire   lamps

firebrands for *pitṛs*
(fire, light in different concrete forms)

(18)   ?

cattle over bonfire ⟷ all under Mārgapālī (rope)
              (purification, protection)

(19) kingship—coronation ⟷ gambling
      (that is, 11 above)

contests

(both gambling and contests related to kingly prosperity)

(20) day   before   Dīvālī   inauspicious   ⟷   "May   evil
disappear
and Bali's empire be restored"

(End of old year   New Year's Day)

If we ignore for the moment the lost symbols and take up the
possible interrelations among the known symbols, we can construct a map of interrelations. If we construct it in such a manner
as to reflect such relations as far as possible by proximity, the path-
ways of association form the following chart:

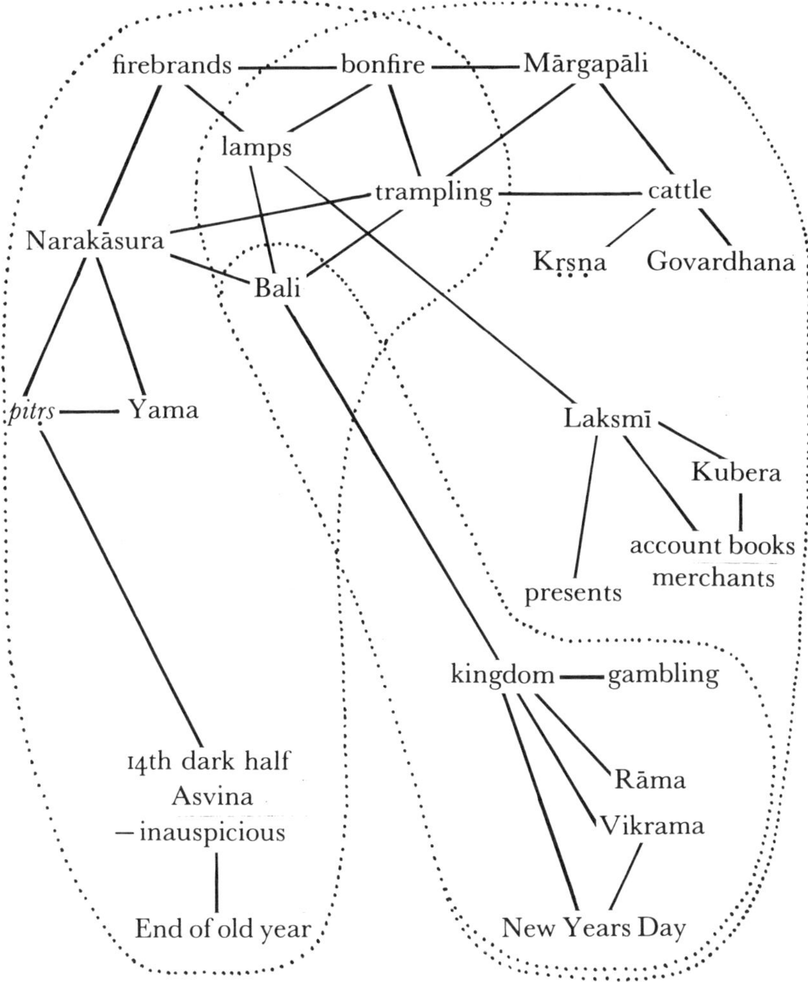

This diagram makes clear:

(1) That Bali and Lakṣmī are of central importance in the sets of possible interconnections.

(2) That there are three overlapping sets of symbols in which each set is grounded in a common theme. These three I would characterize as death or distress; prosperity; and sovereignty.

(3) That Bali is the pivotal symbol common to all three thematic areas.

That Bali holds this pivotal position suggests a development of the festival from one of the areas into the others via his legend. Thus, Dīvālī might have begun as a festival of the dead or of the ancestors, but gradually drifted to become a festival of prosperity. On the other hand, it might have been a festival of prosperity which, because of the ambivalence of the character of Bali, also developed a dimension relating to death. The evidence so far noted is not conclusive enough for either one of these assumptions, or for forming others. To reach a clearer view we must take into account another piece of evidence.

There are two Puranic texts on the celebration of Dīvālī that vie for the position of the earliest text giving details of the festival. These are, *Padma* 6.124, and *Bhaviṣyottara* 140, which has been discussed in detail by J. J. Meyer. It appears that one of them is a copy of the other (though incorporating some decisive changes), for the two texts agree substantially—in large sections word for word. Moreover, the pattern is the same, each text treating in the same sequence the days of the festival, thus:

13th of dark half of Kārtika:[3] *Padma* 6.124.4–5

14th   : *Bhaviṣyottara* 140.7–13
                             Padma 6.124.6–17

New Moon Day   : *Bhaviṣyottara* 140.14–29
                             Padma 6.124.18–33

Next Day (1st of bright half): *Bhaviṣyottara* 140.30–73
                             Padma 6.124.34–70

There are some major points of discrepancy within these parallel sections. The most extensive is the description of New Moon Day *(amāvāsya)*. Verses 18 and 19 of *Padma* and verses 14 and 15 of *Bhaviṣyottara* are the same. What follows in *Padma* is somewhat diffuse, beginning first with the following (6.124.20–25):

Then in the afternoon he (the king) should make the cities and
the assembled people glad by speaking words of praise. Where
there is love of the Pitṛs there is joy in heaven. Formerly when
Hari was still asleep, Lakṣmī was awakened by the women.
After one has wakened Lakṣmī, one should then worship her.
Him who does this Lakṣmī does not leave for the year. Having
with the help of Brāhmans become fearless, those afraid of
Viṣṇu, the enemies of the Devas, knowing that Viṣṇu was
asleep on the milk ocean, repaired to the dwelling of Lakṣmī.
"You are Light, Prosperity, sun, moon, lightning, a golden
star. Of all lights you are the light—and thus the light of the
lamp." This Lakṣmī who is on earth on the holy day of
Dīpāvalī, she in the herd of cows in Kārtika is propitious
towards me.

This is followed by the reference, mentioned above, to the gambling of Śiva and Pārvatī, and then by the section on *Govardhanapūjā* (above, pp. 175–76).

The *Bhaviṣyottara* is much more unified and gives many details
not found in *Padma* relating to Bali (140.16–21):

Then in the afternoon let [the king] proclaim in the city,
"Today, my people, is the reign of Bali. Enjoy yourselves to
your hearts content." And the people shall show their pleasure
in the city so that their courtyards are whitewashed for the
festival. The house and surroundings are decked out with
flowering trees and sandalwood and garlands, etc. With their
hearts thus filled with delight, men and women in high spirits
romp together in games of chance, carousing and coupling.
The house resounds with the sound of dance and instrumental
music and is illuminated by lamps.

There are further details about placing the lights on the house, and
then the text returns to the king and the association with the reign
of Bali (26–29):

About midnight the king himself shall wander slowly through
the city on foot, to the sound of noisy instruments and beneath

flaming torches, in order to behold the enjoyment of his people. So he surveys the city, made splendid, and equipped with means of protecting the people against mundane and demonic dangers. When he sees this great marvel, and his own fortunate magnificence and the joy of Bali's reign, he shall go to his house.

When it is past midnight and the people are almost asleep, then their full joy is expressed by the women of the city with the sound of their winnowing-baskets which they beat like a drum — happy that inauspiciousness has been banished from their own houses and yards.

Later in both *Padma* (6.124.46–55) and *Bhavisyottara* (140.47–56), there is a further section on the worship of Bali, which Kane translates thus:

> The king should at night draw the figure of Bali having two arms on a circle made on the ground with five coloured powders; the image should have all ornaments and should have Vindhyavali [Bali's queen] near him, should be surrounded by asuras like Kusmanda, Bana, Mura and others, should wear a crown and ear ornaments; the king should himself offer worship in the midst of his palace together with his brothers and ministers with several kinds of lotuses and offer sandalwood paste, incense and *naivedya* of food including wine and meat and employ the following mantra 'salutation to you, O king Bali, son of Virocana, enemy of gods and the future Indra, accept this worship.' Having thus worshipped he should keep awake at night by arranging for dramatic spectacles presented by actors based on stories about ksatriyas. Ordinary people also should establish inside their houses on a couch the image of King Bali made with rice grains and worship it with flowers and fruits.

As we have said, given the fact that some sections of these two texts are identical, there appears to be a borrowing by one from the other. And because the *Bhavisyottara* text is unified around Bali, and the *Padma* version is quite diffuse, it makes most sense to see *Bhavisyottara* as reflecting an earlier, simpler stage of the festival, and *Padma* as the production of a later stage when more elements had been linked into the complex of the festival. The fact that *Bhaviṣyottara* holds together logically adds weight to this supposition. It is not entirely beyond all possibility that a skilful writer took a short section from *Padma* on Bali and developed it in order to satisfy the interest of kings vis-à-vis Bali and thus arrived at the *Bhaviṣyottara* version. But this seems historically improbable.

However, even though the primacy of *Bhaviṣyottara* seems likely, one should not thereby assume that the origin of the Dīvālī is to be seen in a celebration of Bali's kingdom. A likelier possibility seems to me to be that Dīvālī is an overlay upon an earlier festival of the New Year. To assess these conjectures we must wait until our final chapter.

7

Mahābali and Ōṇam

Of all the twists and turns that the story of Bali has taken through the ages, the most surprising is one that lives on in the tradition of contemporary Kerala. For here the story of Bali and Vāmana has been linked to the festival called Ōṇam, Kerala's most popular festival, often referred to as its national festival. In this version Bali has become Mahābali, "the great Bali," and is the hero of the story, Vāmana being now merely a functionary for the Devas.

Texts 22 to 25 all refer to the link between the festival and Mahābali. Texts 23 (reproduced above, p. 24) to 25 are from works that are each in some way an introduction to Kerala culture. The first two are from Malayalis, the third by a Canadian. The two Malayalis are Christians. That they are interested enough to reproduce the story and talk of Ōṇam explains why Ōṇam is called the "national festival" of Kerala. It is no longer an exclusively Hindu festival, and in recent years non-Hindus have begun to celebrate it (KDG-E 251).

I have asked many people to tell me the story of Mahābali, and whether they are Hindus, Christians, Muslims, or Jews, they all adhere to the essential outline followed in these three versions.

Text 22 is a much longer piece, quite original (hence I have referred to its central story as Myth C) and holds an important place in attempts to understand the significance of Mahābali for Malayalis. It is a ballad dating probably from the seventeenth century (Krishna Chaitanya, 152).

Text 22
[*Mahābalicaritam*]

> "O lovely, beautiful parrot girl! Please come here
> and sit down near me.
> Honey and bananas and milk — whatever you want —
> all shall be given to you.
> Whence have you come, O parrot child?"
> "From Tṛkkakkara I have come."
> "What is the news in Tṛkkakkara?"
> "It is not easy to tell the story."
> After hearing this,[1] the parrot child
> was very glad, and told the story slowly:
>
> May the holy son of Śaṅkara,[2] and the goddess Sarasvatī,
> and my *guru,* and Lakṣmī bless me.
> And may Kṛṣṇa and the teachers
> come to my heart and bless me.
> May a great number of people hear
> the *līlā*s of Mahādeva[3] of Tṛkkākkara.
> Nārada told of all the *līlā*s of Nārāyaṇa
> and I have listened to him.
>
> 20 When Mahābali ruled the land
> all men were equal.
> At that time people lived in happiness
> and there were no calamities,
> neither were there griefs and diseases.
> And infant mortality was unheard of
> for many thousands of years.
> All forms of farming were there
> giving abundant yields of
> paddy and other crops.
> The wicked were unseen —

in this world all people were good.
On earth all men were equal,
And all houses were equally fine.

36 Women and children and all others
lived at that time with joy
and wore ornaments made of pure gold.
There was no theft and no cheating,
there was no lying at all.
When merchants weighed their goods
the rules were strictly followed,
for malpractice — short measure,
fraud and the like — were unknown.
And good rain fell as needed.
Vaidikas sang Vedic *mantras* and hymns.
And the sacrifice and other rituals
were performed continuously for the protection of the land.
The King named Mahābali told the people:

49 "May you celebrate all
Tiruvōṇam days in every month
for it is the birthday indeed
of Śri Mahādeva.
How the Ōṇam days are to be spent
I will tell you.
Having offered worship
one should celebrate a beautiful festival."

In order to see
the Ōṇam festival of the god of Tṛkkākkara,
children and others
walked the road to Tṛkkākkara
without any sadness.

61 Then Mahābali continued, saying to the men and women:
"We should conduct the festival like this:
From this day all of us
should decorate our houses,
we should clear and sweep the courtyard
and daub it with cow dung.
We must build a mud platform

and construct on it chalk designs
and decorate it
with *tumpa* and other flowers.
This performance beginning from Attam
ten days before Ōnam.
How many celebrations there are
I cannot describe."

71 And they shouted with joy, decorating it and themselves:
"As the sun sets [on the evening before Ōnam]
let Mahādeva make his royal visit.
Let the women, the aged and others
have their baths and their feasts.
And thus the same in every month
Ōnam festival should be performed."

When Mahābali protected his kingdom
At that time all were equal.
At that time a boy came and asked Maveli,
"Three steps of earth please give me."
"You can have earth measured by three steps."
Three steps of earth he began to measure
but the three steps were not completed.

86 Mahābali renounced his kingdom
and Mādhava ruled the land.
At that time he every day gave feasts
to a thousand Brāhmans,
but stopped celebrating Mahābali's Ōnam.
Then Mahābali heard about that
and in his mind he felt grieved
and then spoke to Krṣṇa as follows:
94 "Since you won the entire earth of mine
I renounced my kingdom;
and since then, alas, all men have become distressed.
O son of Devakī, O Vāsudeva—
You who accomplished the killing of your uncle,
and who grew up in Ambati—[4]
You sucked the breast of Pūtanā,

you ate stolen milk and curds and butter,
and stole the clothes of the women;
You walked with the grazing cows,
and held up the mountain as an umbrella;
You ate the beaten rice of Kucela[5]
and made your living by driving the chariot of Arjuna.
You are the one who cheated me in measuring the earth,
who consumed the poison of Kāliya,
and who, at the end of a *kalpa,*
rested with great joy
on the leaf of a banyan tree!
What is now the reason for this distress?"
As Mahābali listened
Mādhava himself replied:
"Desist from grieving in any way
There is a time, one day in a year
For you to come and see your people.
On the day of Ōṇam in the month of Ciṅṅam
you can happily come," he said.
As time went on,
the son of Vasudeva, Mādhava,
and Yudhiṣṭhira son of Dharma,
sat together happily
and Yudhiṣṭhira said as follows:
"Cowherds and *gopīs,*
women and boys and maidens—
Let them all hear what I say:
On the day of Ōṇam in the month of Ciṅṅam
Māvali himself will come here.
120 And all the necessary things shall be properly prepared
better than you did before.
Grass should be cut down in the streets
and they should be cleared
and enclosures and fences should be built.
The floors should be made clean and beautiful.
One should daub the walls with plaster
and build a small platform with red soil.
Having constructed the circles of designs in the courtyard
you should daub all the places with cow dung

and decorate the designs with flowers.
With shouts of joy one should make these decorations.
And everywhere there is happiness.
How many celebrations there are
I cannot describe exhaustively —
bows and arrows made from bamboo shoots,
the *katantuti* drum,
and the sound of *tumburu*,[6] *vīṇā*s, trumpets,
smaddala[7], *ceṇṭa*[8], tabor and small drum
and fine music of trumpets and *vīṇā*s,
and the *rāga*s sung by sailors
and all kinds of sword-throwing and ball games
along with so many kinds of celebrations like this.
And maidens spend their time
with enjoyment in plays and sports.
151 And at that time in all fine cities
trade in many kinds of paddy and rice
should be carried on as necessary.
But there should be an ample supply of elephants,
horses, sheep and goats and cattle.
And there will be enough of
various kinds of cloth, including fine white cloths
and fine *manapātan,*
and clothes from Kāyankula and Pōrkkala
and towels and white cloths
and calico,[9]
and clothes from China will be ample —
as well as from the south and the east —
using designs from sword handles.

And silk clothes for women
in many kinds are in plenty.
And there is no end of
168 mirrors and musk and camphor,
and animal [?] and saffron;
the right kinds of perfumes and sandalwood
and other beautiful things.
There is no end to preparations like these.
Bunches of green and ripe plantains

and bundles of *pappaṭa* are in plentiful supply.

Betel and arecanuts and coconuts
and cumin-seed, mustard and chilly,
jaggery, honey and sugar,
sesame oil, ghee and coconut oil—
there is sufficient of these and countless other things.
All people who are here
engage in buying and selling
all the things they wish.

192 Now hear the words of beautiful women.
One lady said to her husband:
"I wish to have a *sari*.
It should not be too small
lengthwise or breadthwise.
It should be forty-five inches wide.
Make sure it is a superior grade.
If you see a fine one
be sure to get it."
Another lady heard this and
she said to her husband:
"Don't be bashful—
go and choose pieces of good quality."
And hearing this, another lady said:
"I want a cloth that is not for every day
that will not soon wear out."
When she heard this, another
said to her husband:
"Hear what I say!
If you go to buy cloth
you must come back on Paraṭam.
There is a cloth like Vivali silk. . . .
Remember what I say, now!"
Other women made their husbands promise
that they would get them something to wear.

216 And hear the words of the young girls:
"You must have clothes with a blue stripe."
"I must have cloth with the design of *taram*."

"I must have something to wear."
At that time another maiden asked her mother:
"O mother, I have no Ōṇam-cloth:
it causes me great shame."
"If Father brings me cloth I won't take it.
It will be for you, my daughter.
Only when Ōṇam is over
will I take the cloth."
228 Thus are heard the many kinds of talk
of women and girls.
And there is no end to the women
who put on ornaments:
bracelets with earrings,
*tāli*s and rings,
gold hip ornaments and ear ornaments
and bangles,[10]
fine ankle rings and hip strings
golden ornaments and jewels,
pearl necklaces and swinging *tāli*s
and jewels strung on silk-threads.[11]

"I do not have a necklace and a *tāli*, mother."
Having heard these words of her daughter
a woman at once replies:
"You need not worry about that.
You have no need of ornaments.
Clean and polish your marriage-*tāli*
and wear a good garment. That is enough."

Five days after Attam
you should make arrangements of all kinds.
When the sun sets on Utrāṭam
We prepare a feast for Gaṇapati.
Having lit the silver lamp
we should set out incense and lights
and mirrors and many other things —
250 fresh rice and a kind of *oṭṭara* [cake]
jaggery from the *palmyra* tree, and oranges,
cucumber, betel leaf and arecanut.
Having properly decorated the platform

we bring Gaṇapati to it
and cover it with costly silk.
Women bring water in a small pot
and sprinkle on it.
And many children prepare fine bamboo-shoot arrows
and drums
and other kinds of arrows
and stand there.

264 And Śiva and Subrahmaṇya
and Pārvati and other goddesses
come and fill the place.
And we set before the platform
paddy and rice, and fill
the pots with first rate gold,
break coconuts and sprinkle the coconut milk.

269 In all houses at that time
people were happy.
Women and children and others
all took their baths and sang hymns.

At that time
Mahābali and Mahādeva
paid their holy visit to the earth.
Having heard the news of this in the Deva worlds
all the celestial damsels came there.
From the Nāga worlds
all the serpent-women came.
Nārada, playing his *vīṇā* in the star worlds,
came to see the holy visit of Nārāyaṇa.
Rāma and the boys came there to see it,
and the sun and the moon
in their revolutions visited Tṛkkākkara.
There were two white elephants on both sides,
and all the quarters were filled
with the blare of the sound of conches.
Women danced in rows
and sang in rhythm with the dance.
Devas danced and sang

and women danced and sang.

Then Mahābali and Mahādeva
made their holy journey
back to the world of Vaikuṇṭha.
As Mahābali was going away
and the soldiers stood respectfully
one man there also wept.
"Don't be sad," said Mahābali.
"After some time I will return."
On hearing this the men were greatly pleased in their
hearts.

This song is composed by Śaṅkara:
When uneducated men sing it,
let wise men correct the mistakes.
The sorrow of the educated
who sing this story and play it,
and of the uneducated who hear it,
will be removed
and they will acquire happiness;
they will have sons and nephews.
Those who extol God
singing this song,
will attain to the feet of Nārāyaṇa
when the time of death arrives.

Text 24
[Jacob: 112–13]

This festival [Ōṇam] is a very important one, and takes place
in the month of Chingam [August 15 to September 15], which is
the first month of the Malabār year. It is the one festival in
which all Malayalis join, without distinction of caste or creed.
There is an interesting legend connected with it.

Once upon a time, Kerala was ruled by the Asura, Mahābali. It was a period of great prosperity and goodwill. Everybody was happy and contented. There was no injustice, or

exploitation of the poor by the rich. In fact, nobody was poor at that time.

Now, the Devas [the gods] have no love for Asuras. They were all very jealous of the popularity of Mahābali. If it went on like this they would have no place in men's minds and nobody would worship them. So they approached Mahāvishnu and told him of their fear. "I will look into the matter," said the Great God. Mahāvishnu took the form of a young Brāhmin boy, whose name was Vāmanan, and came to the earth. He approached Mahābali, who received him kindly and with respect. He had always respected Brahmins. "What can I do for you?" he asked Vāmanan.

"I want only three feet of earth."

"Three feet of earth? What good will that do?"

"I want to sit there and worship God," said the boy.

"I will certainly give you what you ask," said Mahābali.

The King's Guru, Sukramuni, called him aside. "Mind what you do!" he said. "This is no Brahmin boy, but Mahāvishnu himself come to destroy you."

But Mahābali would not go back on his word. He asked the boy to take three feet of earth, from wherever he liked. Suddenly the boy grew up and became a very great giant. With one foot he measured the whole earth. With another he measured the underworld.

"Now where can I get the third foot?" he asked. "Here," said the King and bowed his head. Vāmana put his foot on Mahābali's head and pushed him down to hell!

But before the good King went down, he asked for a boon.

"Allow me to visit my people once a year," he begged.

This request was granted Mahāvishnu.

So he comes every year, on the Thiru-Onam day, and visits Kerala. All people rejoice on that day. It is the great festival of the year for all Malayalis.

Text 25
[Woodcock: 14–15]

In Kerala the whole perspective of this ancient legend is changed, for Bali becomes Mahābali, the Great Bali, who ruled his realm so well that he aroused the jealousy rather than the fear of the gods, and who gave up his kingdom, not because he was the victim of a trick, but because he was too generous to refuse a request and too honourable not to fulfil a promise. As he withdrew into the underworld, victim of the malice of the gods, he asked one boon for himself, which was granted: that on a single day each year he might be allowed to return and to see how his beloved children, the Malayalis, were faring. That day is Thiru Onam, and Mahābali's ghostly but amiable presence is greeted by a special feast of boiled bananas and by the exchanging of gifts, while in the king's honour the girls put on white skirts and coloured blouses, and dance with flowers in their hair. At the same time the Nairs, the traditional warrior caste of the Malabar Coast, stage sword-fights, and in the wide backwaters the young men race the great snake boats, the *chundan valloms,* with their tall ornamental sterns and their hundred paddlers, whose very name and form look back to the age when the gods of the Brahmins were still unknown to Kerala and the people worshipped the Nagas, the serpent deities who lived, like King Mahābali, in the underworld. The story of Mahābali is a fragment of mythological history, representing the conquest of the native Dravidian culture by the advent of the Aryan teachers from the north who brought with them the Vedic religion and the Sanskrit language, and who imposed on southern India a caste system which had not existed before they came, but which has proved durable enough to bedevil the politics of Kerala even in the mid-20th century. The legend, in other words, presents the Dravidian version of a great social transformation which took place before the historical records began, and this is one of the reasons why King Mahābali, despite the fact that he incurred the wrath of the great gods, is still affectionately remembered by the ordinary people of Kerala as a personification of the losing side in the struggle between cultures.

The Kerala versions of Myth A (Texts 23–25) are all quite brief—largely because they are free from the massive elaborations of the Purāṇas. But they do have certain features that give an indication of their Puranic heritage. The theme of the jealousy of the Devas is found only in *Brahmā* and then very briefly. In these texts it is firmly linked with the traditions about Bali's good rule.

The details of Mahābali's rule in *Mahābalicaritam* contain some details found only in *Skanda* (7.2.14): the fertile earth, and freedom from poverty, pain and untimely death. The portrayal of the earth as paradise (*Skanda* 7.2.14) is reiterated by K. M. George. The theme of Vāmana's taking of the worlds with two steps is generally repeated but the placing of the third step on Bali's head remains specific to *Bhāgavata*. Still, the entirely original picture of the Lord pushing Bali down to Pātāla with his foot is traceable to the *Bhāgavata*.

The most important new motif in these accounts, however, is the association of Mahābali with the festival of Ōṇam — which is celebrated as the occasion to his return to his people.

"Ōṇam" is actually an abbreviated form of Tiruvōṇam, one of the 27 *nakṣatras* (constellations or "asterisms") accepted by Hindus. The term Tirovōṇam came to Malayalam from Tamil and is the equivalent of the Sanskrit *śravaṇa,* or sometimes *śroṇa* (which we have discussed above). The Tiru- suggests that, if the word was taken over from Sanskrit, *śroṇa* was regarded as a short form of *śrī-oṇa,* for *tiru-* is the Tamil-Malayalam equivalent of *śrī*.

The *nakṣatra* Tiruvōṇam appears at least once every month. The festival in Kerala occurs each year on the day it appears in the month of Ciṅṅam (August-September), which is the month of Bhādrapada in the Sanskrit calendar and so called in other parts of contemporary India. In actual fact, the festivities are spread over a number of days, but the culmination of all activities is the day of Tiruvōṇam.

A. *Ōṇam in ancient South India*

Even though Ōṇam is particular today to Kerala, there is evidence that the festival was at once time celebrated across a larger part of South India. The earliest evidence comes from the *Maṭuraikāñci,* one of the *Pattupāṭṭu* ("Ten Songs') dating from the Saṅgam era. The *Maṭuraikāñci* is sometimes dated as early as the second century A.D. (CI-O:6), but a more conservative estimate is the fifth century. The poet Māṅkuti Marutanār describes (*Maṭuraikāñci,* 590–98) the Ōṇam festival as one dedicated to the deity Māyōn who destroyed the *avuṇar,* a Tamil equivalent of the Asuras. It was celebrated in the bright fortnight of the month of Kanni or Āśvina, the Ōṇam day apparently being the full moon day. The actual celebrations lasted for seven days. Marutanār describes how at that time the monsoon waters run over the streets where chariots are driven. The people assemble and worship their own chosen deity, and there are games and duels in front of the temples and in the streets. These are called *cērippōr* (group war) and appear to be the forerunner of various games found more recently in Kerala.

On Ōṇam day a feast was spread before the rural people. The poet describes the fruits and root-crops which were bestowed as a gift on the people. Marutanār compares the food to that given out by the Chera king on his birthday. The festival concluded on the evening of the seventh day with the bathing of the deity *(ārāṭṭu)*. On the morning after the end of the festival, the Pāndya king, Net-unceliyan, presided over an assembly of warriors, chieftans, pundits, and others dependent on him, and gave gifts to them.

There are clearly many similarities between these customs and those of contemporary Kerala (see below, p. 203f). There appears, however, to be no link with Mahābali, the focus of the festival being Māyōn, a name referring usually to Viṣṇu in his form as Kṛṣṇa.

There is further evidence of a widespread celebration of the festival. The writings of the Āḷvars show that it was not confined to Madurai or Kerala. Tirumaḷicai Āḷvār mentions that the star heralding descent of the Lord of Veṅkata is Śravaṇa (Varadachari, 42). More telling references appear in Periyāḷvār (Tiruppallāṇṭu 9; translated from the Malayalam in Elankulam Kunjan Pillai, 35):

> Having put on the yellow cloth discarded by you,
> Having eaten the left-overs of your food,
> And wearing the *tulasi*-garland you have discarded
> We, the servants at your feet,
> performing assiduously all necessary tasks,
> at this time of Tiruvōṇam
> sing eternal years to Thee, the Lord
> who has as his royal couch
> The serpent Ananta.

Here there is not only mention of clothes and food, as in accounts from both ancient Madurai (that is, in the picture from the *Maturaikāñci*) and contemporary Kerala, but a firm linking of these offerings to the worship of Viṣṇu in his form as Anantaśāyin.

Other verses explicitly state that Tiruvōṇam is the Lord's birthday, with the suggestion that it is the birthday specifically of the
Lord as Kṛṣṇa (after Raghava Aiyangar, 94):

> O Lord, there are only seven days
> till Tiruvōṇam your birthday.
> The sweet songs sung by the women
> In praise of you have begun.
> Rice and vegetables and other things
> for the Ōṇam feast
> have been collected and cooked.
> So Lord, tomorrow you should not go
> grazing cattle. Dress yourself lavishly
> in fine clothes
> and remain here.

In another verse the singer of the song appears to be Kṛṣṇa's
fostermother Yaśodā, and the indication is the same—that Tiruvōṇam is Kṛṣṇa's birthday (*Tiruvāymoḻi* 2.4.2):

> O my Lord, don't run away.
> You should bathe on this day
> which is Tiruvōṇam
> the day of your birth.

An indirect assertion of Ōṇam as Kṛṣṇa's birthday appears in
the verse (Elankulam Kunjan Pillai, 37):

> For Vāsudeva Kṛṣṇa was born
> from the womb of Devakī.
> It is the tenth day after Attam.

Not all references are, however, to Kṛṣṇa. We have seen an
example where it is to Anantaśāyana. In the following the implication seems to be that Nṛsiṃha, the Man-lion incarnation, appeared at Tiruvōṇam (Elankulam Kunjan Pillai, 36):

> On the holy festival of Tiruvōṇam
> in the evening when it is dusk—

> O Hari, taking the form of a lion
> you are here.

In contemporary Kerala, Tiruvōṇam remains the birthday of Viṣṇu; not, however, in his Kṛṣṇa form but in his dwarf-form. The earliest clear identification in literature of the birthday of the Dwarf as Śravaṇa-Tiruvōṇam is, as we have seen, in *Bhāgavata Purāṇa* 8.18.5.

B. The Recent Celebration of Ōṇam in Kerala

1. Ōṇam as a "Spring" Festival

The earliest European account of the celebration of Ōṇam in Kerala is that of Fra Bartolomeo in in his *Voyage to the East Indies* (Padmanabha Menon, 4:289–90):

> About the 10th of September the rain ceases in Malabar. All nature seems as if renovated; the flowers again shoot up, and the trees bloom; in a word, this season is the same as that which Europeans call spring. This festival seems, therefore, to have been instituted for the purpose of soliciting from the Gods a happy and fruitful year. It continues eight days.... On this occasion they also put on new clothes, throw aside all their old earthenware and supply its place by new. The men, particularly those who are young, form themselves into two parties and shoot at each other with arrows. The arrows are blunted, but exceeding strong; and are discharged with such force that a considerable number are generally wounded on both sides.

The suggestion that Ōṇam occurs in the Spring is at first confusing, in that the period of the year in which it occurs corresponds more properly to Autumn, since it is in an intermediary position between the hottest and the coldest seasons of the year. (Such comparisons are further complicated by the fact that between the hottest season and the period when Ōṇam occurs there is an extended rainy season.) The analogies with a European spring derive from the following:

(a) The blooming of numerous varieties of flowers makes the

already beautiful countryside of Kerala especially attractive. The association with spring is further strengthened by the extensive use of flowers in the laying of flower-carpets *(athappōvidal)* by the girls of a family in the courtyard of the family compound. Typically the courtyard is swept clean, sprinkled with cowdung, and the flower pattern is laid by the girls who have been out collecting fresh blossoms, accompanying their activities with the singing of traditional Ōṇam songs (see CI–O:29).

In laying the carpets, different customs are followed. In southern Kerala the flowers are laid over mud steps which must be odd in number. The pile of mud with its steps is in the shape of a cone and looks like a pyramid in the round. In the central and northern areas, the flowers are laid on the floor of the courtyard which has been plastered with cowdung (CI–O:14). The designs vary from day to day (KDG-E:251).

(b) The giving of gifts, particularly in the most celebrated form, the providing of new clothes, reminds one of Christian Easter-Spring traditions. On the evening of the day preceding Ōṇam (that is, *Utrātam*), servants and children traditionally give to their masters and parents gifts of rice, yams, pumpkins, and plantain bunches, and the masters reciprocate by giving, in particular, new clothes *(ōṇappuṭava)* to their servants. The context in which this has been traditionally applied is that of the Nayar tarawad *(taravāṭu,* that is, the extended family). It is the *kāraṇavan*, the senior male member of the tarawad, who makes these gifts of new clothes to the junior members of the tarawad and to the servants (HK: 4.295). The traditional colour of these new clothes is yellow, except in South Travancore where it is blue. (HK:4.295) This giving of clothes is carried through all levels of society to the extent that on the morning of Tiruvōṇam day the members of the royal family of Travancore receive new clothes from Śri Padmanābha, the form of the deity at Trivandrum, through the hands of the officiating priest (HK: 4.305).

An important gift often given in the past was the bow. Along with the clothes given by the deity at Trivandrum, the members of the royal family also received bows and arrows (HK:4.305). The Maharajah also traditionally gave the same to leaders of his army. Examples can be seen in the museum at Padmanābhapuram palace near Sucindram. This appears to be correlated with a tradition of placing bows and arrows behind an image of Tṛkkākkara

Appan (see below) in the front courtyard of the house.

This gift giving has taken on wider ramifications over the years. William Logan mentions in his *Malabar Journal* (1:62) an article of agreement between King Areeramuta of Cotiote and Thomas Hodges of the British East India Company.

> For the better preservation of the friendship subsisting between the Company and the King and for the freedom of their commerce in his Dominion, the King promises not to suffer any European nation but them to purchase pepper, cardamoms and sandalwood therein and the Company are annually to present him at the feast of Onam with the sum of fanams 1,2000.

More recently, factories have distributed their annual bonuses to their workers during this time, and government servants have received their salary in advance at this time (CI–O:14).

2. *Ōṇam as a New Year Festival*

(a) In the period immediately before Ōṇam, the women collect their old pots, baskets, broomsticks and other worn-out household implements and dispose of them. This seems replete with the symbolism of spring cleaning, the ushering in of a new year as people respond to the new vitality of the world of plants and animals. Significant in this regard is the fact that in the southern part of Kerala, Ōṇam is thought of as a festival of the New Year. Ciṅnam, the month in which Ōṇam occurs, is the first month of the year in these parts. M. S. A. Rao indicates that the last month of the year, Karkkaṭakam (July-August), is a very inauspicious month for any undertaking. To counteract the evil effects, reading of the *Rāmāyaṇa,* the *Mahābhārata,* and *Bhāgavata Purāṇa* is common. Rao also indicates that part of the house cleaning is a ceremony called "driving out the Cetta,' the Cetta being conceived of as a goddess. All the members of the household shout, "Cetta off you go! Śrīdevī, we welcome you in." Also on the last day of the old year a song is sung; it appears to be a variant of that just cited (CI-O: 14):

> Let the days of scarcity go!
> Let the first month and Ōṇam come.

This points to another dimension of the symbolism of the festival in Kerala. The passage of the year involves a gradual decline in the food supply, and hence much is made of the fact that the arrival of Ōṇam is not just a fresh start psychologically but also a return of prosperity. This dimension is significant because Ōṇam occurs in a lull between the first and second monsoon and coincides approximately with the first harvest of paddy. Thus it is also regularly thought of as a harvest festival. The feasting which is characteristic of Ōṇam day itself reflects the affirmation of the renewed prosperity provided by the harvest. The midday meal on Tiruvōṇam day is traditionally the best meal of the year. Even if one cannot eat well at other seasons of the year it is expected that one will do so during this festival season. As the old saying has it: "*chothikku chothichum nellu pulunganam:* On Choti day (7 days before Tiruvōṇam) paddy should be boiled, even if it is borrowed" (CI-O:13–14).

(b) Another major component of the festival celebration is the variety of games played. These are mainly competitive games, between two teams or two individuals. Among team games are *talappantu,* a variety of football; and *attakalam,* in which the players are divided into two groups with one inside a circle, and the others outside. Those on the outside try to pull the others out. In Travancore (South Kerala) there is another rather complicated team game, called *Kilikaḷi.*

The individuals take part in archery competitions, wrestling matches (in South Malabar), and *kayyānkaḷi,* a person-to-person combat in which there can be serious injuries if the opponents are badly mismatched.

These games may be a survival of, or alternatively, may have once been paralleled by, much more violent games engaged in by Nayar soldiers. That Syrian Christians also took part can be inferred from an order by Archbishop Menasass of Udiyam Perur Sunahados that they not engage in these fights (Ulloor 3.173).

From a number of different accounts it is clear that soldiers were divided into two teams (sometimes from opposing villages). In an account of a fight between the forces of the kings of Cochin and Calicut in 1519, it is said that there were 4,000 soldiers in each group. There are records of the presentation of money to Nayar soldiers (including the wounded) from the treasury of the Sri

Padmanabhaswami Temple in Trivandrum in the years K.E. 941, 943, and 946.

Ulloor thinks the custom was that although the battle was only a mock battle, it had to appear real, and hence it had to include an element of real danger.

He also discusses the comments on such a game given by the poet Śri Nilakaṇṭha of Ceppukaṭu (dated from the late eighth or early ninth century M.E.). The poet suggests that the Ōṇam fights developed from the heroic interests of the soldiers:

> Only if we fight with heroic values
> can we attain to the heaven for heroes.
> If we are killed we attain to *mokṣa*.
> If we don't die from the fight we
>   receive fame and wealth.
> So let us begin to fight.

The poet later describes with pathos the widows' embracing their husbands' corpses and the good times enjoyed by the surviving soldiers: the drinking of coconut milk and the chewing of betel-nut. The poet reports that after the fight the rulers convened a meeting of chieftains and advised them not to continue the fight and not to quarrel. This suggests that these fights allowed fighting men an opportunity to express their aggressiveness in a controlled setting.

3. *Ōṇam and Mahābali*

These Ōṇam customs, however, are often interpreted as a celebration of Mahābali's annual visit to Kerala. Thus, the cleaning and the flower-decorations are seen as a preparation, a royal welcome, for the coming of the returning monarch (CI–O:1):

> Ten days before Onam the people start making preparations for the reception of Bali. Flower-carpets are laid from the "Atham" day and on the eve of Onam, "Onathappan" a symbol of Bali is worshipped. During the Onam days, the people throughout the length and breadth of Kerala go on feasting and merrymaking, so that their beloved King may feel happy to be with his people.

The spirit of the festival in relation to Mahābali can best be gauged from Ōṇam songs. The following song expresses the worry that all the required preparations will not be completed before Mahābali arrives (CI–O:8):

The courtyards are not cleared as yet
O Maveli, why thou art come?
Bananas are not brought from market yet
O Maveli, why thou art come?
Ball games have begun not, nor is the pandal ready.
Uncle has not come, nor have the gifts arrived.
The paddy is not boiled nor is it even dried,
The goldsmith has not come, nor are the ornaments ready.
The little girl's face looks pale,
The older girl's husband has not come yet.

And there is the excitement of the bounty hoped for from the hands of Mahābali:(HK: 4.291):

Chombil house maiden, Little maiden,
What did he give you who yesterday came?
A new dress he gave me, a small dress he gave me.
A lounge likewise on which to recline,
A tank to disport in, a well to draw water from, a compound
to gambol in a big field to sing in,
Freshen up flowers, oh freshen for me.

This is the mood of expectation that reaches fruition in the feasting and merry-making (in war-games, dancing, singing) that are organized "so that their beloved king may feel happy to be with his people" (CI–O:1, Mateer, 187).

In view of so much interest in Mahābali in Kerala one may well ask for the reason for such significance attached to the figure. The answer, from the legendary history of Kerala, is that Mahābali is generally believed to have been King of Kerala with his capital city in Tṛkkākkara. This brings us to yet another tradition of ritual.

On the day before Ōṇam, images of Ōṇattappan (the Lord of Ōṇam), or Tṛkkākkara Appan (Lord of Tṛkkākkara) (KDG–E:251)

are installed in the centre of the flower decorations. In northern
and central Kerala, these are earthen images sold by local potters,
and are in the form of a pyramid about nine inches in height. In
the south, around Trivandrum and towards Cape Comorin, the
upper piece of a grinding stone is used on Tiruvōnam and on other
days, cowdung shaped in a phallic form (CI-O:16,29). Water, flowers, and leaves of *lucas aspera* are offered to the image.

To the question, "Who is Ōnattappan, or Tṛkkākkara Appan?"
Malayalis give no unanimous answer. A beautiful devotional
Ōnam song clearly identifies the dirt image as a deity from the
temple, presumably Viṣṇu (Nambiar: 34):

> When Holy Ōnam dawns
> You come in the form of clay
> even though you are there
> in the form of gold.
> With a sandalwood stick
> in your hand,
> jumping into the flower decorations
> you come to my courtyard.
> Welcome, welcome, welcome!

But many identify Ōnattappan as Mahābali (CI-O: 16; Krishna
Iyer: 2.68). There is an indirect confirmation of this in the practice
of placing a number of figures in the decorations—in Malabar
nine, and eleven around Cochin and Tṛkkākkara. This suggests a
variant on the practices related to Bali at Dīvālī (in Maharashtra,
for example), and hence strengthens the hypothesis that Ōnattappan is Mahābali.

There have also been suggestions, however, that Ōnattappan is
Śiva. The refrain of the song just cited is "Hara," which can be a
welcome, but also is a name of Śiva. Does the song then celebrate
Śiva? The phallic form of the image in Southern Kerala also suggests that possibility. This tradition is related to another which we
shall explore below, that the original deity at Tṛkkākkara was
Śiva.

Also, in the Citralaya Museum in Trivandrum there is a painting by P. I. Itoop entitled "Onappuja" (Stock No. 984). The painting shows a worshipper, apparently a Śaiva, sitting in a yogic pos-

ture, the lotus posture, with his hands held together in *añjali* before what appears at first sight as a large mound. Above the mound is an umbrella, and flowers have been placed around the base of the mound. An oil lamp burns before it and there are a variety of objects before the worshipper, presumably for use in *pūjā*. Looked at closer, however, the "mound" seems to be an image with a cloth covering. If that is so, then the *pūjā* is in accord with the instructions we have seen above in *Garuḍa* (1.136) and *Agni* (189) for the celebration of Śravaṇadvādaśī. The cloth and umbrella would thus indicate that the deity worshipped is Viṣṇu in his form as Vāmana.

This picture seems drawn from a strand different from the others—a high caste strand rooted in Sanskritic materials, such as the Purāṇas. The picture is thus distinct in its ambience from the imagery of the customs so far recorded, customs that exist on the popular level of the lower castes. It is clear that at this level the figure of the Lord of Ōṇam is subject to various interpretations—one of which identifies him as Mahābali.

C. *Questions of Historical Development*

The relationship of Mahābali to the festival of Ōṇam raises for us a number of important historical questions. Given that Ōṇam was observed as the birthday of Viṣṇu-Kṛṣṇa in ancient Tamil Nadu, while Śravaṇa was identified as the birthday of the Dwarf in the *Bhāgavata* and other Purāṇas, it is possible to see clear lines of development: either (a) from Ōṇam, as related to Viṣṇu or Kṛṣṇa, to the Vāmana *avatāra* and finally to Mahābali; or (b) from Ōṇam, as related to Mahābali, to Vāmana, and then to Viṣṇu more generally. There is also the possibility (c)—a variant of (a)— of Ōṇam, being initially related specifically to Vāmana, and then in different contexts being (1) generalized as the birthday of Viṣṇu-Kṛṣṇa, and (2) related to Mahābali. Which of these lines represents the truth remains an open question.

In addition, there is a related question that takes us back to issues raised in Chapter 6. It is obvious that a number of features of the Dīvālī-Bali link are similar to the association between Ōṇam and Mahābali:

(1) A celebration of the return of Bali.

(2) A likening of the conditions of the festival to those in Bali's kingdom.

(3) The constructing of images of Bali (in some cases from cow-dung).

(4) The whitewashing of houses and plastering of floors with cow-dung.

(5) The giving of gifts.

(6) The wearing of new clothes.

(7) The importance of quasi-military contests.

(8) The association of Bali with the new year (Kollam era in Kerala, Vikrama era in North India).

(9) Viewing both festivals as post-monsoon festivals.

(10) A contrast drawn between the privations of the year's end and the prosperity brought in the new year by Śrī.

The number of similarities between the Divāli-Bali association and the Ōṇam-Mahābali one is so great that it is virtually impossible that they could have arisen totally independently of each other. That does not *necessarily* mean that one was borrowed from the other. It is possible that both have drawn from an earlier common source.

In dealing with these questions it seems appropriate to look first at the Ōṇam-Vāmana-Mahābali complex, since a number of Malayalis have considered questions related to this.

(1) Although they have not noted the Puranic details, some Malayali scholars have explored the possibility that the idea of Tiruvōṇam as the birthday of Vāmana developed somewhere in South India and was brought to Kerala. Elankulam Kunjan Pillai has tried to show that the crucial links in the chain of development are Tirupati in the Venkata hills, and Tṛkkākkara, near Cochin in Kerala. In its briefest form, his argument is (39) that the image of the Lord of Venkata is that of Vāmana — as it is also at Tṛkkāk-kara. Tṛkkākkara, he argues, was built as a Tirupati of the west, of the Chera country.

That Tṛkkākkara holds an important place in the development of Ōṇam in Kerala can hardly be doubted. Merely the fact that the clay image in the courtyard of the Kerala home at Ōṇam is called Tṛkkākkara Appan gives a special place to Tṛkkākkara. From ancient inscriptions dating from the year 36 of the Malayalam era (861 A.D.) we know that Ōṇam was celebrated at a number of tem-

ples in Kerala (CI-O:6). But the grandest celebration seems to
have been at Tṛkkākkara, one of the thirteen *divyadeśam*s of Mal-
ainādu (that is Kerala) (Gopalan, 49). This was so primarily
because of the association of Tṛkkākkara with the Kulaśekhara
Empire, the second Chera Empire dating from 800—1102. Under
these emperors, the land was divided into various *nātus*, each ruled
by governors (*nātuvaḻis*) appointed by the Emperor. The festival of
Ōṇam at Tṛkkākkara seems to have served, among other things,
to consolidate the ties between the Emperor and the *nātuvaḻi*s. The
description in the *Kerala District Gazetteer—Ernakulam District*
(104-5) is informative:

> The Onam festival was celebrated here on a fabulous scale
> under imperial auspices. The inscriptions of the period dis-
> covered from Thrikkakkara gives us interesting glimpses into
> the arrangements made for the celebration of the festival
> which lasted for 28 days. It was a festival of both religious and
> political significance. The image of the God of Thrikkakkara is
> believed to be that of Viṣṇu in the form of Vamana *Avatar*.
> This conception has invested the celebration of the Onam fes-
> tival at Thrikkakkara with a special significance because ac-
> cording to tradition Onam is the glorification of the
> achievement of Lord Viṣṇu in his avatar or incarnation as
> Vamana [Dwarf]. This spirituality associated with the festival
> coupled with the festivities that accompanied it helped to boost
> the morale of the Sri Vaishavites and imparted to their creed a
> new vigour, vitality and appeal. Moreover, the festival also
> served to stir feelings of national solidarity, and to uphold the
> political supremacy of the Chera Emperors over the local
> chieftains. The Onam festival at Thrikkakkara was attended
> . . . by all the Naduvazhis of Kerala.

The tradition persisted until recently in Cochin (Kocci) and
Kozhikode (Kōḻikōṭu) that on the Attam day, ten days before
Tiruvōṇam, the Raja set out on a journey which took him around
the town and then back to his palace. This was called *attaccamayam*.
Most scholars feel that this is a relic of a journey formerly made by
the rulers in Cochin and Kozhikode to the assembly of *nātuvāḻi*s in
Tṛkkākkara (CI-O 9; KDG-E 104-5; CSM 378; Krishna Ayyar,

17,24). Related to this is a tradition that the practice of celebrating Ōṇam at home came about because when kings went to Tṛkkāk-kara temple for the Ōṇam festival, they told their subjects to visit the temple also; one citizen could not attend and was told to worship the Lord at home (CI-O:9).

It is, however, uncertain whether or not the image at Tṛkkākkara was always that of Vāmana. It has been suggested that Tṛkkākkhara means Tiru-kāl-kara — "The auspicious place of the feet," (Sharma) or "The place of the divine feet" (CI-O 81) — suggesting the place where Viṣṇu placed his foot on the head of Mahābali. It has also been noted that an alternative name for the place is "Vāmanakṣetra," the field of Vāmana (KDG-E 105). There are, however, some complicating factors. Since the temple at Tṛkkākkara was for some time completely in ruins (HK 4:293), it is not known for certain what the original image was. Nammālvar refers to the place as "Tirukkātkaraï" (Gopalan, 49) which means, literally, "the auspicious bank of the irrigation channel"; and his description of the image suggests the iconography of Kṛṣṇa — "like a cloud" (v.8), "black, graceful cloud-form," (9), though there is a reference also to his "four beautiful, graceful broad shoulders," which may indicate Viṣṇu rather than Kṛṣṇa. (but note *BhG* 11.46). The only reference to the divine activity, the killing of Kaṃsa, again suggests that the image is that of Kṛṣṇa (Nammālvar, *Tiruvāymoli* 9.6).

It is, of course, possible that Nammālvar is wrong, or that the iconographic forms overlap to such an extent that it is not easy to distinguish the image clearly. Again, it is also possible that in referring to the image the poet speaks freely about a wide variety of attributes of Viṣṇu and his avatars.

Possible light is shed on Nammālvar and Tṛkkākkara by one of the traditional Ōṇam songs of Kerala (Nambiar, 34):

> In the space
> between the southern and the northern shore
> the *tumpa* flower flourished.
> By the thousand *tumpa* flowers
> a boat rested.
> At the end of the boat
> a banyan tree sprouted.

> In a hole in the banyan tree
> a small child was born.
> For that child to sing and tap,
> A drum and drum-stick to play with.
> Along with these, O flowers,
> Bloom, blossom, thrive!

This is presumably a song in that stream of Kerala tradition that sees Ōnam as primarily the birthday of Vāmana. But mention of the child also evokes thoughts of Kṛṣṇa. Moreover, the song is reminiscent of one of the stories of the founding of the Sri Padmanabhaswami Temple in Trivandrum.

> The place where Trevandrum now stands was formerly a jungle, called Ananta Kādu. In the centre of this desert dwelt a Pulayan and his wife, who obtained a livelihood by cultivating a large rice-field, near to their hut. One day, as the Pulayan's wife was weeding her grounds, she heard the cry of a babe close to her, and on search, found it so beautiful that she supposed it was a divine infant, and was at first afraid to touch it. However, after washing herself, she fed the babe with milk, and left it again under the shade of a large tree. As soon as she had retired a five-headed cobra came, removed the infant to a hole in the tree, and sheltered it from the sun with its hood. It was an incarnation of the god Vishnu. While there, the Pulayan and his wife used to make offerings to the babe of milk and conjee in a cocoa-nut shell. Tidings of these things reaching the ears of the sovereign of Travancore, orders were issued for the erection of a temple at that place. The natives add that the cocoa-nut shell used by the Pulayan is still preserved in the royal pagoda at Trevandrum. (Mateer, 16)

Other quite different accounts of the founding of the temple also give an important place to the divine child (see *The Temple of Sree Padmanabha*, 2–3, TSM, 1: 82–83) even though the image at Trivandrum is of Padmanābha, the Lord lying on Ananta. The effect of this is to suggest that the common feature of the child (*bāla*), or the youthful one (*kumāran*), may be a crucial point which allows the devotee to identify disparate manifestations of God in the form of a child as really the same. And if Nammālār thinks of the image at Tṛkkākkara as Kṛṣṇa while others hold it to be Vāmana, then a similarly unspecific youthful figure may have been found there. In addition, the text of the *Mahābalicaritam* (lines 93–111) makes clear that the writer had no difficulty in identifying the one who had taken away the earth from Mahābali as Kṛṣṇa.

Considered from the viewpoint of Tirupati too the situation remains unclear. The Lord of Tirupati is known in south India as "Veṅkaṭācalapati," Lord of the Veṅkata mountains. Tirumaḷicai Āḷvār depicts him as eternally youthful (*kumāran*) (Varadachari, 42), and this could fit Vāmana, the Brāhman boy. In the *Tiruvāy-moḷi*, also, it is said (Elankulam Kunjan Pillai, 39): "The Lord who measured the land has reached the Tiruveṅkata mountain." This, too, could indicate that the Lord of Veṅkata is Vāmana who also shows himself as Trivikrama — the Lord of the three strides. Given the strong interest of the Āḷvārs in the measuring of the universe with three strides (Varadachari, 7, 18, 25, 37, 38, 46, etc.), it would not be surprising if an image of Vāmana were given such an important place.

There are, however, still complications. Nowhere is it stated definitively that the Lord of Veṅkata is Vāmana. According to Varadachari (14), Poykai Āḷvār describes Tiruveṅkatam as the place where Kṛṣṇa loves to dwell. Pidatala Sitapati's study, *Sri Venkateswara: The Lord of the Seven Hills, Tirupati*, also shows that the image at Tirupati is enormously more complex, being regarded by some as Śiva and by others as a female form (hence the feminine *bālā* in "Bālājī").

All of this makes it clear that it is impossible to trace definitively the kind of link Elankulam Kunjan Pillai sees between Tṛkkākkara and Tirupati.

(2) Another Malayali scholar, N.V. Krishna Warrier begins his discussion from the fact that a great many cultures have a myth of a past golden age. He attempts to show that the Malayalam version is different in that it is historically based. In developing his theory, Krishna Warrier takes us far afield, going as far as Puranic literature and Mesopotamian history. He identifies the Asuras with the people of Assur, the city in northern Mesopotamia which gave its name to the Assyrian Empire. He argues that the leading members of the family of Asuras are Assyrian kings. Thus Bali

must be one of the kings whose name includes the name "Bela" (Belanisasu, Bel Ulaśa, Belaluśa, Belakudura). Prahlāda is Upallita, and Prahlāda's son Virocana is Upallita's son Uluśad(h). On this basis he then identifies Mahābali definitively as the grandson of Uluśa, Belakudura Usurano. All of these kings lived in a period between 1440 and 1070 B.C. (Krishna Warrier, 22–23). He also identifies the capital of Bali's son, Bāṇa, as the city of Nineveh, on the basis that in the Bible (Nahum 3.1), Nineveh is called the "city of blood," which is also one of the names given to Bāṇa's capital, that is, Śoṇitapuram (Krishna Warrier, 26).

There are clear difficulties to this theory. The book of Nahum is a bitter cry by the Jews against the injustices and bloodshed meted out by a proud empire. It fits the context of the protest, the gloating which the Jewish people are able finally to express when they learn (c.621 B.C.) that Nineveh lies in ruins (Nahum 3.1–4: NEB):

> Ah! blood-stained city, steeped in deceit
> full of pillage, never empty of prey!
> Hark to the crack of the whip,
> the rattle of wheels and stamping of horses
> bounding chariots, chargers rearing,
> swords gleaming, flash of spears!
> The dead are past counting, their bodies
>   lie in heaps,
> corpses innumerable, men stumbling over corpses—
> all for a wanton's monstrous wantonness
> fair-seeming, a mistress of sorcery,
> who beguiled nations and tribes
> by her wantonness and her sorceries.

Given the context in which the epithet "blood-stained" is used in Nahum, one can hardly argue without further evidence that the epithet was used more widely for Nineveh. In addition, the identification of the leading Asuras with Assyrian kings seems fanciful. While words may change in moving from one language to another, or even over a period of time within a language, the differences are too great to be a valid basis for Krishna Warrier's theory.

A third problem has to do with dating. While there is increasing evidence that there were waves of Aryan migration across northern Mesopotamia and east into Iran and the Indian subcontinent, there is no evidence of major Aryan attacks on Assur resulting in the defeat of the Assyrians at the time Krishna Warrier is talking about.

Although Krishna Warrier's theory seems highly debatable, he has undoubtedly succeeded in raising the very pertinent question, whether there is some historical event behind the story of Bali and the Dwarf, that is, a clash of nations or cultures.

(3) Another popular theory has favored the idea that Mahābali represents the original pre-Aryan South Indian tradition in the festival of Tiruvōṇam, and that the overcoming of Mahābali by Vāmana represents the rise of Viṣṇu and the Brāhmans to a dominant position in South Indian religious life. This seems to be a Malayali parallel to the view held in Tamil Nadu (but not in Kerala) that Rāvaṇa was originally a Tamil hero whose demonization was a result of Aryan domination (see Filliozat, 160–62). It is this interpretation of the golden age of Mahābali as a nostalgic remembrance of a pre-Aryan, Pre-Brahmanic South Indian experience that Woodcock (Text 24) accepts.

As we have seen above, Ōṇattappan can be interpreted as Viṣṇu (Vāmana), Mahābali, or Śiva. Similarly, Ōṇam may celebrate principally the birthday of Vāmana, or principally the return of Mahābali to visit his people. But then it becomes obvious that one of these views must have given rise to the other, and if one asks which came first, one is again drawn into questions of historical developments and possible conflict between cultures. The question that in particular becomes essential is: Does the past golden age of Mahābali, celebrated in the festival of Ōṇam, reflect an earlier stage culturally or religiously?

In responding to this question, one has to bear in mind that the various answers available within Kerala may have been influenced by sectarian emphases. Recent traditions from Tṛkkākkara suggest this.

The temple compound at Tṛkkākkara has two major images. The main temple on the north is dedicated to Vāmana, a smaller shrine to the south is dedicated to Śiva; the relationship between the two is significant in its ambivalence (CI–O:8):

Though the Vāmana temple is accepted as the main temple at
the elite level, the local people consider the Shiva temple as the
more important one. They believe that Shiva was the 'Kula-
daivan' [family deity] of Mahābali and that there was no
Vāmana temple at that time. The palace of Mahābali was
situated at the place where the Vāmana temple is at present.
After the fall of Mahābali his palace was destroyed and later
on Vāmana was installed on that spot by the saint Kapila.

There are two ponds in the north of the temple, locally
known as 'Danedeka Poika' [the pond pertaining to alms] and
'Kapilathirtham' [sacred pond of Kapila]. It is believed that
the former existed even at the time of Mahābali. He had taken
water from this pond to sprinkle over the alms given to
Vāmana. The latter came into existence after the construction
of the Vāmana temple. It is said that when the Vāmana idol
was consecrated by Kapila, water flew [sic.] out of the idol in
profuse quantity. This holy water constituted the 'Kapilathirtham.'

It is said that after installing the idol of Vāmana, on the
ruins of the palace of Mahābali, saint Kapila asked the rulers
of Kerala to accept the supremacy of the deity.

It is possible that we have evidence here of a Śaiva component
in the present elevation of Mahābali. If the period when Mahābali
was king was a perfect time, this tradition from Tṛkkākkara identifies that golden age as a time when Śiva was worshipped by
Mahābali. One might then see the tradition about Mahābali's rule
as merely a result of relatively recent sectarian rivalry in Kerala.
It could be that a tradition accepted at Tṛkkākkara, that Vāmana had overcome Mahābali here, gave rise to another tradition,
developed by opponents of the followers of Vāmana, that, as many
Purāṇas say, conditions were good when Bali was king. Subsequently, this tradition was linked by Śaivas to the claim that Śiva
was worshipped at that time.

Another possibility, however, is that the claim that Śiva was at
first worshipped at Tṛkkākkara is historically accurate since it is
known that at least one early Chera king, Cēramāṇ Perumāḷ, was
a Śaiva, while the later Kulaśēkhara was a Vaiṣṇava (in fact most

scholars accept the traditional view that he was the Āḻvār of that name).

Some details that we have noted above are also relevant here. That the Lord of Tṛkkākkara is interpreted in some parts as Śiva and that the one worshipped in the mud image in the courtyard is addressed as Hara both tie in with the tradition that Śiva was once the principal deity at Tṛkkākkara. Some details of the *Mahābalica-ritam* are also of interest here. There are frequent references to Mahādeva, a name by which Śiva is generally known. Ōṇam is called the birthday of Mahādeva (line 49); Mahābali returns to Vaikuṇṭha with Mahādeva (line 297); and there is a mention of "the *līlās* of Mahādeva" (lines 16–19). The last seems clearly a doublet of "the *līlās* of Nārāyaṇa", which strongly urges the identification of Mahādeva as Viṣṇu. Yet the decoration of the platform with *tumpa* flowers (line 67) suggests Śiva, a deity associated with the *tumpa* while Viṣṇu is regularly associated with the *tulasi*.

Ulloor M. Paramesvara Iyer (1943, 11) suggests that the author of *Mahābalicaritam* had a very poor knowledge of the Purāṇas. He is probably correct in that. But the character of the text suggests that the author was not as interested in being true to the Purāṇas as he was in accurately describing the events and details of the Ōṇam festival. The use of *tumpa* flowers, the reference to preparing a feast for Gaṇapati (line 246), the placing of Gaṇapati on the mud platform (line 254), as well as an indication of the presence of Śiva and his son, presumably Subrahmaṇyan, all add up to a picture of a thorough mixing of Śaiva elements with the clear Vaiṣṇava elements.

The reference to Mahādeva in *Mahābalicaritam* may have contributed to the development of a Śaiva component in the traditions about Tṛkkākkara. But more likely, it seems to me, Vaiṣṇava and Śaiva elements were already mixed in the celebration of the festival by the time of this text in which case "Mahādeva of Tṛk-kākkara" may well reflect an earlier identification of Śiva as the deity of the temple there.

Worthy of a more thorough investigation is the possibility that the golden age of Mahābali, before Viṣṇu came at the instigation of the Devas, represents a period before the Nampūtiri Brāhmans came to exercise their spiritual domination over the land. A number of disparate facts of the religious life of Kerala make it a serious possibility:

(a) In one version of the Mahābali legend, narrated to me by a Muslim, the Asuras were described as uncivilized and rough while the Devas were highly civilized.

(b) The relation between the Nampūtiris and other castes works in two contrary directions. The Nampūtiris serve as the ultimate legitimation of the religious complex. The head priest in the temple at Trivandrum is a Nampūtiri as in all other Kerala temples, although Nampūtiris are not responsible for the temple rituals. The structure within which this legitimation works is one in which the Nampūtiri is given an inordinately high place in a hierarchy of ritual purity where cleanliness is maintained by separation from all that is unclean. The result of this is tellingly described by Samuel Mateer (32–33):

> Fixed distances are appointed, within which persons of low caste dare not approach those of higher caste. A Nair, for example, may approach, but must not touch a Nambūri Brahman. A Shānar must remain thirty-six paces off, and a Pulayan slave must stay at a distance of ninety-six paces. Other intervals, according to a graduated scale, are appointed to be observed between the remaining castes; thus, for instance, a Shānar must remain twelve steps away from a Nair, a Pulayan sixty-six steps, and so on.

It was this situation that led Swami Vivekananda to infer that the people of Kerala were "all lunatics; their homes so many lunatic asylums" (3:294–5).

But there is evidence that it was not always like that. There is the ironic fact that, according to the story given above (p. 212) it was a Pūlaya woman who found the divine child and thus was responsible for the founding of the temple at Trivandrum. Yet in the recent past, until 1936, Pūlayas were barred from the temple, and not even allowed to use the roads around the temple. This irony suggests that there was once a time when caste restrictions were much less strict.

(c) The tradition that when Mahābali was king all men were equal (*Mahābalicaritam,* line 20) is uncharacteristic of Indian views of perfection. More usually, everybody follows his own *dharma* in the perfect age. This ideal makes sense in the Indian context only as a protest against a situation where the legitimating hierarchical structure has overextended itself, and hence, at some levels has lost its legitimating power. It may also relate, as does the example in (b) above, to the collective memory of a time when caste hierarchies were much less defined.

Associated evidence for a kind of identification of the Nampūtiris and the Lord comes from the widespread practice of giving land to the temples or to the Brāhmans. A Malayali myth about the origin of Kerala tells us that it was raised out of the sea when Paraśurāma threw his axe. Paraśurāma gave all the land thus created to the Nampūtiris (Woodcock, 41). This myth appears to legitimize what used to be the actual situation in Kerala for several hundreds of years. Although most of the agricultural work was under the control of the Nāyars, and while the latter lived on the plantations in large and impressive houses, the owners of the land were Nampūtiris who were almost always absentee landlords. While it did not diminish their prosperity, the status of the Nāyars was that of liegemen of the Nampūtiris.

A. Sreedhara Menon traces the origins of this system to the Chola-Chera war of the eleventh century A.D. He argues that there was such a mobilization of effort towards the war that attention shifted away from the temples; as a result, unscrupulous Nampūtiris put much of the wealth of the temple endowments into their own hands. (1978, 204–5). In addition,

> In the meantime, it also happened that several ordinary tenants who owned lands and properties transferred them in toto to the Namboothiri Brahmins and the temples. They did so because the lands and properties so transferred came to be regarded as *Devaswoms* and *Brahmaswoms* and enjoyed freedom from devastation by the enemy forces in times of war as well as exemption from the payment of tax to the state. In the above circumstances, the Namboothiri Brahmins came to acquire the status of wealthy and powerful landlords or *Janmis*.

A somewhat similar rationale appears to be involved in another exceedingly important event of the history of this area. When the great ruler of Travancore, Martanda Varman (1729–58), had extended the borders of Travancore and established himself as the most powerful ruler in Kerala, he performed an action which some have seen as an effective deterrent to any kings who might try to win back the land that they had lost: he handed over the kingdom to Lord Padmanābha, the deity of the temple at Trivandrum, and then received the kingdom again as a trust. He vowed to rule the land as "Padmanābhadāsa", the servant of Padmanābha (Menon 1967, 273–74).

But there is an element here which suggests that Sreedhara Menon's picture of the origins of the *janmi* system may be rather one sided. There is no cogent reason to deny that, while Martanda Varman's action was an effective political ploy, he was also quite sincere in offering himself as the servant or slave of the Lord. Indeed, a festival that continues to be celebrated bi-annually in Trivandrum suggests that Martanda Varman's successors as Maharaja of Travancore have been quite sincere in perceiving themselves in such a servile relationship vis-à-vis Lord Padmanābha. This is the Arat (*ārāṭṭu*) festival in which the deities of the temple are taken in procession to the beach and bathed in the waters of the Indian Ocean.

Except that the number of people involved is now much smaller than it was, the event appears not to differ essentially from what it was in the mid-nineteenth century. The point essential to our discussion is that the Maharaja has always walked along with his subjects, barefooted and barechested, carrying a naked sword held vertically and wearing on his head a green and purple cap on which there is a footprint. The sword clearly represents the commitment of the kings of Travancore to their trust of protecting the kingdom on the Lord's behalf. The footprint, given what we have noted above in our discussion of Bali, is a sign that the Maharaja as devotee and servant of Śri Padmanābha has placed his head at the Lord's feet.

But this suggests also that those who earlier handed their lands over to the temples and the Brāhmans may also have perceived this as an act of devotion to the Lord. This thrusts us decisively back into the mythology of Mahābali and the Dwarf. As we have noted, the texts of Phases 2 and 3 emphasize the importance of giving land to Brāhmans by lauding Bali's devotion in giving the entire earth to the Dwarf Brāhman boy. Given the associations we have seen between the Nampūtiris and Viṣṇu in various manifestations (as Paraśurāma, as Padmanābha), it seems highly unlikely that the Vāmana-Mahābali relationship would not have been also used in a similar context.

D. Towards a scenario for the development of the association of Ōṇam and Mahābali

All these customs and beliefs seen against their historical background, present what is — to my mind — the strongest hypothesis concerning the evolution of Ōṇam in Kerala where Mahābali has come to hold such a central place. If, as both the general tradition and the specific picture of the *Mahābalicaritam* indicate, the image of the Lord of Tṛkkākkara was or came to be identified with Vāmana, it would not be surprising if, following the tradition found in the *Bhāgavata,* Tiruvōṇam was celebrated there as the birthday of Vāmana. Nor would it be surprising if devout Chera kings came to perceive themselves as later-day Balis and hence to identify Tṛkkākkara as the capital of Bali's ancient and famous kingdom. This identification was possible because the Purāṇas identify a number of different places as the site of Bali's sacrifice. Accordingly, a variety of traditions about the site could develop. Given the rather tantalizing picture of Bali's kingdom developed in the Purāṇas, it would also not be surprising that an idealization of it should come to play an important part in the conception of the festival; and that it should give rise, under conditions where caste structures were being felt as oppressive, to a nostalgic portrayal of Bali's kingdom as a time when such hierarchies were unknown.

Uloor M. Paramesvara Iyer adds a further suggestion to explain the connection of Mahābali and Tṛkkākkara (1943, II):

> Utiyan Cheral 'Vana-varampam', mentioned in the Sangam work *Patittuppattu,* by which expression is meant the Chera king Utiyan whose territory is bounded by the sky, is metamorphosed into Udayan Banavarman, leading to the glib inference that Bana, the son of Mahabali, was a Chera ruler.

The hypothesis that Ōṇam was initially the birthday of the Lord and later was celebrated also as the return of Mahābali — rather than the major alternative that it was initially a festival associated with Mahābali and thence with Vāmana who overcame Mahābali — is also given a kind of confirmation in the *Mahābalicaritam*. This begins with an account of the celebration by Mahābali of Tiru-vōṇam as the birthday of Mahādeva. There follows the defeat of Mahābali by Vāmana, and then the suggestion that under the Lord's rule things are not as good as they were under Mahābali. Ōṇam is then re-established as a festival celebrating the return of Mahābali in addition to the birthday of Vāmana. The details of this new festival are similar to what they are in the first account, but more elaborate. The story thus effectively provides an explan-ation for a shift from Ōṇam as solely the birthday of Viṣṇu to its close association with Mahābali as well.

If we accept this hypothesis, the question we have earlier raised of a link between Mahābali-Ōṇam and Bali-Dīvālī can now be raised in a new form: Was the development of the introduction of Mahābali into the Ōṇam festival given its impetus by the importa-tion of traditions about Bali and Dīvālī, and a linking of them to Ōṇam? This is a question that can be considered more adequately only when we have examined additional evidence, as we shall in the next chapter.

E. Ramifications of an Image of Perfection

Central to the cultural vitality of Ōṇam is the composite image of human perfection. The components of that image that demand the closest attention are, first, the continuing ramifications of the portrayal of Ōṇam as the return of Mahābali to the people of his kingdom. Next we must also examine the suggestion that in Ōṇam there is a brief recapturing of the glorious age of the past.

As regards the characteristic conditions of Mahābali's kingdom we have already seen how much emphasis there is on prosperity and happiness in the celebration of Ōṇam. In addition to these, two other features — equality and good relations among people — loom large as characteristic emphases of the Ōṇam season and thence flow over to affect the lives of Malayālis more generally.

A movement in the direction of equality and good relations is seen in the relaxation of caste rules reported by Samuel Mateer (Philip, 4):

But on festival days Pulayas and other low castes are permitted a little nearer approach to some Pagodas than usual, at Parechal, etc. At Ochira, in the great sham fights slaves are permitted to join and to give and receive blows equally with the Nayars.

When we remind ourselves again of the normal relations between the castes, as we have seen from Mateer's description above (p. 218), we can see that for a Pūlaya to be able to engage in combat with a Nāyar at close quarters clearly indicated a considerable relaxation of normal rules.

Another dimension of the different approaches to caste relations is seen in the giving of Ōṇam gifts (*ōṇakkāḻca*). On the eve of Tiruvōṇam, as we noted, servants traditionally give their masters gifts of rice, yams, pumpkins, and plantain bunches; the masters responded by giving them new clothes. That the gift-giving is by no means reciprocal in value, in that the cloth is considerably more expensive than the produce, suggests that there is something of an attempt to redress the inequalities inherent in the system. The overall effect of this, along with the relaxation of caste rules, could be seen as an infusion of the caste structures with a more humane quality, a general goodwill in keeping with the vision of equality and good relations expressed via the myth of Mahābali's reign.

Beyond this general note of goodwill, however, there is in some of the traditional Ōṇam songs a protest against prevailing social conditions under which even at Ōṇam the vision of Mahābali's kingdom remains far from realization. The emphasis on prosperity, given symbolic focus in harvest and feasting, becomes a natural impetus to protest against inequalities, although the protest is oblique (translated from Nambiar, 36):

Mahābali has come
and Ōṇam is here!
But Uncle has not come, and so
the granary is not opened;
and Auntie has not come, so
the paddy has not been cooked.
Only you have come,
Mahābali!

The background to this is more explicitly presented in a previous song (Nambiar, 35):

> Ōṇam has come!
> Unto us a child is born!
> But the poor man has his rice pudding
> and no feast.

There is also this lightly amusing piece which seems to have somewhat satirical undertones (from Nambiar, 35):

> A certain man went fishing at Manañceram
> on the day of Attam
> and caught a big fish
> with a long tail.
> He brought it home and cut it into pieces
> and prepared it with salt
> and spices as needed.
> When it was being prepared
> eighteen ladies were there;
> they tasted the salt of the cooked fish.
> Before it could be served up
> it was finished.
> Nobody got any curry,
> or even a handful of rice.
> Every vessel was empty.

These intimations of protest within the context of the Ōṇam festivities again raise the question about the origin of the idea that all men were equal during Mahābali's reign. Some of the suggestions given above can be looked at again. What we know of the strict separation of castes suggests a highly rigid approach to the question of ritual purity. There exists sufficient information on temple customs and myths about the place of the Nampūtiri Brāhmans in Kerala to suggest that the remoteness of Kerala from significant centres and concentrations of Brahmanical power, as well as the presence of a large non-Aryan population, may have contributed to a pattern in which legitimation of religious practices was achieved by means of the strictness of the purity-pollution hierarchy. What we know of the background to the "Upper Cloth" riots in southern Travancore in the 1820's and 1850's (see Hospital 1979) suggests that this concern for purity, when coupled with a hierarchy of privilege, as it almost inevitably was, overreached itself. Such were perhaps the circumstances from which a dream of equality arose. Having once arisen, such a dream could well have contributed to the development of Ōṇam as both an amelioration of the worst inequalities and a protest against them. The forms outlined above embody that protest.

The possible implications of the dream in relation to social change in the contemporary world have been developed only recently. E.M.S. Namboodiripad, Kerala's first Chief Minister (from 1957 till 1959) and leader of the Communist Party of India (Marxist), describes the theoretical base of the party in terms of the reign of Mahābali (8):

> In its campaign for a united Kerala, the Party drew its inspiration from the legendary story of ancient Kerala — the regime of Mahabali when, according to legend, 'all were equal' and there was plenty for everybody. The nostalgic craving of the people of Kerala for the days of Mahabali is today expressed in the national festival Onam, when every family does its best to try to re-live the equality and prosperity of the legendary days of Mahabali. Basing itself on this legend, and the social customs centred around it, the Communist Party raised the slogan of working for the revival of the days of Mahabali in the new international and national set up. In other words, it was as the modern and scientific interpretation of the national aspiration for equality, democracy, and prosperity, contained in the legendary story of Mahabali, that the Communist Party evolved its slogan of a new, united, democratic and prosperous Kerala.

It is of some significance, I think, that the Marxists became so strong in this area where the egalitarian myth was so much a living force. In thinking about a new India freed from the imperial domination of the British, Gandhi had also taken up one of the traditional pictures of an ideal kingdom. He made frequent references to *Rāmrājya,* the kingdom of Rāma, as his ideal. The picture of this in the most popular version of north India, the *Rāmacarit-mānas* of Tulsidās is as follows (Hill, 444–45):

> The bliss and prosperity of Rāma's realm neither Serpent King nor Sarasvatī can describe. All who dwelt therein were generous and charitable and did humble service to the Brāhmans. Each husband was true to one wife, and each wife was loyal to her husband in thought and word and deed.
>
> In Rāmacandra's realm the only rods were those in the hands of ascetics, the only differences were those of tune and measure in the dancers' troupes; the word 'conquer' was only heard to urge self-conquest.
>
> The trees in the forest always bore flowers and fruit; the elephant and the lion dwelt together; birds and beasts all forgot their natual enmities and lived in mutual harmony. Birds sang, and beasts of every kind wandered fearless through the forest in perfect happiness. Cool, fragrant and mild blew the breezes, and bees hummed as they gathered honey. Creepers and trees dropped honey at one's desire, and cows gave all the milk that one could wish. The earth was ever rich in crops; in this Tretāyuga were found all the blessings of the Kritayuga. The hills disclosed all kinds of jewel mines, knowing the Universal Spirit to be king of the world. In all the rivers flowed fair water, cool, pure, delicious and refreshing. The seas remained within their bounds, they cast jewels on the shore and men gathered them. All the ponds were thick with lotuses, and the whole country enjoyed perfect happiness. The moon bathed the earth in radiance; the sun gave as much heat as was needed; the clouds shed rain as men desired in Rāmacandra's realm.
>
> The Lord sacrificed myriads of horses and gave countless gifts to Brāhmans; he preserved the Vedic way and was a pillar of the faith, himself transcending nature's elements, yet a very Indra in luxurious delights. Sītā was ever submissive to her lord, virtuous, modest and of perfect beauty. She recognized the majesty of the Lord of grace and did diligent service to his lotus feet. Though there were numberless menservants and handmaidens in the palace, all accomplished in the performance of their duties, she did the housework with her own

hands and attended to Rāmacandra's orders. Any service that might please the gracious Lord Sītā herself skilfully performed. Kausalyā, too, and all the other queens she served within the palace and felt no pride or any loss of dignity. Ever blameless, O Umā, is Sītā, Mother of the world, adored by Brahmā and the host of heaven! She whose gracious glance the gods desire — but she looks not towards them — forgot her high estate and practised this devotion to Rāma's lotus feet.

All his brothers, too, did him obedient service, showing supreme devotion to Rāma's feet; and they were always watching his lotus face to see if perchance the gracious Lord had any orders to give. Rāma felt great affection for his brothers and gave them much moral instruction.

The people of the city lived very happily and all enjoyed delights to which the gods could scarce attain. Day and night they made their prayer to God, beseeching him to grant them devotion to the feet of the Lord Raghubir.

Here the social ideals are more typically Indian. The people of the various classes retain their proper places within the social hierarchy. Gandhi was antagonistic towards many aspects of what had developed in the caste system and was entirely sympathetic towards the plight of the Untouchables. Yet even he accepted the principle of the *varṇa* system. To this the emphases of the Mahābali myth stand in sharp contrast.

In the context of the use of myths for advancing a social vision, the contrast between northern India and Kerala is only too apparent. In northern India, in recent centuries, the place given to Rāma has been quite major. One can see it in the festival of Dasarā, which culminates in a stupendous portrayal of the victory of Rāma over Rāvaṇa. This festival comes just before Dīvālī, and as we have seen, in some places Dīvālī has come to be primarily a celebration of the perfection of Rāma's kingdom.

In Kerala, Rāma has never been so dominant a portrayal of goodness. It is quite understandable, then, that the vision there of a better world should be mediated via the local myth of Mahābali's kingdom. But also, given the radicalness of the vision in its emphasis on equality we can understand the appeal of the Marxist position. No doubt there are many other features of the economic and social conditions of Kerala that contributed to the acceptance of Marxist ideas by such a large percentage of the population in that area, but the ability of E. M. S. Namboodiripad to use the Mahābali tradition in this way must have given considerable impetus to the movement.

Still, other political parties of Kerala have not been content to let the Communists monopolize the myth or the festival. In 1961, the Government of Kerala — by this time a non-Communist coalition was in power — sponsored the celebration of Ōnam through its Department of Tourism, with the expressed purpose of "fostering emotional integration among people belonging to various religions and regions of Kerala," and with the exhortation that it be "an occasion for sinking past rivalries and for cultivating goodwill among all sections of the people" (CI–O 8). The interest in unification and goodwill given concrete form in the Ōnam festival becomes more significant in view of the fact that Christians and Muslims have increasingly celebrated Ōnam in recent years.

Another side to the impetus towards changing structures is seen in the following report of actions of the lower classes with respect to Ōnam.

> In a convention of Pulayas held at Pallichal near Trivandrum a few years ago, it was decided that in future the Pulayas would not send Ōnam presents to their masters. The political parties, functioning in the area, are also trying to dissuade the agricultural serfs including the Pulayas, from sending Ōnam presents. (CI–O 28)

It can thus be seen that the mythical motif of a perfect age, as exemplified by the tradition of Mahābali's reign, functions in different ways. On the one hand it provides for a creative penetration through limiting social structures and perhaps thereby achieves a kind of humanization of these structures. On the other hand, it becomes the focus for expressions of dissatisfaction and an impetus toward social change.

8

Bali Goes West

The only significant literary treatment of Bali in Western literature is that of Robert Southey in his epic poem, *The Curse of
Kehama.* Since Bali has only a cameo appearance one does not
need to know the story in great detail to understand his role. But
the general setting of the scene is clearly given. Kehama is a great
tyrant who, in a style not uncharacteristic of Indian mythology,
has by means of austerities and sacrifices gained control of all the
worlds excepting Padalon (Pātāla), the nether region, which is
under the control of Yamen (Yama).

Kehama's son, Arvalan, has attempted to ravish Kailyal, a
beautiful low-caste girl. She is saved by her father Ladurlad, who
in doing so, kills the dissolute prince. The prince's spirit returns to
haunt the world as a demon of revenge. Kehama curses his son's
killer to wander the earth cut off from the elements, food, drink,
time, sickness, death, and sleep. But this liberates Ladurlad to
lend aid where in ordinary human life he would be powerless.
Thus he manages to defend his daughter from an attack from
Kehama and he is able, unseen, to disturb Kehama's hundredth
horse sacrifice.

Kailyal is also helped by a "Glendoveer" (Gandharva), Ereenia,
who saves her from various calamities. On the other side, Arvalan

obtains help from Lorrinite, a terrible witch who works for the bloodthirsty "Celis" (no doubt *"Kālis"*). The significant events occuring immediately before the appearance of Bali on the scene are summarized by Ernest Bernhardt-Kabisch as follows (102):

> Action resumes when a band of yogis, in search of a bride for their god Jaga-Naut (Juggernaut), carry Kailyal off to their holy city where she is drawn in procession on the notorious car of the seven-headed idol while frenzied worshippers immolate themselves under its iron wheels. Having been conveyed on to the sacred bridal bed by temple harlots, the girl is beset by a lecherous Brahmin who pretends to impersonate the deity and who in the process becomes possessed by the "accursed soul of Arvalan." Ereenia appears to defend Kailyal but is overpowered by the witch Lorrinite and her crew and is carried to the vaults beneath the ocean. Left once more to face the horrid Arvalan, Kailyal frustrates his renewed attack by suicidally setting fire to the bridal bed and the temple. Luckily, Ladurlad arrives and, shielded by the curse, carries her to safety. Together they search for the kidnapped Ereenia.

At this point, it is interesting to look at the actual text:

Text 26
[Robert Southey, *The Curse of Kehama*]

XV
The City of Baly
I.
KAILYAL

> Then thou knowest
> Where they have borne him?
> LADURLAD
> To the Sepulchres
> Of the Ancient Kings, which Baly, in his power,
> Made in primeval times, and built above them
> A City, like the Cities of the Gods,
> Being like a God himself. For many an age

Hath Ocean warred against his Palaces,
Till, overwhelmed, they lie beneath the waves,
Not overthrown, so well the awful Chief
Had laid their deep foundations. Rightly said
The Accursèd, that no way for Man was there;
But not like Man am I!

2

Up from the ground the Maid exultant sprung,
And clapped her happy hands in attitude
Of thanks to Heaven, and flung
Her arms around her Father's neck, and stood
Struggling awhile for utterance, with excess
Of hope and pious thankfulness.
"Come, come!" she cried. "Oh, let us not delay!
He is in torments there! — away! away!"

3

Long time they travelled on; at dawn of day
Still setting forward with the earliest light,
Nor ceasing from their way
Till darkness closed the night.
Short refuge from the noontide heat,
Reluctantly compelled, the Maiden took,
And ill her indefatigable feet
Could that brief respite brook.
Hope kept her up, and her intense desire
Supports that heart which ne'er at danger quails,
Those feet which never tire,
That frame which never fails.

4

Their talk was of the City of the days
Of old, Earth's wonder once, and of the fame
Of Baly, its great founder, — he whose name,
In ancient story and in poet's praise,
Liveth and flourisheth for endless glory,
Because his might
Put down the wrong, and aye upheld the right;

Till for ambition, as old sages tell,
At length the universal Monarch fell:
For he, too, having made the World his own,
Then in his pride, had driven
The Devetas from Heaven,
And seized triumphantly the Swerga throne.
The Incarnate came before the Mighty One
In dwarfish stature, and in mien obscure:
The sacred cord he bore,
And asked, for Brama's sake, a little boon,
Three steps of Baly's ample reign, — no more.
Poor was the boon required, and poor was he
Who begged, — a little wretch it seemed to be.
But Baly ne'er refused a suppliant's prayer:
He on the Dwarf cast down
A glance of pity in contemptuous mood,
And bade him take the boon,
And measure where he would.

5

"Lo, Son of giant birth,
I take my grant!" the Incarnate Power replies.
With his first step he measured o'er the Earth;
The second spanned the skies.
"Three paces thou hast granted;
Twice have I set my footstep," Vishnu cries;
"Where shall the third be planted?"

6

Then Baly knew the God; and at his feet,
In homage due, he laid his humbled head.
"Mighty art thou, O Lord of Earth and Heaven!
Mighty art thou!" he said;
"Be merciful, and let me be forgiven."
He asked for mercy of the Merciful,
And mercy for his virtue's sake was shown.
For though he was cast down to Padalon,
Yet there, by Yamen's throne,
Doth Baly sit in majesty and might,
To judge the dead, and sentence them aright.

And, forasmuch as he was still the friend
Of righteousness, it is permitted him,
Yearly, from those drear regions to ascend,
And walk the Earth, that he may hear his name
Still hymned and honored by the grateful voice
Of human-kind, and in his fame rejoice.

                              7
Such was the talk they held upon their way,
Of him to whose old City they were bound;
And now, upon their journey, many a day
Had risen and closed, and many a week gone round,
And many a realm and region had they passed,
When now the Ancient Towers appeared at last.

                              8
Their golden summits, in the noonday light,
Shone o'er the dark-green deep that rolled between;
For domes and pinnacles and spires were seen
Peering above the sea—a mournful sight!
Well might the sad beholder ween from thence
What works of wonder the devouring wave
Had swallowed there, when monuments so brave
Bore record of their old magnificence.
And on the sandy shore, beside the verge
Of Ocean, here and there, a rock-hewn fane
Resisted in its strength the surf and surge
That on their deep foundations beat in vain.
In solitude the Ancient Temples stood,
Once resonant with instrument and song;
And solemn dance of festive multitude;
Now, as the weary ages pass along,
Hearing no voice save of the Ocean flood,
Which roars for ever on the restless shores;
Or, visiting their solitary caves,
The lonely sound of winds, that moan around
Accordant to the melancholy waves.

[Ladurlad leaves Kailyal on the shore and descends into the
ocean in search of Ereenia.]

XVI

THE ANCIENT SEPULCHRES

4

Through many a solitary street,
And silent market-place and lonely square,
Armed with the mighty Curse, behold him fare!
And now his feet attain that royal fane
Where Baly held of old his awful reign.
What once had been the Gardens spread around, —
Fair Gardens, once which wore perpetual green,
Where all sweet flowers through all the year were found,
And all fair fruits were through all seasons seen;
A place of Paradise, where each device
Of emulous Art with Nature strove to vie;
And Nature, on her part,
Called forth new powers wherewith to vanquish Art.
The Swerga-god himself, with envious eye,
Surveyed those peerless gardens in their prime;
Nor ever did the Lord of Light,
Who circles Earth and Heaven upon his way,
Behold from eldest time a goodlier sight
Than were the groves which Baly, in his might,
Made for his chosen place of solace and delight.

5

It was a Garden still beyond all price;
Even yet it was a place of Paradise:
For where the mighty Ocean could not spare,
There had he, with his own creation,
Sought to repair his work of devastation.
And here were coral bowers,
And grots of madrepores,
And banks of sponge, as soft and fair to eye
As ere was mossy bed
Whereon the Wood-Nymphs lie
With languid limbs, in summer's sultry hours.
Here, too, were living flowers,

Which, like a bud compacted,
Their purple cups contracted,
And now, in open blossom spread,
Stretched like green anthers many a seeking head.
And arborets of jointed stone were there,
And plants of fibres fine as silkworm's thread;
Yea, beautiful as Mermaid's golden hair
Upon the waves dispread.
Others that, like the broad banana growing,
Raised their long, wrinkled leaves of purple hue,
Like streamers wide outflowing.
And, whatsoe'er the depths of Ocean hide
From human eyes, Ladurlad there espied, —
Trees of the deep, and shrubs and fruits and flowers
As fair as ours,
Wherewith the Sea-Nymphs love their locks to braid,
When to their father's hall, at festival
Repairing, they, in emulous array,
Their charms display
To grace the banquet and the solemn day.

6

The golden fountains had not ceased to flow;
And, where they mingled with the briny Sea,
There was a sight of wonder and delight
To see the fish, like birds in air,
Above Ladurlad flying.
Round those strange waters they repair,
Their scarlet fins outspread and plying;
They float with gentle hovering there;
And now upon those little wings,
As if to dare forbidden things,
With wilful purpose bent,
Swift as an arrow from a bow,
They shoot across, and to and fro,
In rapid glance, like lightning go
Through that unwonted element.

XVII

BALY

I

This is the appointed night,
The night of joy and consecrated mirth,
When from his judgment-seat in Padalon,
By Yamen's throne,
Baly goes forth, that he may walk the Earth
Unseen, and hear his name
Still hymned and honored by the grateful voice
Of human-kind, and in his fame rejoice.
Therefore, from door to door, and street to street,
With willing feet,
Shaking their firebrands, the glad children run:
"Baly! great Baly!" they acclaim;
Where'er they run, they bear the mighty name;
Where'er they meet,
"Baly! great Baly!" still their choral tongues repeat.
Therefore at every door the votive flame
Through pendant lanterns sheds its painted light;
And rockets, hissing upward through the sky,
Fall like a shower of stars
From Heaven's black canopy.
Therefore, on yonder mountain's templed height,
The brazen caldron blazes through the night.
Huge as a Ship that travels the main sea
Is that capacious brass; its wick as tall
As is the mast of some great admiral.
Ten thousand votaries bring
Camphor and ghee to feed the sacred flame;
And while, through regions round, the nations see
Its fiery pillar curling high in heaven,
"Baly! great Baly!" they exclaim;
"For ever hallowed be his blessèd name!
Honor and praise to him for evermore be given!"

2

Why art not thou among the festive throng,
Baly, O righteous Judge! to hear thy fame?
Still, as of yore, with pageantry and song,
The glowing streets along,
They celebrate thy name;
"Baly! great Baly!" still
The grateful habitants of Earth acclaim;
"Baly! great Baly!" still
The ringing walls and echoing towers proclaim.
From yonder mountain the portentous flame
Still blazes to the nations as before;
All things appear to human eyes the same,
As perfect, as of yore;
To human eyes, — but how unlike to thine!
Thine, which were wont to see
The Company divine,
That with their presence came to honour thee
For all the blessèd ones of mortal birth
Who have been clothed with immortality,
From the eight corners of the Earth,
From the Seven Worlds assembling, all
Wont to attend thy solemn festival.
Then did thine eyes behold
The wide air peopled with that glorious train;
Now mayst thou seek the blessèd ones in vain,
For Earth and Air are now beneath the Rajah's reign.

3

Therefore the righteous Judge hath walked the Earth
In sorrow and in solitude to-night.
The sound of human mirth
To him is no delight;
He turns away from that ungrateful sight,
Hallowed not now by visitants divine;
And there he bends his melancholy way,
Where, in yon full-orbed Moon's refulgent light,
The Golden Towers of his old City shine

Above the silver sea. The ancient Chief
There bent his way in grief,
As if sad thoughts indulged would work their own relief.

(As Bali watches, he sees Kailyal standing on the shore as she has done for seven days. Then he sees Arvalan and Lorrinite hovering beside her. Soon Ladurlad appears from the waters bringing with him Ereenia whom he has at last freed from bondage after six days of wrestling with a powerful *naga*. As Kailyal embraces Ladurlad, Arvalon suddenly appears in embodied form, and with the help of Lorrinite, seizes Ladurlad and Ereenia. Then Bali intervenes.)

II

"Hold your accursèd hands!"
A voice exclaimed, whose dread commands
Were feared through all the vaults of Padalon;
And there among them, in the midnight air,
The presence of the mighty Baly shone.
He, making manifest his mightiness,
Put forth on every side an hundred arms,
And seized the Sorceress: maugre all her charms,
Her and her fiendish ministers he caught
With force as uncontrollable as fate;
And that unhappy Soul, to whom
The Almighty Rajah's power availeth not
Living to avert, nor dead to mitigate,
His righteous doom.
"Help, help, Kehama! Father, help!" she cried;
But Baly tarried not to abide
That mightier Power: with irresistible feet
He stamped and cleft the Earth; it opened wide,
And gave him way to his own Judgment-seat.
Down, like a plummet, to the World below
He sunk, and bore his prey
To punishment deserved, and endless woe.

XVIII

KEHAMA'S DESCENT

I

The Earth, by Baly's feet divided,
Closed o'er his way as to the Judgment-seat
He plunged, and bore his prey.
Scarce had the shock subsided,
When, darting from the Swerga's heavenly heights,
Kehama, like a thunder-bolt alights.
In wrath he came: a bickering flame
Flashed from his eyes, which made the moonlight dim;
And passion forcing way from every limb,
Like furnace-smoke, with terrors wrapt him round.
Furious he smote the ground;
Earth trembled underneath the dreadful stroke,
Again in sunder riven;
He hurled in rage his whirling weapon down.
But, lo! the fiery sheckra to his feet
Returned, as if by equal force redriven;
And from the abyss the voice of Baly came:
"Not yet, O Rajah! hast thou won
The realms of Padalon!
Earth and the Swerga are thine own;
But, till Kehama shall subdue the throne
Of Hell, in torments Yamen holds his son."

A. *Southey: Bali and Mahabalipuram*

Southey here shows familiarity with a number of important
aspects of the story of Bali as we have seen it developed through
the texts: his famous kingdom, its paradisal quality, his goodness,
his ambition, his being overthrown by Viṣṇu, his being sent off to
Pātāla, and his return to earth once a year.

In detail this comes closer to the Kerala versions than to any of
the Puranic versions. But there are further details that mark its
difference from the Kerala version. The place of Bali's capital city
is identified in accompanying notes as Mahabalipuram, the an-

cient city whose marvelous remains are still visible on the Coromandel coast, south of Madras. The customs for greeting Bali's
return to earth are also not those of the Kerala area; the fesitival
clearly is not Ōṇam.

In "Notes to The Curse of Kehama," Southey (8:305–6) acknowledges his dependence for some of the details about Bali upon
Pierre Sonnerat's account of his voyages to the East. Sonnerat's
discussion in *Voyage aux Indes et à la Chine* indicates (237–39) that this
festival when Bali returns occurs in the month of Cartigué (Kārtika), and the details suggest Divāli. The following is my translation of the relevant section in Sonnerat:

> The Viṣṇupatis have a very large festival on the same full
> moon day. It differs from the former [the Kārtika festival of
> the Śivapatis referred to in the previous paragraph] only with
> respect to its object, the manner in which the two groups per-
> form their celebration being similar. They light fires to express
> their joy in front of the temples; the streets and the houses are
> illuminated and they carry the gods in procession. The
> Viṣṇupatis say that it was on the day of the full moon of this
> month that Viṣṇu took the form of a Brāhman dwarf and ban-
> ished the powerful giant Mahābali to Pātāla; that the giant
> while he was ruler liked illuminations very much and provided
> for each house a *calon* of oil, in order to satisfy his liking; and
> that in going to Pātāla he prayed Viṣṇu to allow the practice
> he had established to be continued on earth. God promised
> him that he would, and at the same time also permitted him to
> return every year on the same day in order to see for himself if
> God was faithful to his promise. It is for this reason that the
> illumination is carried on, and that the children hold fire in
> their hands and enjoy themselves in the street, crying out,
> "Mahabaliro."

There are some surprising details here. We find certain
elements in common with the portrayals of Dīvālī in *Bhaviṣyottara*
and *Padma,* while others — the name of Mahābali, his returning to
visit his people each year — are closer to the traditions of Kerala.
The tracing of the practice of lighting lamps to Mahābali's love of
"illuminations" is a new motif, though it reflects *Skanda* and *Mahā-*

balicaritam in relating festival practices to what Bali himself did when he was king.

One might be tempted at first to see this primarily as a description of Dīvālī (or Dīpāvalī as it is known in this area), to which the writer has added certain South Indian elements that are found especially in Kerala's Ōṇam. But Dīpāvalī is here associated only with the myth of Kṛṣṇa's defeat of Narakāsura (as is also the case in the southern part of Kerala which shares many Tamil traditions, such sharing dating back at least to the late nineteenth century [Mateer, 188]). A further major problem with this interpretation is that the time of the festival seems uncertain. Sonnerat says that this Vaiṣṇava festival occurred on the same day as the festival of Subrahmaṇya, *Paor-Nomi* (Pūrṇimā), on the full moon day of the month of Kārtika. The location of the festival is equally uncertain. Sonnerat does not indicate his source with any precision, though he identifies the Subrahmaṇya festival with the temple at Tirounamalei (presumably Tiruvannamalai). It would seem that he is speaking of an area that lies today in Tamil Nadu.

How then are we to interpret these details? It is possible that Sonnerat missed or misunderstood some of the facts, that what he describes was really the new moon festival of Dīpāvalī. One would then have to conclude that traditions of the relation of Bali to Dīvālī were once extant in this area but have now been lost.

It is, of course, possible that Sonnerat reports every detail correctly. One would then conclude that Śaivas and Vaiṣṇavas have developed different festivals from a common base. Particularly if one accepts the suggestion of Allchin (below, p. 248) that behind the Dīvālī traditions there is an ancient bonfire practice among pastoralists analagous to the need fires of medieval Europe, it becomes possible to see the complex of Dīvālī traditions in North India and the Kārtikadīpam (along with a parallel Vaiṣṇava festival associated with Bali) of Tamil Nadu as variant developments of an ancient and widespread practice of the pre-winter period.

This latter interpretation is confirmed by the description of Louis Dumont of the religious life of the Pramalai Kallar, a South Indian sub-caste living in an area to the west of Madurai. In his account, Mahābali is integrated into the Śaiva complex of Kārtikai. He regards the lighting of lamps as a variant of the Dīvālī celebrations of north India. I translate the relevant section (375):

> A little later the young people and boys [in fact also even the girls] whirl torches made of grass in front of the houses in all the streets of the village and also in the hills. They burn the remainder the last day.
>
> They make these lights in order that the king *māvili* [*mahābāli*] [sic], conquered by the three steps of Krishna [or rather of Vishnu in the appearance of a dwarf (Sanskrit *Vāmana*)] may be able to see his kingdom conforming to his vow. This king was himself the reincarnation of a rat (māyeli, big rat) which had relit the lamp of Śiva and Pārvatī. This lamp had been on the point of extinguishing itself (this is inauspicious), when the rat went to drink the oil from it.

Going back to Sonnerat, we find that he too pictures Bali as ruling in Pātāla (163). Southey borrows that picture, but takes it further than this and portrays Bali on a number of occasions as a righteous judge in the nether world — with "his judgment-seat in Padalon, / By Yamen's throne." The materials we have surveyed on Dīvālī suggest a possible relationship between Bali and Yama, but nowhere in any of the texts we have looked at is there the idea that Bali, when he is sent off to Pātāla, becomes a judge of people's goodness or lack of it. Southey nowhere indicates the source of this idea; it appears to be an entirely alien view, even though it is constructed out of a variety of traditions about the nether world in Indian mythology. He may have made this inference on the basis of Sonnerat's recording of the portrayal of Bali as "generous, true to his word, compassionate, charitable." ("Notes to The Curse of Kehama," 305). It could be on the same basis that Bali is also portrayed as quite unhappy because Kehama, and not the Devas, is in control of the worlds.

Perhaps the most important new theme in Southey is the identification of the city of Bali as Mahabalipuram together with the suggestion that much of Bali's ancient city has been submerged. For these details Southey acknowledges his dependence upon the writings of Chambers in *Asiatic Researches*. Southey cites at length Chambers' description of Mahabalipuram, including, towards the end, the intriguing idea of the submerged city (308-9):

The great rock is about fifty or one hundred yards from the
sea: but close to the sea are the remains of a pagoda built of
bricks, dedicated to Sib, the greatest part of which has evidently been swallowed up by that element; for the door of the
innermost apartment, in which the idol is placed, and before
which there are always two or three spacious courts surrounded with walls, is now washed by the waves; and the pillar, used to discover the meridian at the time of founding the
pagoda, is seen standing at some distance in the sea. In the
neighborhood of this building there are some detached rocks,
washed also by the waves, on which there appear sculptures,
though now much worn and defaced. And the natives of the
place declared to the writer of this account that the more aged
people among them remembered to have seen the tops of several pagodas far out in the sea, which, being covered with copper [probably gilt], were particularly visible at sunrise, as
their shining surface used then to reflect the sun's rays; but
now that effect was no longer produced, as the copper had
since become incrusted with mould and verdigris.

For the tradition that the conditions of Bali's kingdom were
paradisal, Southey again depends on Chambers. The magnificence of the kingdom finds its way into Southey's imaginative
development of the picture in which he turns the ancient gardens
of Mahābali into a brilliant display of tropical underwater beauty.
Thus, in Southey's version of Chambers ("Notes to The Curse of
Kehama," 310–11):

Malecheren [which is probably another name for Baly], in an
excursion which he made one day alone and in disguise, came
to a garden in the environs of his city Mahabalipoor, where
was a fountain so inviting, that two celestial nymphs had
come down to bathe there. The Rajah became enamoured of
one of them, who condescended to allow of his attachment to
her; and she and her sister nymph used thenceforward to have
frequent interviews with him in that garden. On one of these
occasions, they brought with them a male inhabitant of the
heavenly regions to whom they introduced the Rajah and
between him and Malecheren a strict friendship ensued; in

consequence of which, he agreed, at the Rajah's earnest request, to carry him in disguise to see the court of the divine Inder—a favour never before granted to any mortal. The Rajah returned from thence with new ideas of splendour and magnificence which he immediately adopted in regulating his court and his retinue and in beautifying his seat of government. By this means, Mahabalipoor became soon celebrated beyond all the cities of the earth; and, an account of its magnificence being brought to the gods assembled at the court of Inder, their jealousy was so much excited at it, that they sent orders to the god of the sea to let loose his billows, and overflow a place which impiously pretended to vie in·splendor with the celestial mansions. This command he obeyed, and the city was at once overflowed by that furious element; nor has it ever since been able to rear its head.

It is clear from yet another western investigation, William Young Willets' *Illustrated Annotated Annual Bibliography of Mahabalipuram,* that the marvellous set of sculptures and temple structures of this city has captured the imagination of scholars for a number of different reasons. Willets makes the point that the idea that there is a city or some temples offshore from the present structures is one which dies hard. Exploratory soundings by Mackenzie and Ellis in the early nineteenth century brought no evidence of a submerged city. Nor is it likely, in view of the pattern of currents along the Coromandel coast, that a submerged city has been entirely eroded. Yet there are still reports of aircraft pilots seeing submerged buildings from the air; and so the tradition continues.

Willets also explores the tradition relating the ancient structures and Mahābali. From the earliest period of European contacts, the place has been known by some variant of the name Mahabalipuram (3). But S. Krishna Swami Aiyangar has pointed out that the only concrete association of Mahabalipuram with Bali is a panel in one of the caves depicting the form of Vishnu as Trivikrama. There are no independent references relating the place to Mahābali. It is not known when the first associations of this kind were made.

It is generally accepted nowadays that Mahabalipuram was constructed by one of the kings of the Pallava dynasty. The two

most commonly mentioned are Narasimhavarman I and Rajasimha. Krishna Swami Aiyangar favors the former, and R. Naga-
swamy the latter. Other names by which the city has been known
suggest the possible origin of the name Mahabalipuram. The best
known of these is Mamallapuram (sometimes Mahamallipur).
There are two possible reasons for applying this name: the first is
that the epithet *mahāmalla* is applied in various inscriptions to both
Narsimhavarman and Rajasimha. Thus, since *puram* just means
"city," this would be an indication that the city belongs to one or
other of these great kings. The epithet *mahāmalla* means "exceedingly
powerful." An alternative epithet meaning the same is *mahābalin*
which in compound form would be *mahābalī*. Thus it would take
no great shift for the "city of the very powerful one" to become "the
city of Mahābali."

A variant suggestion of Willets appears untenable. He notes
that, as Krishna Swami Aiyangar (1917) shows, Tirumaṅkai Āḷvār
referred to Mahabalipuram as *kadalmallai talasayanam*. Willets
translates *kadalmallai* as "the hill near the sea," but the Tamil word
for hill is *malai* not *mallai*. Thus his intimation that the name
Mahabalipuram may have originally been "the hill which lies close
to the sea," is untenable unless it can be shown that *mallai* was originally *malai*. In any case, given the more acceptable theory that
mallai refers to the powerful king who founded the city, such an
interpretation is rendered redundant.

All of this is of substantive interest in explaining the association of
the city with Mahābali but does little to aid our understanding of
the mythology. In relation to the latter, however, what is surely
important is the development of an indigenous Indian tradition of
Atlantis, the submerged city, together with elements that one finds
in Western stories concerning the Flood and the Tower of Babel.
For in the version from Chambers that Southey cites (erroneously
as it turns out, for Chambers does not identify Malecheran as
Bali), the city is inundated because it vies in splendour with the
heavenly regions. Southey reflects this idea, referring in the poem
to the city as "A place too god-like to be held by us, / The poor
degenerate children of the earth" (8.144). The theme of the jealousy of the gods, found in the Malayali versions, is used here as
well, but used to a different purpose.

B. Western Analogues — from Kronia to Hallowe'en

The other major Western contributor to the history of Bali is J.J. Meyer in his *Trilogie Altindischer Nächte und Feste der Vegetation.* The second part of the trilogy is devoted to an extensive study of Bali. It focuses mainly on the relation between Bali and Dīvālī. Arguing initially that the *Bhaviṣyottara* version is the earliest, Meyer then goes on to see Dīvālī as originally an agricultural festival, which is also·(as is not infrequently the case in other cultures) a festival of the dead and therefore a festival of lights. He suggests that Bali is essentially an agricultural deity, and concludes by comparing Bali to the ancient Roman god Saturn.

The comparison with Saturn — and one could easily extend this to Saturn's Greek counterpart, Kronos — is a fruitful one to pursue. There are a number of ways in which the nature of Kronos and festivals relating to Kronos and Saturn (Kronia and Saturnalia) are very similar to characteristics of Bali and the festivals associated with him. Thus, in Hesiod's *Work and Days* a past Golden Age is related to Kronos (11):

> First of all the first gods who dwell on Olympus made a golden race of mortal men who lived in the time of Cronos when he was reigning in heaven. And they lived like gods without sorrow of heart, remote and free from toil and grief: miserable age rested not on them; but with legs and arms never failing they made merry with feasting beyond the reach of all evils. When they died, it was as though they were overcome with sleep, and they had all good things; for the fruitful earth unforced bare them fruit abundantly and without stint. They dwelt in ease and peace upon their lands with many good things, rich in flocks and loved by the blessed gods.

Also the festival of Kronia was a harvest festival held on the twelfth of Hekatombaion (June/July), and it is described thus by Rose (67–68):

> On that day masters served their slaves and ate at the same table with them, thus furnishing part of the material for yet another legend, that in the days when Kronos was the

supreme god, there were no social distinctions, but all alike enjoyed peace and plenty.

The Saturnalia also appears to have been originally a harvest festival. As in the case of the Kronia, social distinctions were broken down. The details available to us about Saturnalia are more extensive than in the case of Kronia and are summarized by Rose (225; see also Sir James Frazer, *The Golden Bough*, 8:306–12):

> during it there were no social distinctions, slaves had a holiday and feasted like their masters, and all restrictions were relaxed, one being the prohibition on gambling with dice, which was supposed to be enforced at other times of the year. It was, however, a more thorough-going season of jollity than Kronia, at least in historical times, "the best of all days," says Martial. Civilians and soldiers alike celebrated it, it was usual to choose by lot a Lord of Misrule [*Saturnalicius princeps*, "Leading Man of the Saturnalia"], and gifts were exchanged. Although the date is different, it seems probable that its customs, blending with those of the New Year festival and with the northern Yule had their share in producing the traditional merry-makings of Christmas.

Naturally, in view of these similarities, one wonders whether there was at some distant past some historical connection between these figures and Bali. Are they repositories in different areas of an ancient Indo-European tradition? Nillson (*A History of Greek Religion*, 22–23) argues that the myth of the struggle of the Titans and Kronos with Zeus reflects a conflict between older and later cults within Greece. Given the argument coming from South India, that Bali represents the Dravidian heritage, it is possible that both in Greece and in India, the encounter of the Aryans with groups already in these lands resulted in similar kinds of mythologizing — of a battle between the old and the new, in which the representative of the old (Bali, Kronos) is defeated. Counterpointing that myth there might also exist another that came from a different level of the society, a myth idealizing the earlier historical period as a Golden Age.

Another contribution to the comparative discussion is provided by F. R. Allchin in his *Neolithic Cattle-Keepers of South India*. On the festival of Dīvālī, he says (127):

> From the broad comparative point of view the festival is typical of the autumnal festivals of the Mediterranean: Frazer long ago pointed to the possibility that the Christian feasts of All Souls and All Saints were a continuation of an old pre-Christian autumnal festival of the dead in which the worship of fire, the concept of a new year, of the walking abroad of ghosts and spirits, and even the prophylaxus of cattle by fire, can be traced. . . . Thus in seeking for the heart of such festivals we must penetrate below the Christian stratum to the older core. The coincidence of features of Divali and the old Mediterranean autumnal festival are in themselves remarkable . . .

Allchin goes on to note (129) that in the worship of Mount Govardhana the mountain is modeled in cowdung, often as a flat cone. He also notes that among the Mahadev Kolis of Bombay, cattle are driven over a cowdung cone described as a model of Bali. They are also driven over a small bonfire. Allchin further links these practices with archeological evidence from neolithic times of ash mounds which, he says, were evidently the result of dung dropped by cattle in the pens at night being allowed to accumulate for a period of time and then burned, either by design or by accident. He goes on later to suggest that the burning was not accidental, that the cowdung "may have been fired in connection with seasonal festivals, marking such events as the beginning or end of the annual migration to the forest grazing grounds. Among modern pastoralists in peninsular India, bonfires are still lit for festivals at such times. Cattle are also driven through fires as prophylaxis against disease, just as in the need fires of western Europe" (Allchin 1968, 311).

The reference to the need fires is the most suggestive for understanding the symbolism involved. The need fires, the history of which can be traced back to early medieval times (Frazer 7:270) were utilized when an epidemic broke out among the cattle of an area. The fires were held to have a purifying effect. Allchin's suggestion, however, is that the practices of Dīvālī are also quite closely related to those that one sees in western Europe in such festivals as Halloween. Frazer discusses the point that the Celtic year was divided into two parts, summer from the first of May to the end of October and winter from the first of November to the end of April. He notes that, unlike many other systems for dividing the year, this had nothing whatsoever to do with the position of the sun in the heavens. He goes on to argue that the practices involved in Halloween and May Day reflect an earlier stage than the agricultural life of medieval Europe (7:223):

> Now these particular points of the year . . . while they are of comparatively little moment to the European husbandman, do deeply concern the European herdsman; for it is on the approach of summer that he drives his cattle out into the open to crop the fresh grass, and it is on the approach of winter that he leads them back to the safety and shelter of the stall. Accordingly, it seems not improbable that the Celtic bisection of the year in two parts at the beginning of May and the beginning of November dates from a time when the Celts were mainly a pastoral people dependent for their subsistence on their herds, and when accordingly the great epochs of the year for them were the days on which the cattle went forth from the homestead in early summer and returned to it again in early winter.

The symbolism of the need fires suggests a similar symbolism for the fires at the changing of the seasons. As the pastoralists moved from one place to another, the lighting of fires would appear to represent a burning up of the old, a periodic starting of life in pristine freshness.

It is intriguing that in both Europe and India this period of transition is linked with the dead, that at both Hallowe'en and Dīvālī (that is, immediately preceding the New Year Day) evil and inauspicious forces on one hand, and the dead on the other, were thought to be let loose. Such similarities, of course, again raise the question of a possible common historical background to these practices. On the question of Bali's relationship to this, we may deduce from the depiction of Bali by a cowdung cone which is trampled upon, that the initial linking of him into the complex may well have been as a representation of inauspicious forces that are being symbolically put down at this point in the year.

The positions of Meyer and Allchin are obviously disparate: Meyer traces Bali to an agricultural scenario, while Allchin links him to a pastoral one. The contradiction is not final since Bali could quite easily have been linked into two different milieux.

C.   *Towards the Complete Bali*

The present discussion admittedly gains much of its definition against the background of the writings of people like Meyer and Allchin. But there are certain features of the present study that I think should be emphasized. First, this study is not addressed predominantly, as Meyer's is, to origins. An overweening interest in origins seems to imply that if one can get to the original manifestations in relation to a particular symbol or deity or whatever, one can understand what it/he truly represents. A variant on this is the commonly-held idea that the first manifestations are the best — what Eliade has referred to as "the prestige of origins." One can often see this in studies of Christian history, where a strong interest on the part of scholars in ascertaining the nature of pristine Christianity draws attention to the experience of the church in its earliest years. It is assumed that somehow the forms manifest and the ideas developed there are more truly Christian than what took place later within Christian history.

My own work continues to be developed against the background of the writings of my teacher, Wilfred Cantwell Smith. Among the many ideas of his that I regard as significant breakthroughs in thinking about human religiousness, one that is particularly telling in this context is his emphasis upon "cumulative tradition." He points out that the traditions in which people of faith live out their lives continually undergo change. These changes occur as individuals respond to new elements of the world in which they find themselves. At the same time, they also arise from the inner dynamics within the traditions themselves. By his emphasis upon the creative involvement of each person of faith in either maintaining or changing the tradition, Smith enables us to be aware that tradition is not fixed but is continually in process. He thus alerts us to the possibility that what a symbol becomes may be just as important as or even more important than what it was in its original formulation.

I see this applying particularly to the case of Bali. The transformations that can be traced in Puranic literature are a massive demonstration of the ability of a figure to take on new dimensions.

Smith (1971: 135) has also directed the implications of his understanding of the cumulative religious tradition to a specific area, namely, to the study of Scripture. He has set forward a suggestion, not perhaps generally accepted yet, that it may be less valuable to do what is presently being done in Biblical studies — to look at the origins and backgrounds of ideas — than to see how the ideas have been utilized, or what they have produced, down through the centuries (1976, 48):

> Does the historian need reminding that the ... history of a thing is, rather, its ongoing life, its ramifying results, its development and growth and change, eventually perhaps its disappearance or disintegration [forwards] into parts or its transmutation into something else? By all means let us, with regard to anything, know how it became; but let us study further how and what it went on becoming. The study of history must be in large part the study of creativity.

What Smith is applying principally to the study of the Bible can be equally applied to the study of a figure like Bali. Thus, as I have suggested, it is as important to see what Bali has become in his passage through the centuries of Hindus relating themselves to him in a variety of ways, as it is to know what he was originally. Looking at differing texts through successive phases, we can see new interpretations being incorporated within the story of Bali. This study has largely been an attempt to see the changes that have taken place, to understand the context to which those changes were a response and a contribution, and to realize the incredible ingenuity, diversity, and originality of the Hindu mythmakers. In short, it has been "in large part the study of creativity."

But we must consider also the question of what might be a legitimate contemporary approach to the study of a figure like Bali. I have placed my own approach in the section called "Bali Goes West," because I see it as falling in a line of continuity with other western interpretations of Bali beginning with Southey's. I have been convinced that the legitimate task for me is to allow Bali to come West in a new way — such that a contemplation of him informs how we view the world.

At the same time, it is my hope that the effect of this study will not be simply one of facilitating Bali's coming West in a new way, but also one of Bali's returning to India, to enlighten Indians, and to enable Hindus to be more aware of this part of their religious heritage. In addition, given the times we live in, I hope that the effect of this study will be for Bali to "go global" — that the debates which Bali embodies, and the understanding, insights, and vision that he represents, may not be confined to Hindus or to Western scholars, but reach far beyond into our common human experience.

I am not denying that it is important to try to understand historical developments. Indeed, I shall now attempt to trace Bali's relationship to the great variety of symbols with which he is associated. In relation to the Puranic texts, the development is relatively straightforward. As we have outlined it, Bali begins as a typical opponent of the Lord in one of the Lord's incarnational forms. But under the influence of alternative traditions concerning Bali as the opponent of Indra, and in the light of somewhat more positive portrayals of the opponents of the Devas in certain wisdom traditions in *MBh,* he became a more positive figure. This positive side was then, as also in the case of his grandfather, Prahlāda, co-opted by the devotional movement, so that Bali was eventually portrayed as a great devotee of Viṣṇu.

The really big historical problems, however, are brought to light in the consideration of the traditions of Kerala — most notably in the relation of Bali/Mahābali to Dīvālī and Ōṇam. There is a sufficiently large number of features shared by these two festivals, and by Bali's relationship to them, to suggest a major borrowing of one tradition from the other. The question is, which borrowed from which? Could it be that Bali was at first associated with Dīvālī, but because Dīvālī was alien to Kerala, both the Bali legend and its attendant Dīvālī customs were transposed to Tiruvōṇam? Or was it the other way around? Was Bali originally related to Ōṇam and only later came to be associated with Dīvālī? There is, of course, a third possibility that Bali was associated with some other festival, the remains of which can be seen in both Dīvālī and Ōṇam. Given the tendency in India to continually build new traditions upon old, to take practices which have been accepted for millenia and then to give them new dimensions by introducing into them new myths and symbols, the third possibility is less likely than the first two.

In order to try to decide whether the movement was from Dīvālī to Ōṇam or *vice versa,* it is important to look back to the possible origins of these festivals. In the light of the parallels that Allchin and Meyer have noted, the most striking common feature of these festivals seems to be that they are related quite closely to the new year. I find the fact quite intriguing that both in India and in the near-Eastern and European areas, there have been three traditional periods at which the new year begins. One which can be traced back as far as ancient Mesopotamia occurs in early autumn (August-September). In India, it is this traditional period which is accepted in Kerala and is now used as the basis for the calendar of the Kollam or Malayalam era. Our continuing heritage from Mesopotamia in the West is given in the Jewish celebration of Rosh Hashanah. These are both quite closely associated with the harvest, in the Jewish case the harvest festival itself being some fifteen days later than Rosh Hashanah and called the festival of Sukkoth. But there is evidence tht the festival of Sukkoth, with its focus on the construction of booths or huts, was taken over from the *akītu* festival, the New Year in Mesopotamia (Rowley, 291–93). Consequently, scholars think that this harvest festival was originally the Jewish New Year festival (Schauss, 170) (the festival of Rosh Hashanah is not itself referred to in the biblical text). In the case of India, Ōṇam is still a very significant harvest festival.

The second of these New Year festivals occurs in late autumn (October-November). What is intriguing is the similarity between Dīvālī and the traditions of Hallowe'en and All Saints Day in the West. These festivals bear a number of other features in common, especially the interest in the dead and the lighting of fires. More specifically, Allchin has shown a relation of Dīvālī customs to ancient practices of moving cattle from one place to another, which parallels what Frazer is able to see in ancient Europe.

The third New Year festival found in India and the West occurs in the spring. It too can be traced back to Mesopotamia, since the *akitu* festival appears to have been celebrated in some cities (for example, in Ur and Erech) in both autumn and spring (Rowley, 294). Frankfort (34) suggests that the designation of *akitu* as the "New Year's festival" means the celebration of "a new beginning in the annual cycle." Such a new beginning was important not just after winter but also after summer. The varying traditions of spring festivals are today enshrined in the practices of Mardi Gras in southern Europe, South and Central America, and also in the festival called Holī in North India. The characteristic feature of these festivals has often been an ebullient licentiousness, an irreverent breaking of the rules of the society, and an overturning of the normal hierarchical structures.

The fact that the various systems of dating in India are related to these festivals — that Ōṇam is near the beginning of the Malayalam year, that Dīvālī is at the beginning of the Vikrama year, and that Holī is near the beginning of the year for those who use the Śaka dating — suggests that these different calendars may represent a codification of earlier traditions concerning the beginning of the New Year. The evidence might initially suggest that three different cultural groups moved both into Europe and into India — the first group carrying on Near Eastern traditions of a new year in September; the second bringing pan-Eurasian pastoral traditions of a new year beginning in October-November; and the third, an agriculturally-focussed group, relating the New Year to the coming of new life in the spring. As far as India is concerned, this would mean that variant traditions reflect different migrations of groups of people out of Mesopotamia and central Asia via Iran into the Indian sub-continent.

There are, however, other possibilities. With the continuing contact of Kerala with Mesopotamia (and Mesopotamian Jews), the placing of the Kerala New Year in August-September may have developed under more recent influence from Mesopotamia. Also, the Śaka era is thought by many scholars to date from the beginning of the rule of the Kuṣāna king, Kaniṣka (Rapson, 1: 581–85) in 18 A.D. This is not beyond question, as there is a great deal of debate about the dating of Kaniṣka (see R. C. Majumdar, 144–46); the era might have begun with the coming of Śakas. At any rate, what is significant is that both the Śakas (or Scythians)

and the Kuṣāṇas came into the Indian Northwest out of Bactria in
central Asia, and that both were quite strongly influenced by the
Greeks who had been dominant in these areas not long before.
Thus, the placing of the Śaka new year in the spring may well have
taken place under influence from Greece or Rome. Similarly, the
establishment of the Vikrama era may reflect foreign rather than
indigenous traditions; the historical evidence is complex (Rapson,
1: 702):

> 58 B.C. Initial year of the Vikrama era.
> Traditionally ascribed to a king Vikramāditya of
> Ujjain who is said to have expelled the Çakas from
> India. The tradition may have some historical founda-
> tion; but in any case it seems probable that the sup-
> posed founder of the era has been confused with
> Chandragupta II Vikramāditya [380–414 A.D] who
> finally crushed the Çaka power in Western India [the
> Western Satraps]. It seems more likely that the era
> marks the establishment of the Çaka suzerainty by
> Azes I and that its use was transmitted to posterity by
> the Mālavas and other peoples who had once been feu-
> datories of the Çakas.

Yet another explanation is available as to why the Kerala and
the Vikrama New Years came to be placed at the juncture of the
end of the monsoon period and the beginning of harvest. In
Thailand, there is an association of Dīvālī with the re-awakening
of Viṣṇu, as well as with the overcoming of Bali (ERE: 5,888). In
Padma 6.124.21 (see above p. 183), there is a reference, in connection
with Lakṣmī's part in Dīvālī, to Lakṣmī's formerly having been
wakened by the women while Viṣṇu was still asleep. This motif of
awakening Viṣṇu seems clearly derived from the Indian myth of
Viṣṇu sleeping on the milk ocean during the period of the rains.
The awakening of Lakṣmī and Viṣṇu seem to be a metaphor for
the beginning of the new year. One can then see in Dīvālī a heaping together of symbols of freshness, renewal, and a pristine quality to life — that mark the end of the rainy season and the renewal
of the food supply with the bringing in of the harvest. In Kerala,
the situation is somewhat complicated because it has two rainy

seasons, the South-west monsoon which comes to this area considerably earlier than it does to northern India, and the shorter, less potent North-east monsoon which it shares with the eastern parts of South India. Ōṇam and the Kerala new year occur in a position in the seasonal cycle for that area analogous to that of Dīvālī and the Vikrama new year further north — at the end of the first monsoon, and at the time of the bringing in of the rice harvest.

Alex Wayman has extensively discussed the relation between Dīvālī, Dasarā, and Holī, and ancient Vedic half-yearly sacrifices performed every spring and autumn. He sees Holī as the survival of a ritual of the spring equinox, and Dasarā and Dīvālī as variant survivals of a ritual of the autumnal equinox. He explains the variations from the equinox thus (302):

> But about a millennium and a half ago Indian calendar-makers turned to using the so-called Immovable Zodiac, whereby the sun enters the fixed constellation Meṣa (usually equated with Aries) about April 15; while Western Calendar-makers, and some modern Indian ephemerides, use the so-called Movable Zodiac, whereby the sun now enters the seasonal Aries decided conventionally by the vernal equinox about March 21. The two systems differ in this respect because the traditional Indian system does not take into account the shifts of the vernal equinox due to precession of the earth's axis (approximately 50″ per year). That is why a festival once regularly associated with an equinox became displaced by almost a month, or even more in a year with an intercalary month.

Wayman may well be correct in seeing these as extensions of Vedic equinoctial sacrifices. The total picture of both Dīvālī and Ōṇam suggests a much greater interest in the seasonal cycles as they are related to the pastoral and agricultural life of the people. Of particular interest, is a renewal of the annual cycle at a point related to the end of the monsoon and the prosperity marked by the harvest.

Despite the complexities which this discussion affords, we must return to the question whether Bali was originally related to the festival of Ōṇam in ancient south India. If he was, then he might be seen as a Dravidian deity whose festival was drawn into the

Aryan heritage, since he is portrayed as being overcome by Viṣṇu. There is, however, no evidence of an early relationship of Bali to Śravaṇa-Tiruvōṇam. On the other hand, there is strong evidence that Tiruvōṇam was the birthday of Viṣṇu and that subsequently it became specifically the birthday of the Dwarf.

The fact that there is no indication of a link between Bali and Ōṇam before the seventeenth century also suggests that the traditions of Bali and Dīvālī were developed much earlier than those of Mahābali and Ōṇam, and thus the ideas and practices of the two festivals which are uniquely common to them would seem most likely to come from Dīvālī to Kerala's Ōṇam.

If Allchin is correct, the first relating of Bali to Dīvālī may well have been in the context of Trivikrama and Bali, a portrayal of Bali as representative of negative forces in the universe which are overcome by striding or stamping. This affirmation of life fits into the widespread pattern found in New Year festivals, which relate the end of the old year to inauspiciousness, even death, and the beginning of the new year to prosperity and reinvigoration. This anthithesis explains how Śrī, the embodiment of prosperity, came to be linked with the new positive phase and simultaneously with Bali.

Theodore Gaster, in his discussion of the elements of the seasonal pattern (mortification, purgation, invigoration, jubilation) in ancient Near Eastern ritual, points to a number of features of the *akītu* festival which are very similar to those of Dīvālī, or Ōṇam, or both (62–64):

(1) A suspension of normal order of society (slaves' short-lived authority over master; a temporary king appointed).

(2) Ceremonial purgation (of the temple with water or incense; dispatch of a scapegoat).

(3) Mimetic combats of the divine champion against a monstrous adversary or Dragon (also ceremonial races).

(4) A banquet given by the King.

(5) The return of the dead (funerary offerings; a belief that the dead ascended from the netherworld at the beginning of autumnal year).

Given the fact that the king played a central role in this symbolic transformation from old to new, and given the suggestion of the relation between New Year and enthronement (Rowley, 291–94), it is interesting to observe that in the Vedic *rājasūya yajña*, or royal consecration ritual, the king, striding forth, tramples on a piece of lead placed under a tiger skin "as on the head of Namuci," and later "steps on the skin the steps of Viṣṇu" (Keith, 341). This suggests an assimilation of the actions of the king to those of Indra and Viṣṇu, the great heroic deities of the Vedic period. One can find support for this view in *Aitareya Brāhmaṇa* (8.5.12), where a parallel is drawn between the great consecration of Indra and that of the king.

Moreover, since in *Vāmana* and *Skanda* Bali's festival is referred to as part of Indra's festival, it seems that Dīvālī may have been originally (though it is no longer) principally related to Indra. It would thus be quite suitable as a New Year festival cum royal triumph after the style of the *akītu* festival in which Bali functions initially as a negative figure. In the light of the relation between Śrī and Bali in Myth B, and the positive portrayals of Bali and his kingdom associated with it, one would not be surprised by a shift in which Bali became related to the positive phase of the New Year festival. In relation to this, it is significant that the festival known as Kojāgarī Pūrṇima or Kaumudī Mahotsava is celebrated on the full moon day of Āśvina in honour of Indra and Lakṣmi (Dahl, 170). According to *Bhaviṣyottara* 140.4.60ff. and *Padma* 6.124.56ff., Kaumudī is a name associated with Dīvālī. Thus it appears likely that the present Kaumudī represents a displacement of Indra from Dīvālī.

Such a displacement becomes even more plausible when one considers the portrayal in *Mahābalicaritam* of the time when Viṣṇu had won back the world for the Devas as being not nearly so fine as when Mahābali was king. That is, the present age ruled by Indra is obviously imperfect. If one needs an instrument through which to project one's vision of a time of perfection, the tradition of the greatness of Bali and his reign is there to be utilized.

Bali thus having been accepted as a great king whose kingdom was eminently prosperous, one might also expect kings to identify with Bali in the manner suggested by the *Bhaviṣyottara*. Further, in Kerala, given the fact that there was no Dīvālī, one could readily see that king-devotees—for example, at Tṛkkākkara—might identify themselves with Bali, and then express this identification in the festival related to Vāmana, thus adding a new dimension to the Ōṇam festival. It would not be surprising, then, to find the culture generally drawing upon the traditions relating Bali to Dīvālī in other parts of India.

But while one may speculate in this fairly narrow historical context about developments in relation to Bali, as I have argued, one should also attempt to be sensitive to his significance for the religious history of humankind, that is, to his global significance. In thinking about this, we need to move into a more general discussion of religion. One could, of course, write at great length on such generalities; the present study stops short of a full consideration and is content to suggest possible points of view.

I find it most fruitful to think of religion as a dimension of human life in which the human imagination is directed towards the highest enhancement of life. In looking at religion in this way I am responding to a degree to the thinking of Ernest Becker. Becker (1973, 1975) sees life enhancement as a form of death denial and death denial as the basic drive for human culture and religiousness. It seems to me, however, that this position can be partly reversed; a strong denial of death can be seen as one form that life enhancement has taken within human life.

I see this religious concern, this interest in life enhancement, as deriving from the peculiar nature of the human animal. Unlike other animals, as far as we can observe them, human life is vulnerable to terrible degradation. When we look at animal life, it is difficult for us to think of some animals as being fulfilled and others as not. Dogness consists in being a dog, and animality in being an animal. In the case of humanity, however, the range of possibilities seems to be enormous. It is possible for human life to be inhuman; humanity consists not in existing as human beings but in living in a human or, perhaps, a humane fashion. There is a striking awareness on the part of human beings of positive and negative experiences, and this awareness, combined with our ability to remember the past, our fertile imaginations, and our ability to project into the future, enables us to imagine an enormous range of positive and negative possibilities. Religion is that dimension in life in which people allow themselves to imagine the possibilities, to construct value-systems directed towards the full enhancement of human life, and then on towards the identification of what is valuable, significant, and real.

The essential process involved in determining what is significant, real, and enhancing is an extension of a process at the foundation of human experience, that is, the perceptual process which involves focusing. Focusing involves choice. The whole of life is built upon a process of choosing and clarifying. From the time that we as children first begin to handle the world, we find in ourselves an ability to draw something out of a field of phenomena in such a way that one can identify it and name it. This is the ability to distinguish "a" from "not-a", an ability that we use as the basic technique to structure our world. Religion takes this ability into the area of values. In the primary classifying, ordering, and structuring of our world we continually distinguish between things, people, places, and times; in the area of religion, that is, in relation to the enhancement of life, we are continually evaluating people, things, places, and times.

In this choice between "a" and "not-a" there are two different kinds of mechanisms involved. One may, as I said, focus on a valued aspect, isolate it from the field in which it is set so that the field remains a neutral background; or one may make a sharp distinction between aspects so that one is positive and the other negative. Following these two principles, mankind creates two kinds of structures in the realm of religion. In one there is a considerable focusing on specially valued aspects of life so that the rest of life recedes into something less valued, or something neutral. But there are also structures in which the positive valuation of one aspect is correlated with the negative valuation of something else. These varying structures are exceedingly important for understanding how religious ideas are developed.

I am saying, then, that the process of life enhancement is a process of isolating valued aspects of life and of allowing and making choices for the development of a more meaningful world, a more significant human life. We live in a universe of values and continually create hierarchies of significance.

The articulation of this life enhancement is developed most clearly at the level of thought. Not, however, at the level of conceptual ideas. The basic elements of religious life are found, not in the realms of theology or philosophy but rather in the area of the story. They lie embedded in our "myths"—stories expressing the values that guide an individual or a group.

In looking at myths and how they work in the direction of valuation and towards life enhancement, we may focus on a number of different aspects. The most important, I think, are the *themes* of myths, the *foci* of the mythic imagination, the various *structures* into which most mythic creations fall or on which they depend, and the *symbols* which are strewn through the narratives. It is by looking at the first two aspects that we can most easily discern the wider significance of Bali.

There is a relatively small number of significant basic themes of myth. One of the best places to see an outlining of such themes is in Genesis 2 and 3. Looking at this in its two aspects — an idealized version and a portrayal of the way life actually is in its "fallenness" — one meets essentially six different themes. These themes rise as answers to the questions: What is the essential nature of human life, what is it about? What is the ideal human being like? (This is quite closely correlated with the first in that in a way it answers the first question.) What is the relation between men and women? What is the relation of humanity to work? What is the meaning of death? How do humans relate to the animate and inanimate world? These themes are explored in an astounding variety of stories across the world. Myths, I would suggest in brief, are those products of the human imagination directed towards life enhancement in which these questions are explored and, in various fashions in different cultures, are given their answers.

In arriving at the answers to questions that are basic to the themes of myths (though quite often the questions are not actually asked — one might say that answers are given before questions are asked) there is a limited number of what I have called the *foci* of the mythic imagination, by which I mean figures or conditions of life in which humans have concentrated their imaginations of a fully enhanced, enriched life. Three such *foci* are central to all myths. The first and most widespread is that of the hero. Here the focus is on an individual person who in some way presents basic values for a culture; his life acts as a guide for human experience. Besides this personal focus, there are also foci of a spatial kind (paradise-heaven) and of a temporal kind (a past Golden Age, or a future Perfect Age). In the case of all three, one may see two different kinds of relationships between those who relate themselves to the myths developed around these foci and the myths themselves.

These motifs may enshrine the aims and ideals of the people of a culture and become a positive guide for people's lives. On the other hand, these motifs may be in the nature of a sublimation, substitution, or projection, providing a radical contrast to present experience. For example, in relation to heroes, one is able to see a positive association with the hero (in the style of Joseph Campbell) in which the path of the hero is set forth for all members of a culture to follow: the stories of the hero are then a kind of charter for the people of that culture. On the other hand, following Becker's understanding of the hero, we may see the hero as one who compensates for the lack of heroism, vision, and "divinity" in the ordinary person.

In the "great" traditions there is another focus of the human imagination. This is a conception of the central reality of the universe. This seems to have developed rather late in human history, for the evidence that we have suggests that in primitive and archaic cultures there was no strong interest in a centralized and intellectually unified conception. In the "great" traditions, however, it is actively present and the full enhancement of life is frequently seen to involve a special relationship to this central reality. Typifying this vision Augustine talks of God in a representative voice: "Thou has made us for thyself and our hearts are restless until they rest in thee." In these traditions almost inevitably the imagining of heroes, paradise, or a past or future perfect age is related specifically to conceptions of this central reality of the universe. Thus, the hero figure is portrayed as one who bears a special kind of relationship to this central reality. In some cases there are portrayals of very special hero figures who are so closely related to the central reality that one conceives them as indeed none other than the central reality in human form (hence such concepts as incarnation, *avatāra,* or *trikāya*). In the Christian view, for example, the paradisal conditions are a corollary of being most intimately in the presence of, and centred on, God.

With this background in view we may return to Bali. We can see Bali bearing different kinds of relationships to Indian attempts to conceptualize what is significant, valuable, and real. In the earlier phases of the Epic-Puranic texts, Bali represents forces inimical to a central idealized reality of the universe, that of *dharma* (virtue, righteousness, and order). Thus Viṣṇu, often seen as upholding *dharma*, is portrayed in his Dwarf *avatāra* as overcoming this disorderly and disturbing force.

But gradually the focus shifts, and in the period of the middle and later Purāṇas the total corpus of Bali presents something of a debate or tension between different foci of significance — *dharma, bhakti,* and prosperity. In Bali there is an exploration of the relation between these features, of which the total effect is to suggest that although Bali may be good, and a great devotee, that does not necessarily mean that his kingly role is legitimate. The fact that his kingdom is eminently prosperous may even be seen as problematic. But from another viewpoint within the same arena of debate, Bali can be shown as the true devotee who has learned not to be attached to anything. Bali lost his kingdom but found his Lord.

In yet another context, that of Dīvālī and the festival of Ōṇam, the portrayal of Bali's great kingdom is given a more positive focus. In Kerala we continue to see this envisioning of possibility via the time "when Mahābali was king" as a protest against inequalities of the social system, and beyond protest, a powerful impetus for change.

Hindus, and others beyond the borders of India, have experienced an enhancement of their lives through the contemplation and celebration of this complex figure. It is my hope that the present study may contribute towards the further envisioning of possibilities that Mahābali represents.

Appendix A.

List of Texts

1. *MBh* 12.326.74-76
2. *MBh* 3 App. I (lines 63-82)
3. *Rām* 1.28.1-11
4. *Vāyu* 2.36.74-87 = *Brahmānda* 2.73.75-86
5. *Hariv.* Harivaṃśaparva 31.68-92
6. *MBh* 12.216-18
7. *MBh* 12.220-21
8. *Agni* 4.5-11
9. *Hariv. App.* 42B
10. *Matsya* 244-46 (10a. *Vāmaṇa Saromāhātmyā* 2-4; 6-10)
11. *Vāmana* 48-52
12. *Kūrma* 1.16
13. *Brahma* 73
14. *Bhāgavata* 8.15-23
15. *Padma* 6.266-67
16. *Bṛhannāradīya* 10-11
17. *Skanda* 1.1.17.286-1.1.19
18. *Skanda* 5.1.63.10-270
19. *Skanda* 7.1.114
20. *Skanda* 7.2.14-19
21. *Skanda* 7.4.19
22. *Mahābalicaritam*
23. George, 210-12
24. Jacob, 112-13
25. Woodcock, 14-15
26. Southey, *The Curse of Kehama*

APPENDIX B.
List of Motifs in Myth A

	MBh	MBh App	Rām	Vāyu	Hariv.	Agni	Hariv. App.	Matsya	Vāmana	Kūrma	Brahma	Bhāgavata	Padma	Brhannāradīya	Skanda 1	Skanda 2	Skanda 3	Skanda 4	Skanda 5	George	Jacob	Woodcock
1. Story of Kitava; reborn as Bali															X							
2. Indra and Virocana; Virocana offers head															X							
3. War between Devas and Asuras						X			X	X		X		X	X	X						
4. Bali defeated — revived by Bhrgus												X										
5. Asuras besiege Amarāvatī															X							
6. Brhaspati says Devas invincible															X							
7. Devas from Amarāvatī												X			X							
8. Devas assume bird/animal forms															X							
9. Asuras find Amarāvatī deserted												X			X							
10. Asuras enter Amarāvatī												X			X							
11. Bali virtuous										X	X		X		X					X		X
12. Bali overcomes Indra/Devas	X		X	X		X	X	X	X	X			X	X	X							

13. Bali establishes kingdom	X	X	X		X			X				X	X	
14. Kali(yuga)'s nature "lost"					X					X	X	X	X	X
15. Prahlāda's advice to Bali— good rule						X								
16. Bali renowned through three worlds		X												
17. Bali's kingdom—good conditions				X	X	X	X	X	X					
18. Time given			X			X								
19. Lakṣmī to Bali				X		X								
20. Nārada unhappy—no distress										X	X			
21. Devas jealous							X					X	X	X
22. Devas fear—nobody worships them													X	
23. Devas to Aditi				X					X					
24. (Devas +) Aditi to Kaśyapa					X			X	X					
25. Kaśyapa instructs Aditi to worship Viṣṇu								X	X					
26. . . .on Śravaṇadvādasī (day)									X					
27. Devas + Aditi + Kaśyapa Brahmā				X		X								
28. Brahmā explains Indra's loss of kingdom						X								
29. Brahmā instructs Devas—to Viṣṇu				X		X			X					
30. Brahmā instructs Devas—to worship Viṣṇu—1000 names									X					
31. Brahmā instructs Devas—to Best of tirthas: Viṣṇusaras									X					

No.	Event	MBh	MBh App	Rām	Vāyu	Hariv.	Agni	Hariv. App.	Matsya	Vāmana	Kūrma	Brahma	Bhāgavata	Padma	Brhannāradīya	Skanda 1	Skanda 2	Skanda 3	Skanda 4	Skanda 5	George	Jacob	Woodcock
32.	Indra to Earth — Mahānādi									X													
33.	Nārada to Viṣṇu — report (details)																		X				
34.	Devas to Viṣṇu			X			X	X			X	X	X		X				X			X	
35.	Viṣṇu praised by Devas, Aditi, Kaśyapa						X	X	X	X	X	X	X	X	X								
36.	Viṣṇu praised — *Tapas*							X					X										
37.	Viṣṇu praised — *Payovrata*												X	X									
38.	Viṣṇu manifests himself								X		X		X	X			X						
39.	Description of Viṣṇu										X		X	X			X						
40.	Description of Viṣṇu + Devī													X									
41.	Sravaṇadvādaśī (day of appearance)															X							
42.	Ecstasy of Aditi												X										
43.	Further hymn by Aditi										X		X	X									
44.	Hymn by Kaśyapa												X	X									
45.	Viṣṇu pleased with vow of Aditi														X								
46.	Viṣṇu to Aditi (+ Kaśyapa): "Ask boon."										X		X										
47.	Request by Devas/Aditi/Kaśyapa															X	X						

No.	Event									
48.	Request—Be born as son of Aditi				X			X			
49.	Request—Restoration of Indra to kingdom		X		X						
50.	Assent by Viṣṇu				X		X	X	X		X
51.	Viṣṇu: "Bali is my devotee: no battle."					X					
52.	Viṣṇu disappears						X				X
53.	Aditi goes to Kaśyapa						X				
54.	Hari (to Kaśyapa) to Aditi			X			X				
55.	Hymn by Brahmā						X				
56.	Viṣṇu in womb of Aditi—Portents	X	X		X	X		X			
57.	Bali—question: "Why portents?"		X	X	X						
58.	Prahlāda meditates—Lakṣmī to Devas		X								
59.	Prahlāda meditates: Vision of Hari in womb of Aditi		X	X	X						
60.	Prahlāda praises Viṣṇu		X		X						
61.	Prahlāda explains		X	X							
62.	Bali scorns Viṣṇu		X	X							
63.	Prahlāda curses Bali		X	X							
64.	Bali prays forgiveness		X	X							
65.	Prahlāda—the curse will take effect		X								
66.	Prahlāda instructs Bali—non-attachment										

	MBh	MBh App	Rām	Vāyu	Hariv.	Agni	Hariv. App.	Matsya	Vāmana	Kūrma	Brahma	Bhāgavata	Padma	Brhannāradīya	Skanda 1	Skanda 2	Skanda 3	Skanda 4	Skanda 5	George	Jacob	Woodcock
67. Prahlāda instructs Bali — devotion								X	X	X												
68. Viṣṇu becomes Dwarf														X				X		X	X	
69. Viṣṇu born as son of Aditi and Kaśyapa	X	X	X	X		X	X	X		X		X	X	X								
70. Description of Viṣṇu (4 armed/Vāmana)										X		X	X		X							
71. Born — Sravaṇadvādaśī												X										
72. Birth — Praise of all beings							X	X	X	X		X	X									
73. Viṣṇu to Devas — "Choose what I should do"													X									
74. Dwarf initiated								X	X			X										
75. Paraphernalia from Daityas, Ṛṣis								X	X						X							
76. Description of Dwarf		X		X			X	X	X	X	X	X						X				
77. Dwarf: worship Śiva — *tīrthas*																		X				
78. Nārada to Bali — instruction																		X				
79. Dwarf — yogic study																		X				
80. Nārada's complaint																		X				
81. Dwarf — "Bali sacrificed to me — not slain by me."																		X				

Motif	1	2	3	4	5	6	7	8	9	10	11	12	13	14	15	16	17	18	19	20	21	22	23	24	25	26	27	28
82. Dwarf to weapons—"Kill Bali or not"																X												
83. Bali — Sacrifice	X	X	X						X							X												
84. Bali — Horse Sacrifice(s)									X				X	X				X										
85. Place of Sacrifice						X			X				X															
86. Excursus on Tīrthas									X																			
87. Dwarf to Sacrifice	X		X			X	X		X		X	X				X				X								
88. Dwarf to Sacrifice + Bṛhaspati + Ṛṣis																				X								
89. Earth quivers as Dwarf walks							X																					
90. Dwarf to (enclosure of) Bali		X														X												X
91. Dwarf at entrance						X												X										
92. Dwarf recited Vedas						X					X	X				X	X			X								
93. Bali asks about Portents								X		X																		
94. Śukra explains: Viṣṇu coming								X		X						X												
95. Śukra: "None of share to Devas."											X																	
96. Bali: "What give to Him?"								X																				
97. Śukra: "Nothing" (obstructs)						X		X		X						X	X		X				X					
98. Śukra: "Request should be granted."											X																	
99. Bali: "Blessed am I."								X				X		X									X					
100. Bali: "I'll comply with request." (Never "No" to suppliant)								X		X						X												

		MBh	MBh App	Rām	Vāyu	Hariv.	Agni	Hariv. App.	Matsya	Vāmana	Kūrma	Brahma	Bhāgavata	Padma	Brhannāradīya	Skanda 1	Skanda 2	Skanda 3	Skanda 4	Skanda 5	George	Jacob	Woodcock
101.	"Even if he kills me — to *mokṣa*"									X					X								
102.	Śukra curses/becomes bee.															X	X						
103.	Bali welcomes Dwarf, *arghya*			X					X					X	X	X	X			X			X
104.	Bali offers seat															X							
105.	Bali pleased — offers gift															X							
106.	Bali — "Ask what you want."			X				X	X	X	X			X	X		X	X					
107.	Dwarf — excuse on Demons									X													
108.	Dwarf — on Sacrifices seen by him														X								
109.	Dwarf begs three strides			X	X	X		X		X	X	X	X	X	X						X	X	X
110.	Bali: "Ask more (elephants, etc.)"									X	X		X	X	X								
111.	Dwarf: "No."									X	X			X	X								
112.	Why three strides																						X
113.	Dwarf: "Worship God"																						X
114.	Śukra's warning													X		X		X					X
115.	Śukra clogs pot — blinded — one-eyed														X								
116.	Bali: "Won't go back on word"																		X				X
117.	Bali grants request (3 strides/3 worlds)			X	X	X		X	X	X	X	X	X	X	X	X					X		X

#	Motif	1	2	3	4	5	6	7	8	9	10	11	12	13	14	15	16	17	18	19	20
118.	Bali: "Fortunate am I"												X								
119.	Bali pours water on hand					X		X	X	X	X	X						X			
120.	— — — — golden jar								X	X	X	X									
121.	Bali worships Dwarf										X				X						
122.	Bali washes feet								X		X			X							
123.	Bali causes Viṣṇu to sip water									X											
124.	Dwarf grows (large/great)					X		X		X	X				X					X	X
125.	Dwarf: 4-armed form														X						
126.	Dwarf: Cosmic form (Viśvarūpa)			X					X	X	X	X			X						
127.	Dwarf: Trivikrama form	X						X				X						X			
128.	Dwarf: Brilliant			X																	
129.	Dānavas (named) approach Lord—smashed				X		X	X													
130.	Viṣṇu strides	X	X	X	X	X	X	X		X	X	X						X			
131.	Free Daityas from attachment									X											
132.	Second step — Meru														X						
133.	Second step — Brahmaloka, Satyaloka, top of world egg									X	X	X	X		X	X		X		X	X
134.	Third step not completed									X											
135.	Foot worshipped by Brahmā, Devas									X	X	X			X						
136.	Foot too far — broke shell								X	X			X			X	X				
137.	Water released from foot — "Gaṅgā"								X	X	X	X			X	X		X	X		

		MBh	MBh App	Rām	Vāyu	Hariv.	Agni	Hariv. App.	Matsya	Vāmana	Kūrma	Brahma	Bhāgavata	Padma	Brhannāradīya	Skanda 1	Skanda 2	Skanda 3	Skanda 4	Skanda 5	George	Jacob	Woodcock
138.	Asuras want to fight — Bali discourses on Time											X											
139.	Where third step?											X	X									X	
140.	Viṣṇu — "Garuḍa third step"															X							
141.	Bali: "My back/head"											X	X										
142.	Vindhyāvali: "My/son's/husband's heads"															X							
143.	Bali — *bhakti*										X												
144.	Brahmā/Viṣṇu — "I'm pleased with *bhakti*. Ask boon."											X				X					X	X	X
145.	Bali: nothing/except feet											X				X							
146.	Bali: Return to people once a year																				X	X	X
147.	Viṣṇu — Dwarf/Boy again										X				X	X							
148.	Viṣṇu: "The triple world mine"										X												
149.	Bali again takes water										X												
150.	Discussion by Prahlāda, etc. on punishment												X										
151.	Bali to Pātāla (Sutala, Rasātala)	X			X	X	X	X	X	X	X	X	X	X		X							X
152.	Cruel ones (Prahlāda, etc) killed				X																		

No.	Episode																		
153.	Bali bound/restrained			X	X			X	X	X			X		X	X		X	
154.	Pleasures in Pātāla, etc.							X	X	X			X						
155.	Viṣṇu: "Since Bali gift — long life"							X	X										
156.	Viṣṇu: "Bali will be Indra"							X	X				X						
157.	Bali — "How?" — Misguided Rituals							X	X					X					
158.	Brahmā/Indra/Devas praise Hari						X				X		X		X				
159.	Prahlāda praises Hari												X						
160.	Three Worlds to Indra	X	X			X	X	X		X	X	X	X	X			X		X
161.	Praise of Viṣṇu by various other beings												X		X				
162.	Bali in Pātāla with Prahlāda										X		X						
163.	Viṣṇu — Boon to Bali							X											
164.	Sudarśana									X									
165.	Instruction in *bhakti*							X		X	X								
166.	Nārada: "Free Bali"							X											
167.	Garuḍa releases Bali							X											
168.	Bali: "How *darśana* and *pūjā* of feet?"																X		
169.	Viṣṇu: "I abide in your heart"																X		
170.	Bali and Durvasas																	X	
171.	Bali: "I will not leave feet" — Viṣṇu leaves feet behind																X		
172.	Vāmanadvādaśī (Bhādra)														X				

No.	Entry	MBh	MBh App	Rām	Vāyu	Hariv.	Agni	Hariv. App.	Matsya	Vāmana	Kūrma	Brahma	Bhāgavata	Padma	Brhannāradīya	Skanda 1	Skanda 2	Skanda 3	Skanda 4	Skanda 5	George	Jacob	Woodcock
173.	Tīrtha—Vāmanakṣetra/-Puṣkara																X	X					
174.	Festival—Dvārapratipadā, Dīpapratipad									X									X				
175.	"Kings shall worship Bali"									X									X				
176.	Festival will be like Bali's kingdom									X									X				
177.	Festival of Oṇam—Visit of Mahābali																				X	X	X

NOTES

Chapter 1

1. Others who are the subject of a somewhat similar exploration are Vṛtra, Śiśupāla, and Prahlāda. For a brief discussion of Śiśupāla, see my 1978 article. Prahlāda has been the subject of a major discussion by Paul Hacker.

2. I have followed the pattern of capitalizing the names of all major classes of beings such as Asuras, Rākṣasas, and Devas.

Chapter 2

1. The name of the text derives from the beginning words of the text in Akkadian, words which mean "when on high." For a translation of the central part of the text, see Pritchard: 31–39.

2. See *Ṛg Veda* 10.72.3: "In the first age of the gods, *sat* was born from the *asat*."

3. See *Ṛg Veda* 10.121.1,7; and 10.82.6

4. See *Ṛg Veda* 10.129.3.

5. See *Ṛg Veda* 10.90.

6. Thus one can see in the *Bhāgavata* 3.5–12 a highly developed version of the creation of the world.

7. See the many examples in O'Flaherty 1975, pp. 330–38.

8. The correlation of good and evil with light and darkness is quite widespread across much of the ancient civilized world.

9. In the *Bṛhadāraṇyaka* version, the breath sings the Udgītha, while in the *Chāndogya*, the Udgītha is reverenced as the breath.

10. For one of the earliest systematizations of this see *Mānavadharmaśāstra* 2.90.

11. Tripura may mean either triple city or three-fold citadel.

12. It is, however, worth noting that even as early as *Śatapatha* there is an association of Mleccas and Asuras. The Devas cut off Vac from the Asuras, and thus, deprived of speech the Asuras are able only to cry out unintelligibly. Thence the conclusion that he who speaks thus is a Mlecca (*Śatapatha* 3.2.1.32).

13. Appendix I (42.1–660).

14. For a discussion of some related views on the danger of divine power, see O'Flaherty, 1976: 139–73.

Chapter 3

1. It should be noted that in *MBh* 12.124.54–60, there is a similar account of Śrī's leaving Prahlāda and going to Indra (see Hiltebeitel:157).

2. Two periods have often been characterized by the two great goals of human life, *mokṣa* and *dharma*. On the relation between these, see Ingalls (1957) and Van Buitenen. The *dharmasūtras* and the *Mānavadharmaśāstra* appear to represent a new emphasis on *dharma* in which the life style focused on *mokṣa*, that is,

saṃnyāsa, is incorporated in the system of *dharma* as one of the four stages of life (*āśrama*).

3. It also has the effect of revealing all of the earlier myths in the set in a similar light.

Chapter 4

1. Some exceptions to the generalization have already been mentioned in Chapter 2 (p.51) where examples of substantively significant hymns are afforded by *Bhāgavata* 7.8.40–56.

2. In the section on conventional elaboration, since the passages do not provide substantively new ideas, it seems convenient to include as well examples from Phase 3 accounts at this point, for clearly this conventional elaboration is to go on throughout Puranic literature.

3. For a discussion of Indra's sin, see O'Flaherty 1976: 146–53.

4. For a discussion of the four Yugas in Hindu mythology see Cornelia Church (1971, 1974); and Mircea Eliade (1959): 112–18.

5. For a discussion of the Manvantaras and the relation between these and Yugas and Kalpas see Dimmitt and Van Buitenen 56–58. See also Mankad. There are also descriptions of the Manvantaras in *Bhāgavata* 8.1 and 8.13.

6. See SBE 30, pp. 305–306

Chapter 6

1. There is one exceedingly brief mention in which it is indicated that Bali achieved salvation: *Garuḍa* 1.87.36–37.

2. This compound comprised two parts: *dīpa* = lamp; and *pratipad* = the first day of a lunar fortnight. Thus the whole word indicates an identification of this first day of the lunar fortnight by reference to lamps.

3. Kane points out (195) that this is according to *pūrṇimānta* reckoning, that is, a reckoning in which the month is calculated from full moon to full moon.

Chapter 7

1. It should be noted that *Mahābalicaritam*, like other popular texts of this kind has many inconsistencies.

2. That is, Gaṇapati or Gaṇeśa.

3. Although this epithet most often refers to Śiva, it seems almost certain that this line and the next are referring to the same activity—hence Mahādeva would refer to Viṣṇnu.

4. that is, Gokula.

5. that is, Sudāmā, a boyhood friend of Kṛṣṇa.

6. A kind of flute.

7, 8. Different kinds of drums.

9. That is, material from Kōlikōṭu (Calicut).

10, 11. The text is corrupt at this point; it is impossible to make sense of it.

BIBLIOGRAPHY

Abbreviations

AITM	Ancient India Tradition and Mythology
ASS	Ānandāśrama Sanskrit Series
Bib Ind	Bibliotheca Indica
CSS	Chowkhamba Sanskrit Series
HOS	Harvard Oriental Series
HR	History of Religions
IHQ	Indian Historical Quarterly
JAAR	Journal of the American Academy of Religion
JAOS	Journal of the American Oriental Society
POS	Poona Oriental Series
SBE	Sacred Books of the East
SBH	Sacred Books of the Hindus

A. *Primary texts in Sanskrit, Tamil, and Malayalam* by title; with translations into European languages.

Agni Purāṇa. ASS 41. 1900. Poona. Translation: Manmatha Nath Dutt. 2nd ed. *CSS* 54. 2 vols. 1967. Varanasi.

Aitareya Brāhmaṇa with the commentary of Sayana. *Bib. Ind.* 1896. Calcutta. Translation: Arthur Berriedale Keith. *HOS*, 25. 1920. Cambridge.

Atharva Veda with the commentary of Sāyaṇa. 1896. Bombay. Translations: Maurice Bloomfield. *SBE* 42. 1897. Oxford. Reprinted 1964. Delhi; William Dwight Whitney. *HOS* 7–8. 1905. Cambridge.

Bhagavad Gītā with the commentary of Śaṅkara. Dinkar Vishnu Gokhale, ed. *POS* 1. 1950. Poona.

Bhāgavata Purāṇa with the commentary of Cūrmika. 1910. Bombay. Translations: into English: M.N. Dutt. 1895–96. Calcutta. J. M. Sanyal. 1930–34. . Calcutta. A. C. Bhaktivedanta Swami Prabhupada. 1972–77. New York; into French: Eugène Burnouf. 5 vols. 1840–98. Paris.

Bhaviṣyottara Purāṇa. 1910. Bombay

Brahma Purāṇa. ASS 28. 1895. Poona.

Brahmavaivarta Purāṇa. ASS 102. 4 vols. 1935. Poona. Translation: Rajendra Nath Sen. *SBH* 24. 2 vols. 1919–22 Allahabad. Reprinted 1973. New York.

Bṛhadāraṇyaka Upaniṣad. ASS 15. 1953. Poona. Translation: Robert Hume. *The Thirteen Principal Upanishads.* 1921. Oxford. Reprinted 1958. Madras.

Bṛhannāradīya Purāṇa. Bib. Ind. 562. 1891. Calcutta.

Chāndogya Upaniṣad with the commentary of Śaṅkara. 1927. Poona.

Garuḍa Purāṇa. 1903. Bombay. Translations: Manmatha Nath Dutt. 1908. Calcutta. J. L. Shastri. *AITM* 12–14. 1978–79.

Harivaṃśa. V. S. Sukthankar, S. K. Velvalkar, and P. L. Vaidya, eds. 1969–71. Poona. Translations: into English: H. C. Das. 1897. Calcutta.; into French: Simon Alexandre Langlois. 1834–35. London.

Hiraṇyakeśin Gṛhya Sūtra. J. Kirste, ed. 1889. Vienna. Translation: H. Oldenberg. *SBE* 30. 1892. Oxford.

Kūrma Purāṇa. 1972. Varanasi. Translation: A. S. Gupta, ed. 1972. Varanasi.

Mahābalicaritam; in *Pāṭṭukaḷ.* K. Raghavan Pillai, ed. 1964. Trivandrum.

Mahābhārata. Critical edition. 1933–69. Poona. *Mahābhārata* with the commentary of Nīlakaṇṭha. 1862. Bombay. Translations: Pratap Chandra Roy. 2nd ed. 11 vols. 1927–32. Calcutta. Manmatha Nath Dutt. 7 vols. 1895–1905. Calcutta. J. A. B. van Buitenen. 7 vols. 1974. Chicago.

Mahābhāṣya of Patañjali. Vedavrata, ed. 6 vols. 1963. Jhajjar.

Mānavadharmaśāstra with the commentary of Medhātithi. *Bib. Ind.* 1932. Calcutta. Translation: Georg Bühler. *SBE* 25, 1886. Oxford.

Matsya Purāṇa. *ASS* 54. 1907. Poona Translation: a Taluqdar of Oudh. *SBH* 17. 1916–17. Allahabad.

Maturaikāñci. In *Pattupāṭṭu, Ten Tamil Idylls.* J. V. Chelliah, trans. 1962. Madras.

Padma Purāṇa. *ASS* 131. 1893. Poona.

Pañcaviṃśa Brāhamaṇa. Translation: W. Caland. 1931. Calcutta

Rāmāyaṇa of Vālmīki. 1960–. Baroda. Translation: Hari Prasad Shastri. 3 vols. 1962. London.

Ṛgveda with the commentary of Sāyaṇa. 6 vols. 1890–92. London. Translations: into German: Karl Friedrich Geldner. 3 vols. *HOS* 33–35. 1951. Cambridge, Mass.; into French: Louis Renou. *Etudes Védiques et Pāṇineénnes.* 1955–69. Paris; into English: Horace Hayman Wilson. 1866. London; R. T. H. Griffith. 1896. Benares.

Śatapatha Brāhmaṇa. *CSS* 96. 1964. Benares. Translation: Julius Eggeling. *SBE* 12, 26, 41, 43, 44. 1882. Oxford. Reprinted 1964. New Delhi.

Skanda Purāṇa. 1908–9. Bombay.

Vāmana Purāṇa. 1968. Varanasi. Translation: Anand Swarup Gupta. 1968. Varanasi.

Vāyu Purāṇa. (or *Brahmāṇḍa Purāṇa*) *ASS* 49. 1905. Poona

Viṣṇu Purāṇa. 1967. Gorakhpur. Translation: Horace Hayman Wilson. 3rd ed. 1840. London. Reprinted 1961. Calcutta.

B. *Secondary Texts*

Achyuta Menon, C. *Cochin State Manual.* 1911. Ernakulam.
Agrawala, V. S. *Vamana Purana, A Study.* 1964. Benares.

Allchin, F. R. *Neolithic Cattle-Keepers of South India.* 1963. Cambridge.

Allchin, Bridget, and Raymond. *The Birth of Indian Civilization.* 1968. Harmondsworth.

Allegro. J. M. *The Sacred Mushroom and the Cross.* 1970. London.

Angus, Samuel. *The Mystery-religions and Christianity.* 1966. New York.

Archer, W.G. *Indian Paintings from the Punjab Hills.* 2 Vols. 1973. London.

Becker, Ernest *The Denial of Death.* 1973. New York.

————. *Escape from Evil.* 1975. New York.

Bernhardt-Kabisch, Ernest. *Robert Southey.* 1977. New York.

Biardeau, Madelaine. "Some More Considerations about Textual Criticism." *Purāṇa* 10. 1968.

————"The Story of Arjuna Kārtavīrya without Reconstruction." *Purāṇā* 12. 1970.

Boyd, James W. *Satan and Mara: Christian and Buddhist Symbols of Evil.* 1975. Leiden.

Brandon, S. G. F. *Jesus and the Zealots.* 1967. Manchester.

Brown, W. Norman. "The Creation Myth of the *Rig Veda.*" *JAOS* 62: 85–98. 1942.

————. "Theories of Creation in the Rig Veda." *JAOS* 85:23–34. 1965.

Bussagli, Mario, and Calembus Sivaramamamurti. *5000 Years of the Art of India.* n.d. New York.

Campbell, Joseph. *The Hero with a Thousand Faces.* 2nd ed. Bollingen Series 17. 1968. Princeton.

————. *The Masks of God.* 4 vols. 1959–68. New York.

Carman, John Braisted. *The Theology of Rāmānuja.* 1974. New Haven.

Carstairs, G. Morris. *The Twice-Born.* 1958. Bloomington.

Chambers, William. "An Account of the Sculptures and Ruins at Mavalipuram." *Asiatic Researches* 1:144–71. 1788.

Church, Cornelia. "The Puranic Myth of the Four Yugas." *Purāṇa* 13: 151–59. 1971.

————. "The Myth of the Four Yugas in the Sanskrit Purāṇas — a Dimensional Study." *Purāṇa* 16: 5–25. 1974.

Coburn, Thomas B. "The Study of the Purāṇas and the Study of Religion." *Religious Studies* 16:341–52. 1980.

Coomarswamy, Ananda K. "Angels and Titans, an Essay in Vedic Ontology." *JAOS* 55:373–419. 1935.

Dahl, Upendra Narth, *Goddess Laksmi: Origin and Development.* 1978. New Delhi.

Daniélou, Alain. *Hindu Polytheism.* 1964. London.

Dimmitt, Cornelia, and J.A.B. van Buitenen, ed. & trans. *Classical Hindu Mythology.* Philadelphia.

Douglas, Mary. *Purity and Danger: An Analysis of Conceptions of Pollution and Taboo.* 1966. London.

Dubois, Abbé Jean Antoine. *Hindu Manners, Customs and Ceremonies.* 3rd ed. Henry Beauchamp, trans. 1959. Oxford.

Dumont, Louis. *Une Sous-caste de l'Inde du Sud.* 1957. Paris.

Eliade, Mircea. *Cosmos and History.* 1959. New York.

————. *The Two and the One.* 1965. London.

Eliot, T. S. *Collected Poems 1909–1935.* 1936. London.

Filliozat, Jean. *La Doctrine classique de la Médécine Indienne.* 1949. Paris.

Frankfort, Henry, et. al. *Before Philosophy.* 1947. Harmondsworth.

Frazer, Sir James. *The Golden Bough.* 3rd ed. 1907–15. London.

Gail, Adalbert. *Bhakti im Bhāgavata Purāṇa.* 1969. Wiesbaden.

Gaster, Theodore. *Thespis: Ritual, Myth and Drama in the Ancient Near East.* 1966. New York.

Geertz, Clifford. "The Cerebral Savage" *Encounter* 28 (April): 25–32. 1967.

George, K.M. *Malayalam Grammar and Reader.* 1971. Kottayam.

Goldman, Robert P. *Gods, Priests and Warriors.* Studies in Oriental Culture 12. 1977. New York.

Gonda, Jan. *Aspects of Early Viṣṇuism.* 1954. Utrecht.

———. *Change and Continuity in Indian Religion.* 1965. The Hague.

———. *Ancient Indian Kingship from the Religious Point of View.* 1966. Leiden.

———. *Viṣṇuism and Śivaism: A Comparison.* 1970. London.

Gopalan, Lakshmipuram V. *Sri Vaishnava Divya Desams.* 1972. Madras.

Griswold, H.D. *The Religion of the Rigveda.* 1923. London.

Gupte, Rai Bahadur. *Hindu Holidays and Ceremonials.* 1919. Calcutta.

Hacker, Paul. *Prahlāda: Werden und Wandlungen einer Idealgestalt.* 1960. Wiesbaden.

Hanson, R.P.C., A.R.C. Leaney, and J. Posen. *A Guide to the Scrolls.* 1958. London.

Hara, Minoru. "A Note on the Rākṣasa Form of Marriage," *JAOS* 94: 296–306. 1974.

Hastings, James, ed. *Encyclopedia of Religions and Ethics.* 1911. Edinburgh.

Hawley, John Stratton. "Krishna's Cosmic Victories," *JAAR* 47: 201–221. 1979.

Hazra, Rajendra Chandra. *Studies in the Puranic Records on Hindu Rites and Customs.* 2nd ed. 1975. Delhi.

Hengel, Martin. *Die Zealoten.* 1961. Leiden.

Hesiod, *The Homeric Hymns and Homerica.* With an English translation by Hugh G. Evelyn-White. Revised edition. 1936. Cambridge, MA.

Hiltebeitel, Alf. *The Ritual of Battle: Krishna in the Mahabharata.* 1936. Ithaca, N.Y.

Hooper, J.S.M. *Hymns of the Alvars.* 1929. Calcutta.

Hopkins, E. Washburn. *Epic Mythology.* 1915. Strassbourg.

Hopkins, Thomas J. *The Hindu Religious Tradition.* 1971. Encino.

Hospital, Clifford G. "The Enemy Transformed: Opponents of the Lord in the Bhāgavata Purāṇa." *JAAR* 46. Supplement: 200–215. 1978.

———. "Clothes and Caste in Nineteenth Century Kerala." *Indian Church History Review* 13: 146–56. 1979.

Hughes, Robert. *Heaven and Hell in Western Art.* 1968. London.

Ingalls, Daniel H.H. "Dharma and Mokṣa." *Philosophy East and West* 7: 41–48. 1957.

Jacob, K. *Folk Tales of Kerala.* 1972. New Delhi.

Kane, P.V. *History of Dharmaśāstra.* 9 Vols. 2nd edn. 1968. Poona.

Keith, Arthur Berriedale. *The Religion and Philosophy of the Vedas and Upanishads.* HOS 31–32. 1925. Cambridge, Mass.

Krishna Ayyar, K.V. *Zamorins of Calicut.* 1938.

Krishna Chaitanya, *History of Malayalam Literature.* 1971. New Delhi.

Krishna Iyer, L.A. *Kerala and Her People.* 1961. Palghab.

Krishna Warrier, N.V. *Kalotsavam: Lakhaṇṇaḷ.* 1968. Trichur.

Kunjan Pillai, Elankulam. *Kēralacaritrapraśnaṇṇaḷ.* 1958. Kottayam.

Lévi-Strauss, Claude. *Structural Anthropology.* 1963. New York.

—————. *The Raw and the Cooked. Introduction to a Science of Mythology: I* John and Doreen Weightmen, trans. 1969. New York.

Logan, William. *Malabar.* 2 vols. 1951. Madras.

Long, J. Bruce. "Life out of Death: A Structural Analysis of the Myth of the Churning of the Ocean of Milk." In Bardwell Smith, ed. *Hinduism: New Essays in the History of Religion.* 1975. The Hague.

Macdonell, A.A. *Vedic Mythology.* 1898. Strasbourg.

Majumdar, R.C., et al. *The History and Culture of the Indian People.* 11 vols. 1951–69. Bombay.

Mankad, D.R. "Manvantara." *IHQ* 18: 208–30.

Mankodi, K.L. "Vāmana-Trivikrama in Indian Art." *Purāṇa* 12:48–53. 1970.

Mateer, Samuel. *The Land of Charity.* 1871. London.

Meyer, Johann Jakob. *Trilogie Altindischer Machte und Feste der Vegetation.* 1837. Zurich.

Miller, Barbara Stoler, ed. & trans. *Love Song of the Dark Lord: Jayadeva's Gītagovinda.* 1977. New York.

Murray, Henry. *Myth and Mythmaking.* 1968. Boston.

Nambiar (Nampyar), A.K. "Ōṇavum Ōṇappāṭṭukaḷum." *Sāhityasamita Māasika* (Sept.): 30–36. 1977.

Nagam Aiya, V. *Travancore State Manual.* 3 vols. 1906. Trivandrum.

Namboodiripad, E.M.S. *Kerala: Problems and Possibilities.* 1957. New Delhi.

New English Bible.

Nilsson, Martin P. *A History of Greek Religion.* 1964. New York.

Nock, Arthur Darby. *Conversion.* 1961. Oxford.

O'Flaherty, Wendy Doniger. *Asceticism and Eroticism in the Mythology of Śiva.* 1973. London.

—————. *The Origins of Evil in Hindu Mythology.* 1976. Berkeley.

Onam: A Festival of Kerala. Census of India 1961 Part 8B Monograph Series 1. 1961. New Delhi.

Padmanabha Menon, K.P. *History of Kerala.* 4 vols. T.K. Krishna Menon, ed., 1924–37. Ernakulam.

Pagels, Elaine. *The Gnostic Gospels.* 1979. New York.

Paramesvara Iyer, Ulloor S. *Vijñāna Dīpika.* 4 vols. 1935–68.

—————. "Onam" in *Travancore Information and Listener* 4:10–14. 1943.

Pargiter, Frederick Eden. *Ancient Indian Historical Tradition.* 1922. Oxford.

Philip, Mathew. "Transition of Social Life in Kerala." In *Church, Society and State in Kerala.* 1960. Bangalore.

Pritchard, James B., ed. *The Ancient Near East.* 1958. Princeton.

Raghava Aiyangar, M. *Some Aspects of Kerala and Tamil Literature.* 1973. Trivandrum.

Rai, Ganga S. "Vāmana Legend: In the *Vedas,* Epics and *Purāṇas.* " *Purāṇa* 12:102–140. 1970.

Rao, M.S.A. *Social Change in Malabar.* 1957. Bombay.

Rapson, Edward James. *The Cambridge History of India.* 6 vols. 1922–68. Cambridge.

Rawson, Philip. *The Art of Tantra.* 1973. London.

Rose, H. J. *Religion in Greece and Rome.* 1959. New York.

Rosenberg, Alfons. *Engel und Damonen.* 1967. Munich.

Rowley, H.H., ed. *The Old Testament and Modern Study.* 1951. Oxford.

Ruether, Rosemary Radford. *Liberation Theology.* 1972. New York.

Sachau, Edward C., ed. and trans. *Alberuni's India.* 2 vols. 1962. Lahore.

Sitapati, Pidatala. *Sri Venkateswara: The Lord of the Seven Hills, Tirupati.* 1977. Bombay.

Smith, Morton. *Jesus the Magician.* 1978. New York.

Smith, Wilfred Cantwell. *The Faith of Other Men.* 1963. New York.

————. *The Meaning and End of Religion.* 1963. New York.

————. *Relgious Diversity.* 1976. New York.

Sonnerat, Pierre. *Voyage aux Indes Orientales et a la Chine.* 1782. Paris.

Southey, Robert. *The Poetical Works of Robert Southey.* 1863. Boston.

Spink, Walter M. *Krishnamandala: A Devotional Theme in Indian Art.* 1971. Ann Arbor.

Sreedhara Menon, A. *Kerala District Gazeteer—Ernakulam District.* 1962. Trivandrum.

————. *A Survey of Kerala History.* 1967. Kottayam. ·

————. *Cultural Heritage of Kerala: An Introduction.* 1978. Cochin.

Stevenson, Mrs. Sinclair. *The Rites of the Twice-born.* 1920. London.

The Temple of Sree Padmanabha. 1977. Trivandrum.

Thomas, Paul. *Epics, Myths and Legends of India.* 1948. Bombay.

Les Tres Riches Heures du Duc deBerry. 1969. London.

Tripathi, Gaya Charan. *Der Úrsprung und die Entwicklung der Vamana-legende in der Indischen Literatur.* 1968. Wiesbaden.

Ulloor. *See* Paramesvara Iyer, Ulloor S.

Van Buitenen, J.A.B. "Dharma and Mokṣa." *Philosophy East and West* 7: 33–40. 1957.

Varadachari, K.C. *Alvars of South India.* 2nd ed. 1970. Bombay.

Vivekananda, Swami. *The Complete Works of Swami Vivekananda.* 8 vols. 1971–73. Calcutta.

Wadley, Susan Snow. *Shakti: Power in the Conceptual Structure of Karimpur Religion.* 1975. Chicago.

Walker, Benjamin. *Hindu World.* 2 vols. 1968. London.

Wayman, Alexander. "Climactic Times in Indian Mythology and Religion." *HR* 4: 295–318. 1965.

Welch, Anthony. *Artists for the Shah.* 1976. New Haven.

Welch, Stuart Cary. *Persian Painting.* 1976. London.

Willets, William Young. *An Illustrated Annotated Annual Bibliography of Mahabalipuram.* 1966. Kuala Lumpur.

Winternitz, Moriz. *A History of Indian Literature.* Vol. I, Part 2, *Epics and Puranas.* 1963. Calcutta.

Woodcock, George. *Kerala: A Portrait of the Malabar Coast.* 1967. London.
Zimmer, Heinrich. *The Art of Indian Asia.* 1955. New York.
———. *Myths and Symbols in Indian Art and Civilization.* 1962. New York.
Zvelebil, Kamil Veith. *Tamil Literature.* 1974. Wiesbaden.

GLOSSARY AND INDEX